Garland Studies
in Medieval Literature

Editors

Christopher Kleinhenz,
University of Wisconsin-Madison

Paul E. Szarmach,
State University of New York at Binghamton

Garland Studies
in Medieval Literature

THE *ALEXIS* IN THE SAINT ALBANS PSALTER
A Look into the Heart of the Matter

by
RACHEL BULLINGTON

Volume 4
GARLAND STUDIES IN MEDIEVAL LITERATURE

Garland Publishing, Inc.
New York & London
1991

Library of Congress Cataloging-in-Publication Data

Bullington, Rachel, 1930–
    The Alexis in the Saint Albans psalter : a look into the heart of
the matter / by Rachel Bullington.
        p.   cm. — (Garland studies in medieval literature ; v. 4)
    Includes bibliographical references.
    ISBN 0–8240–4038–4
    1. Vie de saint Alexis—Manuscripts. 2. Alexius, Saint, in
fiction, drama, poetry, etc. 3. Manuscripts, Medieval—England—
Saint Albans. 4. Psalters—England—Saint Albans—Manuscripts.
6. Christian poetry, French—Manuscripts. 6. Bible. O.T. Psalms—
Manuscripts. 7. St. Albans psalter. I. Title. II. Series.
PQ1424.A7B84   1991
841'.1—dc20   91–22717
                                                      CIP

Printed on acid-free, 250-year-life paper
Manufactured in the United States of America

for

James C. Atkinson

In deep gratitude for introducing me to
amiables chansons.

CONTENTS

  I   The St. Albans Psalter: Description, after Francis
        Wormald
  II-a P. 57, The St. Albans Psalter: "Title page," *Alexis*
  II-b P. 58, The St. Albans Psalter: first page of poem. "Bons
        fut ..."
  II-c P. 72, The St. Albans Psalter: *Beatus Vir*
  II-d P. 68, The St. Albans Psalter: Gregorian letter
  II-e Christina's World
  III-a The Book as Symbol: "St. Augustine vs. Felicianus"
  III-b The Book as Symbol: Frontispiece: " Alpha and Omega"
  IV   Epître farcie: "In Die S. Stephani Epistola"
  V   Scenes from Luke XVI, Echternach Codex aureus
        Epernacensis. Nuremberg, Germanisches National-
        museum, Hs. 2 ° 15642, Folio 79 r°

Preface of the General Editors

Garland Studies in Medieval Literature (GSML) is a series of interpretative and analytic studies of the Western European literatures of the Middle Ages. It includes both outstanding recent dissertations and book-length studies, giving junior scholars and their senior colleagues the opportunity to publish their research.

The editors welcome submissions representing any of the various schools of criticism and interpretation. Western medieval literature, with its broad historical span, multiplicity and complexity of language and literary traditions, and special problems of textual transmission and preservation as well as varying historical contexts, is both forbidding and inviting to scholars. It continues to offer rich materials for virtually every kind of literary approach that maintains a historical dimension. In establishing a series in an eclectic literature, the editors acknowledge and respect the variety of texts and textual possibilities and the "resisting reality" that confronts medievalists in several forms: on parchment, in mortar, or through icon. It is no mere imitative fallacy to be eclectic, empirical, and pragmatic in the face of this varied literary tradition that has so far defied easy formulation. The cultural landscape of the twentieth century is littered with the debris of broken monomyths predicated on the Middle Ages, for example, the autocratic Church and the Dark Ages or, conversely, the romanticized versions of love and chivalry.

The openness of the series means in turn that scholars, and particularly beginning scholars, need not pass an *a priori* test of "correctness" in their ideology, method, or critical position. The studies published in GSML must be true to their premises, complete within their articulated limits, and accessible to a multiple readership. Each study will advance the knowledge of the literature under discussion, opening it up for further consideration and creating intellectual value. It is also hoped that each volume, while bridging the gap between contemporary perspective and past reality, will make old texts new again. In this way the literature will remain primary, the method secondary.

In this fourth volume of the series, Rachel Bullington studies the complex relationship between the *Alexis* and a Psalter from St. Albans (now held in the church of St. Godehards in Hildesheim), which contains what critics generally consider to be the earliest extant version of the Old French poem. Examining the merits and ramifications of the proposal that the *Alexis* in the St. Albans Psalter may indeed be *the original version* of the poem, Bullington notes that, in this case, the poem would have been composed "expressly for Christina of Markyate for whom the Psalter was designed." In this study she surveys a vast array of topics of interest to medievalists in a number of disciplines, ranging from the nature and place of the psalter in the Middle Ages, the special character of the St. Albans Psalter and St. Albans Abbey in its historical milieu to considerations of Gallican liturgy and the figure of Lazarus. In all these areas Bullington weaves the story of Alexis—the true center of the Psalter—with a fine critical eye both to detail and to the larger picture. Through a careful analysis of the numerical and arithmetical structure of the Old French poem, she shows how this reliance on the special character of the number three also informs the structure of the Psalter itself—the pictorial cycle, the *Alexis*, and the Psalms.

Those who wish more information about submitting their manuscripts to GSML may write to either of the series editors, but in general submission in English and Germanic literatures should be addressed to Paul E. Szarmach and those in Romance literatures to Christopher Kleinhenz.

Christopher Kleinhenz   Paul E. Szarmach
University of Wisconsin-Madison   SUNY-Binghamton

PREFACE

My thanks are due to many: their names are legion. First, I acknowledge my unending debt to James C. Atkinson, who introduced me to Old French letters, and, especially, to the *Alexis*. He should not be held responsible, however, for errors of my making. In addition, I am indebted to the Fulbright Commission, who allowed me to perform my research for this book during 1981-82 as holder of an Advanced Student Award. Both my research and my personal comfort were enhanced by the excellent guidance of the Fulbright's Madame Geneviève Ramos-Acker, who so ably accomplishes the installation of Americans in Paris. I also benefited greatly from the guidance of Madame Janine Renaudineau, Bibliothécaire, Centre Georges Pompidou: she directed me to invaluable manuscripts and to their keepers. M. Jacques Monfrin was of great help in arranging for me to take part in a seminar on Codicology at l'Ecole des Hautes Etudes, under the direction of M. Jean Vezin: my appreciation of the physical manuscript increased greatly through this experience. The Bibliothèque Nationale became my home away from home during this year of scholarship, and I remain deeply grateful to its personnel, especially to M. François Avril and his colleagues in the Département des Manuscrits. Colleagues at l'Institut de Recherches et d'Histoire de Textes were unfailingly helpful and ingenious, as well, in locating precious manuscripts. The St. Albans Psalter, central to this study, was made available to me through the kindness of the Pastor of St. Godehards in Hildesheim, both during my 1981-82 Fulbright year and during other pilgrimages: my deepest thanks are due to St. Godehards.

I am also grateful to the editors of the St. Albans Psalter for their monumental study of this manuscript, and to the Warburg Institute for its permission to make use of their findings. In addition, colleagues on all sides have generously granted me permission to avail myself of their scholarship: I thank them one and all.

Grateful acknowledgement is also rendered to Cornell College for its support of this project in the form of a Faculty Development Grant. My thanks are due as well to colleagues at Erskine College who have kindly effected the manuscript's final preparation; they are

James Gettys, Dennis Erickson, Franklin Mitchell, and Mark Armstrong.

Finally, my deepest thanks are due to my editor, Christopher Kleinhenz. His expertise in medieval scholarship and in scholarly publishing has been put unstintedly at my disposal throughout the editing process.

The *L* manuscript of the *Alexis*, which is in the St. Albans Psalter, is generally regarded as the earliest extant version of the Old French poem. In the wake of Gaston Paris, literary scholars have been in agreement that its prototype would have been composed in eleventh-century France, and that intermediate versions would have lain between the original poem (lost) and the twelfth-century English manuscript. An editor of the St. Albans Psalter, Otto Pächt, proposes, however, that the poem as found in this manuscript may, rather, be the Old French original: it would have been composed at St. Albans expressly for Christina of Markyate for whom the Psalter was designed.

In this work, I have undertaken a study of the *Alexis* as an integral part of the St. Albans Psalter and an evaluation of Otto Pächt's arguments for its English origin. While the original *Alexis* poem cannot be ascribed to the "Alexis Master," I find, it would nonetheless seem to have furnished him with the central element of a conceptual triptych: (I) the christological cycle; (II) the *Alexis*; (III) the Psalms. In such a design, the numen of Christ would inform both his *praefigura*, David, and his imitator, Alexis. Moreover, as a Christ figure, Alexis would duplicate his model's example in taking on himself the 'leprosy' of the world. This, I propose, was understood by the poem's medieval audience, and is specifically expressed in the text's *mezre*, an apparent *hapax legomenon* which I propose should be understood as "miserable leper". The prototype for the Poor Leper at the Rich Man's door, St. Lazarus, may, indeed, have occasioned the presentation of the *Alexis* as the vernacular text for an '*épître farcie*', as occurred first of all for St. Stephen, proto-martyr, and, later, for such saints as Blaise and Thomas of Canterbury.

Such an interpretation allows for a deeper understanding of the *Alexis*: it is *caritas* which motivates and which suffuses the more readily perceived *askesis*. The understanding of Alexis as a 'leper' permits an appreciation of a greater love, wherein a man gives up his life for his friends in a *separatio leprosi* at once the more charitable and the more ironic because it is unperceived by those who know him best.

xiii

The *Alexis* in the
Saint Albans Psalter

CHAPTER I

PROLOGUE

This study explores the reasons for the inclusion of the Old French Life of St. Alexis in the St. Albans Psalter. This version of the *Alexis*, the **L** manuscript, is generally accepted as the earliest of the four major manuscripts extant.[1] As manifestation of the first major literary work in the Old French language, it well deserves the wealth of scholarship long devoted to its textual study.[2] It merits as well the consideration that it might have originated, as Otto Pächt suggests, at St. Albans Abbey, where it would have been written expressly for the celebrated St. Albans Psalter.[3]

Since only the **L** manuscript of the *Alexis* is furnished with a separate preface, the "Prologue," attributed to the Alexis Master, it would seem valid to consider why this short piece should have been composed to precede the poem. As such, it might serve as the key to understanding the significance of an *Old French* Life in a *Latin* psalter —the practical reason for this particular Life's being there recorded, and the use to which it was put at St. Albans.

In an earlier study of the *Alexis* Prologue, I compared its language, vocabulary and style to those of the Poem proper, in response to Pächt's judgment that such an evaluation was wanting.[4] If, he proposed, it could be shown that the *Zeitstil* of the Prologue was the same as that of the Poem, then there would be good grounds for considering St. Albans as the site of their common origin.[5]

My conclusion was that Prologue and Poem stem from different authors and from different periods. The phonological and morphological forms, the prosodic features, the tone and emphasis of the Prologue indicate an Anglo-Norman author whose *Zeitstil* is markedly different from that of the Poem: phonological forms are more evolved, neologisms are more prevalent, morphological disintegration abounds.[6] And, of special significance for the St. Albans Psalter, the Prologue's essential raison d'être, like its accompanying miniatures, is 'marital' rather than ascetic: in both of these elements,

Alexis remains a 'Declining Bridegroom,' never becoming the 'Reclining Pauper' of the Poem proper.

If it had been possible to establish that the language of the Prologue and of the Poem are the same, it would, indeed, have strengthened the positing of the *Alexiusmeister* and St. Albans as the *fons et origo* of the Old French Life. But even if Prologue and Poem issue from different authors this does not necessarily rule out a St. Albans origin for both of them. It is not inconceivable that there were two 'Masters' flourishing at this abbey in the first half of the twelfth century: the Alexis Master, to whom are due the pictorial cycle and the *Alexis* Prologue, as Pächt judges, and yet another Master, who could have been the writer of the Old French Life. At any rate, it would seem that a Master is evident in the conception of the Psalter, whose over-all design and individual components seem thought out with care and executed with grace: him let us call the *Albanimeister*, the "St. Albans Master."

My investigation of the *Alexis* as a purposeful part of the St. Albans Psalter has led me into all the disciplines of which a medieval religious manuscript partakes: paleography, codicology and art history; liturgical and monastic history; hagiography and its related areas of pilgrimage and relics; and, in this instance, the basic *matière* informing the literary text —the Alexis legend, tradition and numen. Such a synthetic approach has occasioned my drawing extensively from the works of a host of scholars in these respective fields: I gratefully acknowledge my indebtedness to all of them. While it has often been necessary to summarize their findings, I trust that I have done so with discernment and fairness.

Having considered all those factors which enter into a holistic understanding of the *Alexis* and its significance both as a part of the St. Albans Psalter and in its own right, I have arrived at a new theory for its raison d'être. Given the circumstances of its St. Albans genesis and its analogues in other *opera*, a new interpretation of the Saint's Life appears warranted. With such an interpretation, moreover, it is conceivable that this poem represents a 'Sacred Bridge' between liturgy and liturgical drama.

Crucial to this interpretation is the appreciation of an Alexis who represented significantly more to a medieval audience than to modern readers. For Alexis is

2

bigger than his Life itself in representing a conflation of personages: the Eastern *Mar Riscia* and the Western St. John the Calybite, as has been long recognized, and, according to my understanding, the Biblical Christ-types, Job and Lazarus as well.[7] Underlying this latter identification is the understanding that Alexis, like Job and Lazarus, was seen to be afflicted with that "Sacred Malady," leprosy; like his divine model, Alexis took upon himself this affliction for our salvation, bearing our infirmities and carrying our sorrows as a 'leper'--"*quasi leprosum*," as Isaiah had 'foretold' of Christ (Isaiah 53:4).

Furthermore, as a Confessor saint, Alexis might readily be identified with Lazarus, whose intercession the Wicked Rich Man so urgently besought of God. I propose that Lazarus was seen as the Proto-Confessor, in tandem with Stephen, the Proto-Martyr. And just as the Passion of St. Stephen was the matter of an *Epître farcie*, so the Life of the Poor Man, Lazarus/Alexis, sitting outside the Rich Man's door, may well have farced an 'Epistle,' as did the Lives of St. Blaise, of St. Nicholas, and of St. Thomas of Canterbury.[8] Significantly, one of the earliest *Epîtres farcies* —of St. Stephen— is found in another twelfth-century psalter, that of Troyes (Paris, B.N. ms. lat. 238).[9] Moreover, one of its versions closes with this *explicit* : "Ci falt *la vie* saint Estiene." (Here ends *the life* of St. Stephen.) (Phillips MS. 6664, now Bruxelles, Bibl. roy. IV, 1005.) [Emphasis mine.] Such thrilling *matière de farce* , whether concerned with scriptural saint or with para-scriptural saint of *historia*, would have been, per se, the very stuff of which dramatic representation is made. Thus, for example, did the subject matter of the tenth-century Clermont *Passion* find its elaborate and prolonged presentation in the ubiquitous Passion dramas.

A saint's life, so thoroughly impregnated with dramatic elements, might thus partake of both liturgy and drama.[10] Indeed, among the earliest liturgical dramas is the Hilarius *Lazarus*, whose protagonist we have proposed as a model for Alexis. In this play, moreover, vernacular lamentations 'farce' the Latin script: they are notably reminiscent of the *planctus* so remarkable in the Old French *Alexis* .[11]

Para-liturgical and para-dramatic, such a Saint's Life would be ideally suited for such *representationes* as are associated with the cloister, and, sometimes, with

3

cloisters of nuns.[12] Such was the *locus* of Christina of Markyate, *sponsa intacta* , for whom the St. Albans Psalter was apparently made; its Alexis miniatures and Prologue, significantly, show a *Virgo Christi* rationale. And it is especially noteworthy that the earliest recorded performance of a miracle play, the *Ludus Sanctae Catharinae*, is associated with St. Albans through Geoffrey of Maine, who would become its Abbot, and the close friend of Christina. The closing lines of the *Alexis*, invoking a recitation of the Pater Noster, strongly imply a liturgical setting.[13] The wide dissemination and later *ethos* of the Old French poem, evolving from suffering saint to pathetic bridegroom, indicate a popular exposure beyond the cloister walls. Such a movement —from clerical hagiography through secular hagiography to popular 'romance'— could well be occasioned by means of public performance, as within an Abbey church.

Aside from the practical reasons for the presence of the *Alexis* in the St. Albans Psalter, it is important to take note of the esthetic rationale: the conceptual design of the Psalter would seem to include this Life as one of the components vital to its structure. I propose that the design of the St. Albans Psalter was expressly and symbolically tri-partite, embracing (1) the forty-page pictorial cycle, (2) the *Alexis*, and (3) the Psalms, as the three essential components.

In summary, these are the proposals which this study will entertain:

> 1. The St. Albans Psalter is of a basic ternary design: the *Alexis*, in central position, looks, Janus-like, to the Old and New Adams of the 'christological' pictorial cycle which opens the Psalter, and to the prime *praefigura Christi* , the David of the Psalms which follow the Old French Life.

> 2. The Alexis of the Old French poem, a Christ type, functions both as an image of his divine model, the suffering *Agnus Dei* , and of his human one, Lazarus, *Leprosus mundi* : 'quod Lazarus velat Alexii vita revelat.'[14]

4

3. In the company of the saints of Scripture —St. Stephen, proto-martyr, and St. Lazarus, herein understood as proto-confessor—, the *Alexis* would be prime material for a dramatic reading to 'farce' the 'Epistle' of the day.

4. The Old French Life takes on a new and fuller meaning when 'glossed' with the understanding of Alexis as a willing leper: *caritas* suffuses and illuminates *askesis*. Such an interpretation permits an appreciation of a greater love, in which a man gives up his life for his friends in a *separatio leprosi* at once the more charitable and the more ironic because it is unperceived by those who knew him best.

While many of my intermediate findings must remain in the realm of conjecture, their *mise ensemble* would seem to justify a new interpretation for the *Alexis* and to elucidate its inclusion within the St. Albans Psalter.[15]

[1] There are some seventeen extant manuscripts which preserve, in whole or fragmentary form, the Old French version of the Life of St. Alexis. Those of major importance remain the four which Gaston Paris examined in his 1872 critical edition of the poem. (The twelfth-century Vatican manuscript (V), published by Pio Rajna in 1929, offers only the last two hundred lines and no important new readings.) These are the four primary manuscripts:

1. L forms part of the celebrated St. Albans Psalter, executed at the Benedictine abbey of that name in England in the twelfth century. It was brought to Lamspringe Abbey, Germany, by English monks, at some time prior to 1643. It moved to St. Godehard's Church in Hildesheim around 1803 when Lamspringe Abbey was presumably suppressed, and remains the property of St. Godehard's.

2. A (Paris, B.N. fr. 4503) also appears to be of twelfth-century English provenance. The Life of St. Alexis appears in this manuscript among the Lives of St. Brandan and St. Catherine and the Assumption of the Virgin. Paris judges this version inferior to L in quality as well as in quantity (by 21 strophes and 31 single lines). We shall consider this quantitative difference between L and A in Chapter VI.

3. P (Paris, B.N. fr. 19525) is likewise judged to be of English extraction, ca. 13th c. More complete in content than A, it also offers better readings, G. Paris judges. Konrad Hofmann studied this manuscript in depth, utilizing it in

his 1868 critical edition of *St. Alexius*. Included in **P** are sermons on the Pater Noster and on St. John I, both of which I believe have bearing on the *Alexis* .

4. **S** (Paris, B.N. fr. 12471) is a twelfth-century French manuscript. The poem as it appears therein has been greatly augmented and altered in comparison with its above counterparts. It was edited by L. Pannier and published in the 1872 edition of the *Alexis* by Gaston Paris.

Of lesser importance are the following three manuscripts, as described by Christopher Storey (*La Vie de Saint Alexis*, 1968):

1. **V** (Vatican, Cod. Vat. lat. 5334. fo. 125) was discovered in 1925 by Msgr. Mercatic. It is the work of a French copyist, and is judged to have been executed in the twelfth century. It is fragmentary, containing only lines 425-625, with the omission of three lines and the addition of one. Pio Rajna, who published this version in 1929 (*Archivum Romanicum*, XIII), places its date between 1140 and 1160.

2. **Ma** (Paris, B.N. Ms. fr. 1553) is a French manuscript ascribed to the late thirteenth or early fourteenth century. This version was published by Gaston Paris in 1887, and has been edited by Daniele Gatto-Pyko ("*La Vie de saint Alexis, version M- édition critique* ." Dissertation, Florida State University, 1973). Storey describes it as 'poorly copied and of no great interest.'

3. **Mb** (Carlisle, The Cathedral Library) is a thirteenth-century rhymed version of **Ma**. It has been partially published by Gaston Paris (*Romania*, 1888), and by Gatto-Pyko (1973), and fully edited by Alison Goddard Elliott (Chapel Hill, 1983).

2 The bibliography is of course enormous. A thorough and exhaustive listing is kept current at the Bureau d'Histoire et de Recherches de Textes, Paris, whose personnel have been unstintedly helpful to me in this study. For a useful summary, see Karl Uitti, *Story, Myth and Celebration in Old French Narrative Poetry. 1050-1200* . (Princeton: Princeton Univ. Pr., 1972), and Charles Stebbins, "Les Grandes versions de la légende de Saint Alexis," *Revue belge de philologie et d'histoire*, LIII (1975), pp. 679-95.

3 O. Pächt, C. R. Dodwell, F. Wormald, *The St. Albans Psalter* (London: The Warburg Institute, 1960), p. 143, n. 1.

4 R. Bullington, "The Prologue to the Old French *Vie de Saint Alexis* : a Linguistic Study, with Considerations of its Prosodic and Conceptual Features," Thesis, the University of North Carolina at Greensboro, 1971.

5 See Note 3, supra.

6 Such archaisms and neologisms of phonology and of morphology as are characteristic of the Anglo-Norman dialect are best documented by J. Vising, *Anglo-Norman Language & Literature* (London: Oxford Univ. Press, H. Milford, 1923). See as well Mildred K. Pope, *From Latin to Modern French with especial consideration of Anglo-Norman* (Manchester: Manchester Univ. Press, rev. ed., 1952).

The language of the Prologue is characterized throughout by such coexistent archaisms and neologisms as are typical of Anglo-Norman. So the Prologue shows later forms unknown to the Poem, e.g. *pere, mere* vs. the Poem's *pedra, medra.*

While Norman and Anglo-Norman share many phonological and morphological characteristics, the distinguishing factor being their earlier and fuller development in England, there are some features which are seen as peculiarly Anglo-Norman. The Prologue abounds in these forms:

(Phonology)
th for δ: methime, castethet.

__ for δ: vie, oit [oït], pere, mere.
u for o: nus, sul, raisun, barun,
    avum, iuvente, surerain,
    spuse, cumandat, sue,
    suverain, consulaciun,
    sulunc.
ie for e: trinitiet.
e for ie: amistet, certet.
m for n before f: sum filz, emfes.
s for ss: naisance.
g for j: goies.
c for ch: cancun, canter, certet.
iceol for icel; sulunc for selunc;
    avum for avons:
    characteristically Anglo-
    Norman.

added proclitic (analogical) vowel:
    icesta.
lacking proclitic vowel: _spus,
    _spuse.
(archaic) a for e(ə): icesta.

an for en (also a Norman
    characteristic): angendrat;
    an (trinitiet).

(Morphology)

le for la: le naisance, le. . .volentet,
    del. . .pietet.
nominative for accusative: de sum
    filz boneuret, icel sul filz
    angendrat.
accusative for nominative: un sul
    faitur; nurrit; amet.

masculine adjectives with feminine
nouns; suverain consulaciun.
apparent confusion as to gender
(both article and adjective in
wrong form): par le divine
volentet; a cascun memorie
spiritel.

The degree to which the Prologue exhibits an
Anglo-Norman nature may be assessed by a comparison of
the text as found in the St. Albans Psalter with Gaston
Paris' recasting of the passage in 'standard' eleventh-century *Norman* French. I have rendered **L** manuscript's "u" as
"v" where appropriate [*vie, avum, volentet, iuvente, vif,
veritet, suverain, vivent, virginels*], separated its run-
together word [*espiritel, lavie, ecanter, deumethime,
delsurerain, lasue, alspus, unsul, esuverain, acascun*], and
italicized the forms under consideration in both texts:

(Original, **L**. ms.): Ici *cumencet*
amiable *cancun* e spiritel *raisun*
diceol no/ble *barun* eufemien par
num. e de la *vie* de *sum filz*
boneu/ret del quel *nus avum oït* lire
e *canter*. par *le* divine/ volentet. il
desirrables icel *sul filz angendrat*.
Apres *le naisance*/ co fut *emfes* de
deu methime amet. e de *pere* e de
mere /par grant *certet nurrit*. la *sue
iuvente* fut honeste e spiritel./ par
lamistet del *surerain pietet* la *sue
spuse iuvene cuman/dat* al *spus* vif
de veritet Ki est *un sul faitur* e
regnet/ *an trinitiet. Icesta istorie*
est amiable grace *e suverain/
consulaciun* a *cascun* memorie
spiritel. les quels vivent/ purement
sulunc castethet. e dignement sei
delitent/ es goies del ciel & es noces
virginels.

(Gaston Paris, 1872 ed., *La Vie de Saint Alexis* , pp. 177-8.):

Ici *comencet* amiable *chancon* e spiritel *raison d'icel* noble *baron*, Eufemien par *non*, e de la vide de *son* fil_ boneuret, del quel nos avon*s* o*d*it lire e *chanter.* Par *la* divine volentet il desirrables icel *sol* fil_ *engendrat.* Apres *la* naissance co fut e*n*fes de Deu me*d*isme amez e de pe*d*re e de me*d*re par grant *chier*tet no*d*riz. La *soe* jo*v*ente fut honeste e spiritel. Par l'amist*iet* del *so*verain *pedre* [for *pietet*] la *soe* es*p*ose jo*v*ene comandat al *e*spos vif de veritet qui est uns sols *faitre* [for *faitur*] e regnet *en* trinit_*et*. _Ceste *h*istorie est amiable grace e *s*ov*e*raine consolac*io*n a *c*hascu*ne* memorie spiritel, les quels vivent purement s*e*lonc *c*haste*d*et e dignement sei delitent es goies del ciel et es noces virginels.

7 The Old Testament Job and the New Testament Lazarus are typologically paired in various medieval theological and literary works such as *Li Romans de Carite* by le Renclus de Moiliens (Hamel ed., Paris, 1885), for example. Their iconography is linked with that of Alexis by Louis Réau, *Iconographie de l'art chrétien* , Tome 3, *Iconographie des Saints* (Paris, 1955), pp. 52-53. See also Appendix VIII-b and -c for their pairing in popular song. The Christ-symbolism of Job is most notably enounced in the *Expositio in librum beati Job sive Moralia* (*PL*, LXXV-LXXVI) of Pope St. Gregory the Great, who recognized Job and his sons as prefigurations of Christ and his persecutors as heretic-types. This commentary was one of the most influential and highly-revered exegetic texts throughout the Middle Ages, to the point that it was referred to as '*The Job* .'

8 See l'Abbé Lebeuf, *Traité historique et pratique sur le chant ecclésiastique* (Paris, 1741), pp. 132 ss., for the farced epistles (annotated) of Saints Stephen, Blaise, and

12

Thomas of Canterbury. See also Edelestand Du Méril, *Les Origines latines du théâtre moderne* (Paris/Leipzig, 1897), pp. 410-417, for those of St. Stephen and St. Thomas of Canterbury. For St. Thomas of Canterbury, the 'Epistle' cited is the Book of Wisdom ("Lectio libri Sapientiae"), but, as Du Méril notes, the Latin text cited is drawn, rather, from the *Ecclesiasticus* of Jesus, Son of Sirach. See Appendix IV for Lebeuf's musical notation of an *Epître farcie*.

9 This Psalter, *Psalterium ad usum ecclesiae Trecensis* (Paris B.N. Ms. lat 238) is dated as late 12th-early 13th century.

10 Karl D. Uitti has made a penetrating analysis of how the saint's Life partakes of both the "celebration" and the "mythic" to such a degree that "a kind of performance is at issue here." (Uitti, p. 25)

11 In the Hilarius *Lazarus* there is the *planctus* of Mary and that of Martha; each comprises four stanzas of six lines each, of which the beginning three lines are in Latin and the remaining three in Old French. These are repeated in each stanza.

The *planctus* of Mary:

> Hor ai dolor,
> hor est mis frere morz;
> por que gei plor.

> (Now have I sorrow,
> now is my brother dead;
> wherefore I weep.)

that of Martha:

> Lase, cativi!
> Desque mis frere est morz,
> porque sue vive?

13

(Woe is me, wretch!
Since my brother is dead,
why am I alive?)

These *planctus* bear comparison with the pro-
tracted lament of the mother in strophe 89 of the
Alexis:

A! lasse, mezre, cum oi fort aventure!
Or vei jo morte tute ma porteüre.
Ma lunga atente a grant duel est venude.
Pur quei[t] portai, dolente, malfeüde?
Co'st granz merveile que li mens quors tant duret.

(Ah! woe is me, [*mezre*] what a hard blow have I had!
Now see I dead all my progeny.
My long waiting has come to such sorrow
Why did I— poor wretched woman— [ever] bear thee?
It is a great wonder that my heart lasts so long.)

All these laments are reminiscent, as well, of those of the
Foolish Virgins in the *Sponsus* drama:

Dolentas! Chaitivas! Trop i avem dormit.

(Mourners! Wretches! Too long have we slept here.)

12 Without getting into the thorny question as to
whether the dramas of Hrotsvitha of Gandersheim were
pièces à jouer vs. à lire , we find more conclusive evidence
in the case of the five plays recorded by Sister Katherine
Bourlet at the convent of Huy (near Liège). Gustave Cohen
assesses their *mise en scène* as follows: "...Jouées dans un
couvent des femmes, les deux premières Nativités ont bien
pu avoir aussi des religieuses de Huy pour actrices, même
dans certains rôles d'hommes: ce serait l'inverse de ce que
nous avons d'ordinaire, les rôles de femmes étant
généralement tenus par des jeunes gens..." (...Performed in
a convent of women, the first two Nativities [of Cohen's
study] could well have had nuns of Huy for actressses as
well, even in certain men's roles: this would be the reverse
of what we have ordinarily, the roles of women being
generally played by young men.) (*Mystères et Moralités du
MS. 617 de Chantilly*, Paris. Librairie ancienne Edouard
Champion, 1920, pp.CXXI-II.)

14

[13] Msgr. J. Meunier, *La Vie de Saint Alexis* (Paris, 1933), p. 71, emphasizes most strongly that the poem's closing line, "In ipse verbe sin dimes: *Pater noster* . , " indicates a liturgical setting. Later on, we shall relate this to the closing exhortation to incant the *Te Deum* following bona fide liturgical *drama* . Cf. the Hilarius *Lazarus*: "Quo finito, si factum fuerit ad Matutinus, Lazarus incipiat: Te Deum laudamus; si vero ad Vesperas: Magnificat anima mea Dominum . " (Once this has ended, if it will have been done at Matins, let Lazarus begin: Te Deum laudamus; if, however, at Vespers: Magnificat anima mea Dominum.)

[14] This is my paraphrase of the Abbot Suger's paraphrase of the formula of St. Augustine. In one of the windows of St. Denis is inscribed Suger's "Quod Moyses velat Christi doctrina revelat," (What Moses conceals, the doctrine of Christ reveals) by reference to St. Augustine's "In Vetere Testamento Novum latet, in Novo Vetus patet . " (In the Old Testament is the New [Testament] latent, in the New is the Old patent.) (Quaest. in Hept. , LXXIII, *PL* XXIV, 623.)

[15] References to the L *Alexis*, unless otherwise indicated, are to the edition of Christopher Storey, *La Vie de Saint Alexis, texte du manuscrit de Hildesheim* (L), Geneva: Droz, 1968.

15

CHAPTER II

THE PSALTER IN THE MIDDLE AGES

The psalter was the book most frequently used in the Middle Ages by clergy and laity alike. As the earliest service book of the Christian cult, it was a heritage from the Jewish ritual, in which the antiphonal singing of the Psalms was one of the essential elements of worship in the synagogue.[1] It was natural that this practice should be adopted, though not without some controversy, by the early Christians,[2] whose assemblies were of the simplest nature: an informal gathering together of believers for the chanting of Psalms, the sharing of bread, the giving of alms, the exchanging of the kiss of peace.[3] As the Church's organization and liturgy developed and expanded, the prominence of the Psalms not only persisted but increased: as early as 200 A.D., they were deemed the acceptable musical offering *par excellence*, to the exclusion of earlier Christian hymns, accused of being tainted with the excesses of Gnosticism.[4]

Moreover, whereas the psalter had served primarily a musical function in the synagogue, the Church early extended its use and endowed it with a typological significance as well. Basic to this allegorical interpretation was the certitude that the Old Testament anticipated, in word and in deed, the New Testament and its Gospel of salvation.

Such a belief found scriptural authentication; St. Paul, in referring to Old Testament events, had asserted: "Haec autem omnia in figura contingebant illis: scripta sunt autem ad correctionem nostram." (Now all these things happened to them in figure: and they are written for our correction. I Cor. 10:11).[5] The figurative interpretation was again enounced in Galatians 4:22-28, where Abraham's two sons, the one born of a slave, the other of a free woman, are cited as representing the Old Covenant and the New Promise:

> Scriptum est enim: Quoniam
> Abraham duos filios habuit: unum
> de ancilla, et unum de libera. Sed
> qui de ancilla, secundum carnem
> natus est: qui autem de libera, per

17

repromissionem: quae sunt per allegoriam dicta. Haec enim sunt duo testamenta. Unum quidem in monte Sina, in servitutem generans: quae est Agar. Sina enim mons est in Arabia, qui coniunctus est ei que nunc est Ierusalem, et servit cum filiis suis. Illa autem, quae sursum est Ierusalem, libera est, quae est mater nostra. . . . Nos autem fratres secundum Isaac promissionis filii sumus.

(For it is written that Abraham had two sons, one by a slave and one by a free woman. But the son of the slave was born according to the flesh, the son of the free woman through promise. Now this is an allegory: these women are two covenants. One is from Mount Sinai, bearing children for slavery; she is Hagar. Now Hagar is Mount Sinai in Arabia; she corresponds to the present Jerusalem, for she is in slavery with her children. But the Jerusalem above is free, and she is our mother. . . . Now we, brethren, like Isaac, are children of promise.)[6]

The viewing of the Scripture on three levels—the literal, the allegorical, and the moral or instructive—had been formulated by Origen, introduced to the West by Hilary, and firmly established by St. Jerome: "Scripturas sanctas intelligamus tripliciter. Primum, juxta litteram, secundo, medie per tropologiam, tertio, sublimius ut mystica quaeque noscamus." (*Comm. in Ezech, PL* XXV, 147). ("We understand the Holy Scriptures in three ways: first, in a literal sense, secondly in a tropological [i.e., moral] one; and thirdly, in a more sublime way so that we understand all mysteries.")[7] To these three levels was added a fourth, the anagogical or spiritual interpretation. Cassian's analysis of these four senses of Scripture became a model in the Middle Ages; it is well summarized, as Dodwell demonstrates, in the *Quo Ordine Sermo fieri debeat* of Guilbert de Nogent (1052-1130):

Quatuor sunt regulae Scripturarum, quibus quasi quibusdam rotis volvitur omnis sacra pagina: hoc est historia, quae res gestas loquitur; allegoria, in qua ex alio aliud intelligitur; tropologia, id est moralis locutio, in qua de moribus componendis ordinandisque tractatur; anagoge, spiritualis scilicet intellectus, per quem de summis et coelestibus tractaturi ad superiora ducimur. Verbi gratia Hierusalem secundum historiam civitas est quaedam; secundum allegoriam, sanctam Ecclesiam significans; secundum tropologiam, id est moralitatem, anima fidelis cuiuslibet qui ad visionem pacis aeternae anhelat; secundum anagogem, coelestium civium vitam, qui Deum deorum facie revelata in Sion vident signat. (*PL* CLVI, 25)

(There are four rules of the Scriptures, which actuate every page of the holy text like certain wheels. There is the historical rule, which speaks of the deeds which have been done; the allegorical one, by which something is understood from something else; the tropological one, which speaks of the moral and treats of the ordering of moral things; the anagogical, or spiritual one, by which we are led to higher things since it treats of heaven and of the things above. Take, for instance, the word 'Jerusalem.' In the historical sense, it denotes a certain city; in the allegorical sense, the Holy Church; in the

19

tropological, or moral, sense, the soul of one of the faithful who gasps at the vision of peace eternal; in the anagogical sense, the life of the citizens of Heaven, who see the God of gods face to face in Sion.)[8]

Reduced to its simplest terms, according to this view, the sacred text has two essential meanings: a literal one —the "cortex", and a spiritual one —the "nucleus". Such an understanding would be most insistently set forth by St. Augustine, and by his preponderant influence, it would assume the nature of Holy Truth. Claudius of Turin (12th c.) well sums up this patristic tradition; for him: "The Word is incarnate in Scripture, which like man has a body and soul. The body is the words of the sacred text, the 'letter,' and the literal meaning; the soul is the spiritual sense."[9] In Claudius' own words:

Verbum Dei ex Maria carne vestitum processit in mundum; et aliud quidem erat quod videbantur in eo, aliud quod intelligebatur (carnis namque aspectus in eo patebat omnibus, paucis vero et electis dabatur divinitatis agnitio) ita et cum per prophetas vel legislatorem Verbum Dei profertur ad homines, non absque competentibus profertur indumentis. Nam sicut ibi carnis, ita hic litterae velamine tegitur: ut littera quidem aspicitur tanquam caro, latens vero spiritalis intrinsecus sensus tanquam divinitas sentitur. . . beati sunt illi oculi qui velamen litterae obtectum intrinsecus divinum spiritum vident.

(The Word came into the world by Mary, clad in flesh; and seeing was not understanding; all saw the flesh; knowledge of the divinity was given to a chosen few. So when the Word was shown to men through the

20

lawgiver and the prophets, it was
not shown them without suitable
vesture. There it is covered by the
veil of flesh, here of the letter. The
letter appears as flesh; but the
spiritual sense within is known as
divinity. . . . Blessed are the eyes
which see divine spirit through the
letter's veil.)[10]

Claudius's words are but an amplification of those
of St. Augustine, which would become the formula for
medieval exegesis of the Old Testament: "In Vetere
Testamento Novum latet, in Novo Vetus patet." (In the Old
Testament is the New latent, in the New [is] the Old
patent.)[11]   St. Augustine had 'very adroitly' reconciled, as
Louis Réau puts it, 'the historical reality and the symbolic
significance of the facts related in the Old Testament.'[12]
Thus St. Augustine explains that 'Abraham really lived;
what Scripture relates about Abraham really did take
place. But God made of the Patriarchs and the Prophets
the announcers and heralds of his Son: that is why we can,
in everything which they said and did, search and find the
Saviour.'[13]
Nowhere was the movement from the text's surface
to its substance more assiduously invoked than for the
Book of Psalms; it was early and thoroughly explicated,
most notably by St. Augustine and Cassiodorus, and by
Origen, Hilary, Jerome and Cassian as well. According to
the patristic interpretation, the Book of Psalms was,
above all, a prophecy of Christ, and David, his royal
progenitor, was his prophet. Thus does David appear in
the *Ordo Prophetarum* of the twelfth-century Anglo-
Norman *Jeu d'Adam*:

Post hunc accedat DAVID, regis
insignis et diademate ornatus et
dicat: "Veritas de terra orta est, et
justicia de celo prospexit. Et enim
Dominus dabit benignitatem, et
terra nostra dabit fructum suum."

De terre istra la verite
E justice, de majeste.

21

Deus durra benignite,
Nostra terre dorra son ble;

De son furment dorra son pain,
Qui salvera le filz Evain.
Cil iert sire de tote terre,
Cil fera pais, destruira guere.[14]

(Following this, let David come
forth, with the insignia of a king
and crowned with a diadem, and let
him say: 'Truth has arisen from the
earth, and justice has gazed forth
out of heaven. For God will grant
blessing, and our earth will give
forth its fruit.'

Out of the earth will come forth
truth
And justice [will spring] from
majesty.
God will grant [his] blessing;
Our earth will give forth its grain.

From its increase will it yield its
Bread,
Which will save the sons of Eve.
This One will be Lord of all the
earth,
This One will bring peace, will
vanquish war.)

Likewise, with the Passion play fully developed,
David is still cast as a prophet; in the fourteenth-century
Passionspiele from Brixen, he appears in the Crucifixion
scene to point out that the most crucial one of his
prophecies has just been realized:

Als ich am 21 psalm zwar
Gesprochen hab frey offenwar:
Seine hend und fues sy haben
Gar jemerlich durch graben,
Das im alle seine gepain
Gezelt sein worden allain:

22

Secht Nu all zu diser frist,
Ob ietz sölichs nit geschechen ist![15]

(As I indeed said clearly and openly
in my 21st Psalm, 'They have quite
pitifully pierced his hands and feet,'
so that even all his bones have been
counted.' Look now, all of you,
whether such has not happened at
this very moment!)

Thus did the Psalms countervail with the Gospels,
the cornerstone of the faith, to furnish Prophecy for the
fulfillment: 'Novum Testamentum in Vetere latet, Vetus in
Nove patet.'[16] And thus did David, *Rex et Propheta*, enjoy
a special esteem, for he was commonly perceived as the
author of all the Psalms.

This prestige was all the more enhanced by the
understanding that David was not only the prophet and
royal forefather of Christ, but one of his principal
praefigurae as well.[17] So perfected was this association
that it allowed the recognition of Christ himself speaking
through David, sweet singer of the Psalms of Israel. Hence
Jerome found that David sang all the Psalms,but
variously: in the person of Christ, or of the Church, or of
the Prophet himself.[18] Similarly, in his *Enarrationes in
Psalmos* —his longest work, it should be noted— St.
Augustine demonstrated that David represented not only
himself, but the Church, and, above all, the divine
Mediator:

David rex unus homo fuit, sed non
unum hominem figuravit: quando
scilicet figuravit Ecclesiam ex
multis constantem, distentam
usque ad fines terrae; quando autem
unum hominem figuravit, illum
figuravit qui est mediator Dei et
hominum, homo Christus Jesus
(I Tim. 2:5).[19]

(David the King was one man, but he
did not represent only one; that is to
say, he sometimes represented the

23

> Church, which consists of many,
> extending to the ends of the earth;
> sometimes, however, he represented
> that One who is mediator between
> God and men, the man Christ Jesus.)

St. Jerome's and St. Augustine's christological interpretation of the Psalms would remain the Church's traditional one, with many a reiteration: Albertus Magnus, "Totus liber iste de Christo est" (All this book is about Christ); Honorius Augustodunensis, "omnes (sc. psalmi) de Christo intelliguntur" (All [of the psalms] are understood to refer to Christ); Bellarmin, "quod sit psalmus ad Christum pertinens, qui est finis legis et prophetarum" (. . . which is a psalm pertaining to Christ, who is the fulfillment of the Law and Prophets).[20]

The ultimate justification for viewing the Psalms as christological had been found in the words of the very Author and Finisher of the faith: "Necesse est impleri omnia quae scripta sunt in lege Moysi, et prophetis, et Psalmis de me," (For it is necessary that all things be fulfilled which are written of me in the law of Moses, and in the prophets, and in the Psalms.) (Luke 24:44). On such authority, the conflation of David and Christ was to be expected. The son of Jesse, anointed by Samuel the prophet, prefigured the Messiah (the "Anointed One") heralded by John the Baptist; the crown of Israel foretold the diadem of the King of Kings. Thus the Good Shepherd was readily perceived in the Shepherd Boy; the New Adam was implicit in the righteous *Beatus Vir* of the first Psalm.[21] A choice example of this association is furnished in the two historiated initials for the *Beatus Vir* of the Winchester Psalter (12th c.), as noted by Cook and Herzman:

> The Beatus initials . . . are
> illuminated so as to suggest the
> relationship between David . . . and
> Christ. In the loops of the first "B"
> David rescues the sheep from the
> bear and from the lion. In the sec-
> ond "B", Christ, the Good Shepherd,
> expels an evil spirit from the boy
> possessed by a demon . . . , and

Christ delivers souls from hell.
Thus events in the life of David
prefigure events in the life of
Christ.[22]

Hence does this typology furnish the subcode for a great body of art and literature. It informs such iconography as the Tree of Jesse, both in stained glass and in the *Liber generationis* illustrations of Gospel manuscripts;[23] it explains the christological pictures which either accompany the Psalms per se or appear separately within various Psalters.[24]

Moreover, since words from the Psalms were constantly on Christ's lips during the Passion, this Old Testament book constituted prime matter for a staurocentric reading: thus did Psalm 21 come to represent a 'quasi-Passion,' as Thomas Aquinas termed it, and, ultimately, to receive its Vulgate title, "Messiae extrema passio eiusque fructus," (The Final Passion of the Messiah and its Fruits).[25]

Indeed, so perfected was this analogy that it extended to the objects emblematic of the Psalmist, who 'was' the Saviour: the harp of David was the most influential of all Christian symbols of the Cross, by F. P. Pickering's reckoning.[26] Noting that the organs of speech had been systematically compared to the various parts of a stringed instrument in Antiquity, Pickering demonstrates the christianization of this analogy and its long survival: a twelfth-century German Psalter shows David's psaltery superimposed on his body as a "type" of the Crucifixion; sixteenth-century representations of the Cross continue to feature a 'crossbow' (= harp) for its arms.[27] The viewing of David's harp and psaltery as christological symbols had been enounced by St. Augustine: 'everywhere in the Psalms where there is reference to the harp, we are to understand Christ as man in his suffering: *caro humana patiens*; the psaltery is to be understood as expressing Christ's divine nature, and his healing power.'[28] In the light of this understanding, the twenty-first Psalm's opening "Deus, Deus meus . . . quare me dereliquisti?" was clearly a rehearsal for the "Eli Eli, lamma sabacthani?" of the Passion.[29]

With David so well established as the Christ archetype *par excellence*, it is to be expected that a vast number of medieval psalters would be 'glossed' with christological illustrations, the Word making flesh, as it were, the 'prophetic' words of David. Due in great part to the prominence accorded the Psalter by this association, it would remain one of the most frequently produced religious books throughout the Middle Ages, for it was the *sine qua non* both of exegesis and of liturgy.

As the Christian cult had expanded, its liturgy had changed along with its changes in meeting places, shifting from the synagogue to the homes of believers, to the tombs of martyrs, and, finally, to a bona fide house of worship. Accordingly, the liturgy had moved from a celebration by the group-at-large to a formalized ritual in which the priesthood officiated.[30] With this latter development, there was an attendant specialization of the elements of the Mass, and various service books evolved for their appropriate usage: the Sacramentary for the Celebrant, the Evangeliary for the Deacon, the Epistolary for the Subdeacon, the Gradual (or Antiphonary) for the Schola.[31]

Among these liturgical books, the Gospel Book received special veneration, as is evidenced by the magnificent volumes yet extant and by the reverence still accorded to it in the celebration of the Mass. Both by the splendor of its appearance and by the special dignity of its presentation, the Evangeliary has ever been conspicuous; its reading consitutes "le moment, l'acte suprême," as Schmidt describes:

> . . . les processions avec le livre des évangiles à l'entrée et avant la lecture, vers l'ambon, tandis que le célébrant donne la bénédiction au nom du Christ, le salut "Le Seigneur soit avec vous" avant la lecture de l'évangile, le signe de croix tracé sur le livre des évangiles et sur le front, les lèvres et la poitrine du lecteur, le baisement du livre des évangiles par le célébrant après la lecture. L'usage d'un livre spécial contenant les évangiles a également une signification symbolique ainsi que le fait de se tenir debout pendant la

lecture tandis qu'on reste assis
pendant les autres lectures.[32]

(. . . the processions with the Gospel
book upon entering and before the
Reading, toward the ambo, while the
celebrant gives the benediction in
the name of Christ, the greeting "The
Lord be with you" before the reading
of the Gospel, the sign of the cross
traced on the Gospel book and on the
forehead, lips and chest of the
reader, the kissing of the Gospel
book by the celebrant following the
Reading. The use of a special book
containing the Gospels similarly
holds a symbolic significance, along
with the fact that one stands during
its reading, whereas one remains
seated during the other readings.)

Prefiguring the Gospel reading, in accordance with
St. Augustine's formula—"In vetere Testamento Novum
latet"—the Psalms were equally notable. Beginning with
the *Judica me*, recited by the pontiff before vesting as early
as St. Gregory, the Psalms have served as guiding stars to
orient the various parts of the Mass and to light up the way
for the Gospel. [33] Thereby could the Psalter suffice as a
book of common worship and of private devotion for the
laity; from it would evolve the Hours, that 'best-seller of
the late Middle Ages,'[34] with its extensive use of
Psalms.[35] It is small wonder that this was the most
beloved Old Testament book among the people.[36]

By dint of its preponderant liturgical usage, the
Psalms provided the comfort of the familiar within an
aura of sanctity; hence it moved increasingly into the
domain of the laity and was put both to para-liturgical
and to pragmatic uses, as Leroquais richly
demonstrates.[37] So it served as an abecedary so commonly as to equate "to psalm" with "to read," *psalteratus*
with *litteratus*, as witnessed by a note in the Leyde Psalter
(Leyde, Ms. 318): "Cist psaultiers fu monseigneur saint
Loys qui fu roys de France, auquel il aprist en s'enfance."
(This psalter belonged to my Lord St. Louis, who was King

27

of France; from it he learned in his childhood.) The psalter was also employed, like Vergil's works, for the *sortes sanctorum*: when one was in a quandary, the psalter was opened at random to furnish guidance. And when one had sinned, it was the psalter that frequently supplied the acts of penance: the recitation of the Seven Penitential Psalms was routinely prescribed, but more heinous sins might be assigned many more, sometimes in lieu of fasting on dry bread and water.[38] The Penitential of Egbert of York (735-766), for example, stipulates that seven days of fasting may be replaced by reciting twelve hundred psalms on one's knees, or by reciting sixteen hundred and eighty psalms in the standing or seated position. The psalms were commonly evoked to banish the spectres of fear: the perils of shipwreck, the onslaught of disease, the travail of childbirth, the pain of toothache might be brought to naught by the incantation of the appropriate psalm. And it was with this Word of the Lord that the dying were armed in their final struggle, as was St. Augustine, who had the Penitential Psalms (*psalmos Davidicos qui sunt paucissimi de poenitentia*) transcribed to parchment and mounted the length of the wall, under his eyes, during his final illness.[39] Especially in the monastery was death confronted with the psalms: the brothers wove a singing shroud of psalms around the body in death's final throes and throughout its wait for burial.[40] Indeed, if the psalms were the bulwark of defense against sin and death for the lay folk, how much more indispensable were they for those in the religious life. St. Benedict's *Regula* provided the order for the chanting of the entire psalter every week; one might vary that order, he granted, but never fall short of accomplishing the weekly recitation of the entire Book of Psalms:

> Si cui forte haec distributio psalmorum displicuerit, ordinet, si melius aliter judicaverit: dum omnimodis id attendatur, ut omni hebdomada Psalterium ex integro, numero centum quinquaginta psalmorum psallatur. Et dominico die semper a capite repetatur ad vigilias: quia nimis iners

devotionis suae servitium ostendunt monachi, qui minus a Psalterio cum canticis consuetudinariis per septimanae circulum psallunt: cum legamus q. sanctos Patres nostros uno die hoc strenue implesse, quod nos tepidi utinam septimana integra persolvamus.

(If this arrangement is unsatisfactory to anyone, he may do otherwise if he has thought of a better one. No matter what, all 150 psalms must be chanted during the week so that on Sunday Matins the service may start afresh. Monks who chant less than the entire Psalter, with canticles, each week are slothful in their service to God. Our spiritual fathers performed in one day what we now take a week to do.)[41]

With the Hours told by the chanting of the appropriate psalms and with the liturgical year set forth in the Calendar of its opening pages, the Psalter was the *sine qua non* for the ordering of the temporal as well as the spiritual life of those committed to the *Opus Dei.* Not only was it the clock and the calendar, but the almanac as well: the Calendar indicated the *Dies aegyptiaci (Dies mali)*[42]—the days unfavorable for planting, purging or bloodletting— along with the traditional Labors of the Months;[43] the Computistical Tables directed the reckoning of the date of Easter and, thereby, of the opening of Lent, and of the Feastday of Pentecost. Obviously, this was a book which nobody, and certainly not a body of Benedictines, could be without.

In view of the fact that each Benedictine abbey is self-governing, being bound only to the *Regula*, and existing as a member of a confederation rather than of an Order per se,[44] it is to be expected that individual differences should attach to each of its houses. Thus, as a Benedictine house, St. Albans was its own arbiter of what was fit and proper. And its own particular ambience under Norman supremacy was conducive to the inno-

29

vative, a trait especially associated with its Abbot Geoffrey and encouraged by his absolute authority under the Rule.[45] It is then not astounding that the St. Albans scriptorium should custom-produce so atypical a book as the St. Albans Psalter for one of its family.

[1] L. Duchesne, *Origines du culte chrétien* (Paris: Boccard, 1925), p. 9. Msgr. Duchesne emphasizes the need to distinguish between the worship in the temple of Jerusalem and that in the synagogues: it is from the synagogue worship, i.e., the Diaspora, that the Christian rites developed. The essential elements of synagogue worship comprised collective prayer, reading from the sacred books —the *Law* and the *Prophets*— and the singing of the Psalms. A fourth exercise, less essential, was the homily, the *midrasch*. These four elements —readings, chants, prayers, homilies— were adopted without difficulty by the Christian churches, which supplemented the books of the Jewish Bible with New Testament writings, especially the Gospels.

[2] Old Testament writings were sporadically viewed as unacceptable because they were for and from the Jews, 'crucifiers' of the Christian Lord. See Vigourous, ed., *Dictionnaire de la Bible, Supplément*, tome 9 (Paris, 1979), "Psaumes," col. 211.

[3] Duchesne, p. 10.

[4] See Vigourous, ed., *Dictionnaire de la Bible, Supplément* (Paris, 1979), col. 212, for an account of the accusations of Gnostic contamination.

Hymn singing is cited for Christ and his disciples on the night of the Betrayal (Matt. 26:30); their hymn was probably the Hallel (Psalms 113-118), sung by the Jews at the celebration of the Passover. New Testament Christians sang hymns collectively and privately, according to the Epistles (Acts 16:25; I Cor. 14:26; Eph. 5:19; Col. 3:16), and as advocated by St. Paul: "But be filled with the Spirit, addressing one another in psalms and hymns and spiritual songs, singing and making melody to the Lord with all your heart . . ." (Eph. 5:18-19). In his well-known letter to the Emperor Trajan written in 112-113, Pliny the Younger reports that the Christians of Bithynia were singing hymns to Christ, 'as to a God' (Pliny, *Epis.* X, 96).

A Psalm is itself, of course, a hymn, by definition: "A spiritual meditation designed, or at least suitable for, singing or chanting in the worship of God. [Hence,] the book of Psalms is the earliest hymnbook in existence." (Davis and Gehman, *The Westminster Dictionary of the Bible*, Philadelphia, 1944, p. 261). Other Old Testament 'hymns' include the songs of Moses, Deborah, Hannah, Ezekiel, etc.; New Testament examples are those of Mary (the *Magnificat*) and Zacharias (the *Benedictus*): these find their rightful place in the Psalter as "*Canticles.*"

5 See the excellent summary by C. R. Dodwell, "The Mediaeval Interpretation of the Scriptures" in *The St. Albans Psalter* (London, 1960), Chapter XII, pp. 181-184.

6 Dodwell's translation, *The St. Albans Psalter*, p. 182, Note 1.

7 Dodwell, p. 181.

8 Dodwell, pp. 181-182.

9 Beryl Smalley, *The Study of the Bible in the Middle Ages* (Oxford: Clarendon Press, 1941), p. 1.

10 *In Libros Informationum Litterae et Spiritus super Leviticum Praefatio, PL* CIV, 615-17. Smalley's translation.

11 *Quaest. in Hept.*, II, lxxiii (*PL* XXXVI, 623). The full quotation is: "Multum et solide significatur, ad Vetus Testamentum timorem potius pertinere, sicut ad Novum delectionem: quanquam et in Vetere Novum lateat, et in Novo Vetus pateat." (It is frequently and strongly indicated that fear belongs more to the Old Testament, whereas delight pertains to the New : through and through in the Old Testament is the New Testament concealed, and in the New is the Old revealed). This passage seems to have

been universally quoted without its introductory "*quanquam*", hence, with its verbs in the indicative.

12 Louis Réau, *L'Art du Moyen Age* (Paris: La Renaissance du livre, 1935), p. 26.

13 Cited by Réau, p. 26.

14 *Das Altfranzösische Adamsspiel*, Uda Ebel, ed. (Munich, 1970), p. 118.

15 J. E. Wackernell, *Altdeutsche Passionspiele aus dem Tyrol* (Graz, 1897), p. 409. Wackernell notes that the manuscript in which this play appears bears a date of 1511.

See the discussion of David's appearance in Passion plays by F. P. Pickering, *Literature and Art in the Middle Ages* (Coral Gables: Univ. of Miami Press, 1970), pp. 242-243.

16 See Note 11 and *supra*.

17 The Old Testament abounds, of course, in Christ 'types,' among whom the following are noteworthy: Adam, Job on his dunghill, Isaac on the sacrificial altar, Jonah in the belly of the whale, Daniel in the lions' den.

Comparable to the ambivalence permitting the lion to represent both Christ, the Lion of Judah, and Satan, 'seeking whom he may devour' (I Pet. 5:8), is that casting David both as a Christ 'type' and as a model of the sinning and penitent King, as he is represented in royal psalters. So is he shown in his crimes of murder and adultery on the ivory cover of the Psalter of Charles the Bald (Paris, B.N. MS. lat. 1152).

18 "Quamvis David omnes psalmos cantasset . . . per titulum intelligitur, in cujus persona cantatur, aut in persona Christi, aut in persona Ecclesiae, aut in persona prophetae." Prologue to *Breviarium in Psalmos, PL, XXVI,*

824. (Although David sang all the psalms, it can be known by the title in whose person he was singing, whether in the person of Christ, or in the person of the Church, or in the person of the prophet.)

[19] *Enarratio in Ps. LIX. PL* XXXVI, 713.

[20] Cited in J. J. Tikkanen, *Die Psalterillustration im Mittelalter* (Helsingfors, 1895-1900. Rpt. Soerst: Davaco, 1975), pp. 4- 5.

[21] The contrasting of the Old Adam and of the New Adam is ubiquitous in medieval exegesis. Thus is the first Adam contrasted with the *Beatus Vir* —Christ/David— in the Commentary on the Psalms of Pierre Lombard, Bishop of Paris (d. 1160). The French translation of this gloss, as found in the great B.N. Psalter 8846, for example, begins as follows: "Adam nostre premer pere ne fu mie *beatus vir,* kar il alat al conseil des feluns, del serpent et de Eve, ki li firent la obedience Deu enfreindre; et il estut en la veie des peccheurs quant il se delitat en co ke li serpens et Eve l'a deceu . . .". (Adam, our first father, was not at all a 'blessed man,' for he went according to the counsel of evil-doers, of the serpent and of Eve, who made him break his obedience to God; and he set himself in the ways of sinners when he delighted himself in what the serpent and Eve deceived him [into doing].)

The Latin version (i.e. the original) of this commentary, known as "*la Grande Glose,*" was eminently famous and popular, as is shown by its appearance in a wealth of medieval Parisian manuscripts (see *Albrici chronica*, a. 1156. *Mon. Germ., Script.,* XXXIII, p. 843). On the French translations, see P. Meyer, *Rapport, Archives des Missions*, 1971, pp. 84, 89.

[22] Cook and Herzman, *The Medieval World View* (New York: Oxford Univ. Press, 1983), p. 102.

[23] For the 'genealogy' of the Tree of Jesse, see E. Mâle, *L'Art religieux du XII*[e] *siècle en France* (Paris: A.

Colin, 1924), pp. 168-175. Its appearance in stained glass is exemplified in the windows of Saint-Denis, to which the Abbé Suger devoted such careful attention, and in the northern lancet of Chartres, which Viollet-le-Duc put "at the head of all glassware whatever." (Henry Adams, *Mont-Saint-Michel & Chartres*, 1913. Repr. Garden City: Doubleday, 1959, pp. 142-43.)

Magnificent examples of the *Liber generationis* Tree of Jesse in manuscript are furnished by the following, *inter alia*: the great Paris Psalter, B.N. MS. lat. 8846, folio 6 R; the renowned Gospel Book, Paris B.N. MS. lat. 8892, folios 13R and 19R; the Psalter of Blanche de Castille, Paris Bibl. Ars. MS. 1186.

24 Psalters with preceding pictorial cycles include the eleventh-century Tiberius Psalter (B.M. Cotton MS Tiberius C. iv) and the following twelfth-century manuscripts: the Shaftesbury Psalter (B.M. Lansdowne MS. 383); the Winchester Psalter (also known as the Psalter of Henry of Blois, B.M. Cotton MS. Nero. C. iv); the Glasgow Psalter (Hunterian Mus. MS. 229); the Copenhagen Psalter (Motts Smlg. 143. 2); the Fécamp Psalter (The Hague, Roy. Lib. MS. 76713); the Ingeborg Psalter (Chantilly, Mus. Cond, MS. lat. 1695), along with the fountainhead, the St.Albans Psalter (Hildesheim, Church of St. Godehard.)

The St. Albans Psalter and the B.N. Psalter, lat. 8846, for example, demonstrate christological scenes in the historiated initials of the psalms; on this, see J. J. Tikkanen, *Die Psalterillustration im Mittelalter* (Soest, repr., 1975) and Anton Springer, *Die Psalter-Illustration...im Mittelalter* (Leipzig, 1880).

An example of psalters in which christological illustrations are interspersed among the psalms is furnished by the Troyes Psalter (Paris, B.N. MS. lat. 238).

25 Other Psalms with messianic titles in the Vulgate are the following:

Psalm 2: "*Messias rex Sion
omnisque terrae.*"
(The Messiah, King of
Zion and of all the
earth.)
Psalm 44: "*Carmen nuptiale regis
Messiae.*"
(Nuptial song of the
Messiah King.)
Psalm 71: "*Regnum Messiae.*"
(The Kingdom of the
Messiah.)
Psalm 109: "*Messias rex, sacerdos
victor.*"
(The Messiah: King,
Priest, Victor.)

The identification of Christ as the 'singer' of the
Psalms was evidenced early on by the Church's Psalm
titles, as Louis Jacquet summarizes:

> *Continuer la prière* du Christ, à
> travers les Psaumes, voilà bien la
> façon idéale d'user, aujourd'hui
> comme hier, du psautier.
>
> Dès l'origine de l'Eglise, ce fut le
> souci majeur des fidèles, comme en
> témoignent, après les Pères eux-
> mêmes, les diverses séries des
> "Tituli Psalmorum" des manuscrits
> latins qui, sous leur influx,
> introduisent fréquemment les Ps.—
> avec des variantes— par cette
> mention-type: "Vox Christi (ou
> Ecclesiae) ad Patrem." [Emphasis is
> Jacquet's.]
>
> (*To continue the prayer* of Christ
> through the Psalms, this is indeed

the ideal way to use the psalter,
today as in the past.

At the very origin of the Church,
this was the major concern of the
faithful, as is evidenced, according
to the Fathers themselves, by the
different series of "Psalm Titles" in
Latin manuscripts; under their
influence, the Psalms are frequently
introduced by this typical
designation, [sometimes] with
certain variations: "The Voice of
Christ (or of the Church) to the
Father.")
(L. Jacquet, *Les Psaumes et le coeur
de l'homme*; Belgium: Duculot, 1975,
p. 188).

See also P. Salmon, *Les Tituli Psalmorum des
manuscrits latins* (Paris: Edit. du Cerf, 1959), p. 55 *et
passim.*

26 F. P. Pickering, *Literature & Art in the Middle
Ages* (Coral Gables: Univ. of Miami Press, 1970), p. 285.

27 Pickering, Plates 29b, 30a, 30b.

28 *Enarrat. in Psalmos*, PL XXXVI, 671-2, cited in
Pickering, p. 292

29 This Psalm was for all the Fathers a literal
account of the Crucifixion, especially so because Christ
quoted it while on the Cross, as the Gospel writers
emphasize. St. John in particular stresses that the casting
of lots for Christ's garments took place in order to fulfill
the scripture—Psalm 21:19—, which he quotes verbatim:

Dixerunt ergo ad invicem: Non
scindamus eam [sc. tunicam] sed
sortiamur de illa cuius sit. Ut

Scriptura impleretur, dicens:
Partiti sunt vestimenta mea sibi: et
in vestem meam miserunt sortem.
Et milites quidem haec fecerunt.
(John 19:24)

(They said therefore among
themselves, Let us not rend it, but
cast lots for it, whose it shall be:
that the scripture might be fulfilled,
which saith, They parted my
raiment among them, and for my
vesture they did cast lots. These
things therefore the soldiers did.)

The Mocking, the Thirst, the utter enervation of
Christ in his Passion were all found divinely expressed in
Psalm 21, and the Seventh Last Word, though occurring
literally in Psalm 30:5, was found in essence in Psalm 21.

The basis for the staurocentric interpretation of
this "Passion Psalm" will be readily apparent in the
following excerpts:

Deus, Deus meus, respice in me, quare me
dereliquisti?
Longe a salute mea verba delictorum
meorum.
Deus meus, clamabo per diem, et non
exaudies;
Et nocte, et non ad insipientiam mihi ...
Ego autem sum vermis, et non homo;
Opprobrium hominum, et abiectio plebis.
Omnes vedentes me deriserunt me;
Locuti sunt labiis, et moverunt caput.
Speravit in Domino, eripiat eum:
Salvum faciat eum, quoniam vult eum ...
Circumdederunt me vituli multi;
Tauri pingues obsederunt me.
Aperuerunt super me os suum,
Sicut leo rapiens et rugiens.
Sicut aqua effusus sum;

Et dispersa sunt omnia ossa mea.
Factum est cor meum tanquam cera
liquescens in medio ventris mei.
Aruit tanquam testa virtus mea,
Et lingua mea adhaesit faucibus meis,
Et in pulverem mortis deduxisti me.
Quoniam circumdederunt me canes multi;
Concilium malignantium obsedit me.
Foderunt manus meas et pedes meos,
Dinumeraverunt omnia ossa mea.
Ipsi vero consideraverunt et inspexerunt
me.
Diviserunt sibi vestimenta mea,
Et super vestem meam miserunt sortem.
Tu autem, Domine, ne elongaveris
auxilium tuum a me;
Ad defensionem meam conspice.
Erue a framea, Deus, animam meam,
Et de manu canis unicam meam.
Salva me ex ore leonis,
Et a cornibus unicornium humilitatem
meam ...
      (Ps. 21:1-3;7-9;13-22.)

(My God, my God, why hast thou forsaken me?
Why art thou so far from helping
me, and from the words of my
roaring?
O my God, I cry in the daytime, but
thou hearest not;
And in the night season, and am not
silent ...
But I am a worm, and no man;
a reproach of men, and despised of
the people.
All that see me laugh me to scorn:
they shoot out the lip, they shake
the head, saying,
He trusted on the Lord that he would
deliver him:

Let him deliver him, seeing he
delighted in him ...
Many bulls have compassed me:
strong bulls of Bashan have beset
me round.
They gaped upon me with their
mouths,
as a ravening and a roaring lion.
I am poured out like water,
and all my bones are out of joint:
my heart is like wax; it is melted in
the midst of my bowels.
My strength is dried up like a
potsherd;
and my tongue cleaveth to my jaws;
and thou hast brought me into the
dust of death.
For dogs have compassed me:
the assembly of the wicked have in-
closed me:
they pierced my hands and my feet.
I may tell* all my bones: they look
and stare at me. [* = count]
They part my garments among
them,
and cast lots upon my vesture.
But be not thou far from me, O Lord:
O my strength, haste thee to help me.
Deliver my soul from the sword;
my darling from the power of the
dog.
Save me from the lion's mouth:
for thou hast heard me from the
horns of the unicorns ...)
  (King James Version.)

For a summary of the Patristic tradition for this
psalm and its manifestation in art, see Pickering, pp. 280
et passim.

30 See Duchesne, *Origines du culte chrétien*, pp. 110-23.

31 V. Leroquais, *Les Sacramentaires et les Missels manuscrits des bibliothèques publiques en France* (Paris: Mâcon, Protat, 1924), p. xi.

32 Herman Schmidt, *"Les lectures scripturaires dans la liturgie," Concilium* 112 (1976), pp. 125-243.

33 Andrew Hughes, *Medieval Manuscripts for Mass and Office* (Toronto: Univ. of Toronto Press, 1982), p. 83.

34 So described by Dr. L. M. J. Delaissé, as quoted by John Harthan, *The Book of Hours* (New York: Park Lane, repr. 1977), p. 9.

35 See Leroquais, *Les Livres d'heures manuscrits de la Bibliothèque Nationale*, vol. I, *"L'Histoire du livre d'heures,"* pp. ix- xxxviii, wherein he traces the evolution of the Hours from the Psalter: "J'aurais pu intituler ce chapitre: Du psautier au livre d'Heures ... Or, à l' époque carolingienne et jusqu'au XIIIe siècle, le livre de prière des fidèles était le psautier ... En réalité, les premiers livres d'Heures sont une combinaison du psautier et du livre d'Heures ..." (I could have entitled this chapter "From the psalter to the Book of Hours". . . For, from the Carolingian era onward, up to the thirteenth century, the layman's book of prayer was the psalter . . . In fact, the first Books of Hours are a combination of the psalter and the Book of Hours.) (pp. ix, x, xi).

36 Cook and Herzman, p. 6.

37 Chanoine V. Leroquais, *Les Psautiers manuscrits latins des bibliothèques de France* (Mâcon, 1940-41). Msgr. Leroquais' Introduction, in Vol. I of this work, furnishes the best summary of the importance of the psalter in the Middle Ages; his remarks in reference to the evolution of the Hours from the Psalter in Vol. I, *Les Livres d'heures manuscrits de la Bibliothèque Nationale* (Paris,

1927) are also of great value. See also Pierre Riché, *Les Ecoles et l'Enseignement dans l'Occident Chrétien* (Paris: Aubier Montaigne, 1979), pp. 223-225. Riché shows that the psalter, though originally used only in monastic schools, became *the* primary textbook everywhere: it was used to teach reading, writing and chanting. Moreover, it provided moral as well as practical instruction:

En même temps qu'il lisait, l'élève devait savoir par coeur les psaumes. Les hagiographes aiment à représenter l'enfant sur les genoux de sa mère, d'une religieuse, ou auprès d'un moine, répétant les versets les uns après les autres au point de s'endormir, et se réveillant, connaissant parfaitement le texte. Ainsi s'appliquait la parole du psalmiste: "Ego somnio et cor meum vigilat ..." La culture du Haut Moyen Age est une culture que l'on pourrait appeler psalmodique. (pp. 223-24).

(At the same time that he was reading [them], the pupil was supposed to learn the psalms by heart. Hagiographers love to picture the child on the knees of his mother, or of a nun, or beside a monk, [there] repeating the verses one after another, to the point of falling asleep, and, upon awakening, knowing the text perfectly. Thus was accomplished the words of the psalmist: "I sleep and my heart keeps watch. . . "

The culture of the High Middle Ages is a culture which could be called psalmodic.)

[38] Leroquais, *Les Psautiers* ..., p. xi.

[39] Leroquais, *Les Livres d'heures* ..., pp. xx-xxi, is referring to Possidius' *Vita sancti Augustini episcopi PL*, XXXII, 576. "[N]am sibi jusserat Psalmos Davidicos, qui sunt paucissimi de poenitentia, scribi, ipsosque quaterniones jacens in lecto contra parietem positos diebus suae infirmitatis intuebatur, et legebat, et jugiter ac ubertim flebat." (For he ordered that the Psalms of David which are those few Penitential Psalms be written out for him, in order that while lying in bed during his final illness he could look upon them, mounted the length of the four walls, and read them; and he wept constantly and copiously.) The Seven Penitential Psalms, as established by Cassiadorus, are VI, XXXI, XXXVII, L, CI, CXXIX, CXLII.

[40] Leroquais, *Les Psautiers* ..., p. ix.

[41] *Benedicti Regula, S.*, Cap. XVIII. Tr., *The Rule of St. Benedict*, Meisel and Mastro (Garden City: Image, 1975), p. 68.

[42] See R. Steele, *"Dies Aegyptiaci"* in *Proceedings of the Royal Society of Medicine* (History of Medicine Section), vol. XII, 1919, pp. 108-121.

[43] See Henry Webster, *The Labors of the Months in Antique and Medieval Art to the End of the Twelfth Century* (Princeton: Princeton Univ. Press, 1938).

[44] Cf. Cabrol and Leclercq, *Dictionnaire d'archéologie chrétienne et de liturgie* (Paris, 1925), col. 663-670: "D'après ce qui précède, on a vu que, dans l'esprit de saint Benoît, le monastère doit se suffire à lui-même; il forme un petit Etat ..." (According to what precedes, it is evident that, in St. Benedict's mind, the monastery must suffice unto itself; it forms one small State . . .) (666). See also *New Catholic Encyclopedia* (New York/St. Louis, 1967), Vol. II: 'The Order of St. Benedict (OSB) signifies not a centralized institute but the confederated congregations

of the monks and nuns following the Rule of St. Benedict .... Each monastery is an autonomous family, bound by only weak links to other monasteries of the same congregation and by no juridical ties to the rest of the confederation." (p. 288).

[45] In accordance with the *Regula*, the Benedictine community was seen as a family, whose abbot was the father: "Abba, Pater" (c. II); "Abbas autem, quia vices Christi agit, Dominus et abbas vocetur." (The Abbot, indeed, who acts as the vicar of Christ, is to be called Lord and [Father] Abbot.) (c. LXIII). So, as Cabrol and Leclercq point out, his person is omnipotent:

> Celui-ci est élu par le suffrage de toute la communauté; ses pouvoirs sont à vie; son autorité sur le monastère est très étendue; il gouverne, il administre, il régit, il instruit; il est chargé de gérer les intérêts financiers du monastère, aussi bien que ses intérêts spirituels. Il nomme ses officiers auxquels il distribue toutes les charges du monastère, et peut les destituer. Il commande directement ou indirectement à tous ceux qui vivent dans le monastère. Il a le droit de punir, d'excommuniquer et même de chasser du monastère les rebelles et les mécréants ...
> (DACL, Vol. II, col. 668-69)

> (This one is elected by the vote of the entire community; his powers are for life; his authority over the monastery is exceedingly far-reaching; he governs, he administers, he rules, he instructs; he is charged with administering the financial matters of the

monastery as well as attending to its spiritual interests. He names his [own] officers, to whom he distributes all the assignments of the monastery, and he can dismiss them. He is in command, directly or indirectly, over all who live in the monastery. He has the right to punish, to excommunicate rebels and miscreants, and even to evict them from the monastery.)

CHAPTER III

THE SAINT ALBANS PSALTER

The St. Albans Psalter constitutes a landmark both in English art and in French literature. It is remarkable both for its opening forty-page pictorial cycle and for its *Alexis*, the first major literary work in the French language.[1] It is cross-cultural in its peregrinations as well as in its contents. The Psalter was most probably executed at the Benedictine Abbey of St. Albans, some forty miles northwest of London, ca. 1123. Sometime prior to 1657, it journeyed to Lamspringe Abbey in Germany with English Benedictines, and, following the suppression of Lamspringe (ca. 1803), finally came to the Church of St. Godehard in Hildesheim, whose property it remains.[2] The St. Albans Psalter was first studied as an *objet d'art* by Adolph Goldschmidt in his 1895 work, *Der Albanipsalter in Hildesheim*; this is viewed as "a classic in the history of the study of manuscripts."[3] It was in this study that Goldschmidt established the birthplace of the St. Albans Psalter and dubbed its leading artist *"der Alexiusmeister."* More recently, the Warburg Institute has published its facsimile edition, the work of Otto Pächt, C. H. Dodwell and Francis Wormald.[4] Their study embraces not only an analysis of all the artistic elements of the Psalter, but considers, as well, the circumstances of its composition, including an evaluation of the inclusion of the Old French poem. Crucial to Pächt's assessment of the Psalter is the twelfth-century anchorite Christina of Huntingdon, who was an inmate and, later, Prioress, of Markyate, a cell of St. Albans: it is for her, it would appear from entries in the Calendar, that the St. Albans Psalter was produced. Like Alexis of the Old French poem, Christina had fled the marriage bed for a life of chastity: it is for her vindication, Pächt deduces, that *la Vie de Saint Alexis* was included, as *une pièce justificative*, in the Psalter. Thus would it seem that any over-all study of the St. Albans Psalter must take into account the presence therein of the Old French poem. And any consideration of the Alexis *matière* —legend, cult, and poem— must likewise include the St. Albans Psalter and the special purpose which the *Alexis* served therein.

This twelfth-century Anglo-Saxon manuscript is, by all accounts, a landmark in art history. Pächt cites its importance as the only extant pre-Romanesque (English) example starting with a cycle of pictures. As such, he finds, it represents a startling break from its contemporaries in English art. For the Normans had extended their 'conquest' into the realm of art, transplanting their own style of illumination —the inhabited scroll—[5]and imposing, thereby, a virtual ban on pictorial narration in religious art. The sudden appearance of a full-fledged picture cycle is, then, of an epoch-making magnitude, which Pächt describes as follows:

> This unparalleled outburst of pictorial narrative is one of the most astonishing phenomena in the history of medieval art, second in importance only to the sudden rise of monumental sculpture.[6]

The result of this innovation was to change the course of all Western devotional manuscripts, for this fountainhead gave rise to the long line of English psalters —and, by their influence, of Continental ones— in which the image so profusely illuminates the text.[7] Such celebrated volumes as the St. Louis Psalter, the Psalter of Blanche de Castille and the Fécamp Psalter are among those which follow in its tradition.[8] These, in turn, would give rise to the enormously popular Hours, so universally aspired to by all estates —from sturdy Burgermeister to royal bibliophile— that they form the largest single category of manuscripts that now exists.[9]

The Albani Psalter, from which derives such a profusion of pictured books of course had certain English precedents.[10] The famed Utrecht Psalter (ca. 830 A.D.),[11] for example, having migrated to England before the year 1000, had been copied at least three times in Canterbury, notably in the Harley Psalter (Brit. Mus. Harley 603).[12] A native English psalter, the Cotton Tiberius (Brit. Mus. Cotton Tiberius, C. VI), was produced, probably in Winchester, before the Conquest, thus pre-dating the Albani volume by about a century.[13] But the St. Albans Psalter differs markedly, in make-up, style, medium or scope, from such predecessors.

Unlike the Utrecht Psalter (and its copies), which illustrates the Psalms phrase by phrase in monochromic line drawings, the Albani Psalter presents forty full-page miniatures in painted color, their subjects and placement far distant from the Psalms. Its scope surpasses that of the Tiberius Psalter, whose nineteen illustrations, while preceding the Psalms, are executed in outline drawing, and are more limited in the range of subjects —the Ancient of Days, scenes of David, an abbreviated christological series, and the archangel Michael doing battle with the Dragon.[14]

The St. Albans Psalter, by contrast, is revolutionary in its bold exploitation of the pictorial narrative. Its forty full-page paintings stand separate, and completely on their own merits, without a word of authenticating text; and they range from *Principio* —the story of Adam and Eve in the Garden— to the current *seculum* —the legend of St. Martin. So revolutionary, indeed, was such a procedure that the Albani designer apparently felt behooved to place further on in the Psalter a letter of St. Gregory in defense of such gratuitous art. And to leave no doubt, he furnished its Old French translation as well.

One's initial glimpse of the St. Albans Psalter[15] does not suggest that it is of such pre-eminence: it is a small volume (27.6 x 18.4 cm.) of much-mended pigskin over wooden boards, thus lacking both the dimensions and the magnificent covers of such volumes as the Paris Gospel Book (B.N. lat. 8894), for example. But the viewing of its 418 vellum pages (209 folios) confirms art historians' judgment that the St. Albans Psalter is an exceptional work, both for the choice of its contents and for the quality of their execution.[16]

The Psalter contains, of course, the standard elements of a work of its genre: a Calendar, Computistical Tables, the Psalms, the Canticles, the Litany, the Creeds and Prayers. But there is more. Immediately after the practical matter of the Calendar and the Computistical Tables, there unfold forty full-page miniatures, painted in full color, now mellowed to gentle tones of blue, green, brown and mauve.[17]

This forty-page segment is followed by a page (f° 57r°) whose top half is devoted to tinted drawings of scenes from the life of St. Alexis, inscribed with Latin *tituli*;[18] its

49

lower half contains the 'Prologue' to the Old French poem (untitled) which follows (beg. f° 58v°). Its own initial B[ons] (*fut li secles*) is gracefully ornamented. On the last page of the *Alexis*, there appears another unusual element: the well-known reply of St. Gregory to 'Secundinus'[19] in defense of religious art, and its translation into Old French ("*Aliud est picturam adorare . . . /Altra cose est aurier la painture . . . "*). Following this letter there appear three more full-page tinted drawings, of the Supper at Emmaus. All of these highly unusual pictorial elements — the forty-page 'christological' series, the *Alexis* illustrations, the Emmaus cycle— are held to be the creation of the Alexis Master, whose handiwork continues on the first page of the next component, the Gallican Psalter.[20]

Here appears the celebrated *Beatus Vir* historiated initial, which so emphasizes its story as to make it, rather, a letter-framed picture. Herein, King David is majestically enthroned within the lower portion of the *B*. Above him, a strong and wonderful bird, as befits the Holy Spirit, arches in half to speak into the ear of the King. David is playing a harp with his right hand; with his left, he holds an open book whose words reveal it to be his Psalter: *Annunciationem sancti spiritus eructavit beatus david psalmista quem deus legit* (the blessed David as psalmist indited the Annunciation of the Holy Spirit). Thus, as Pächt notes, "we are shown simultaneously the act of composing the psalms and the finished work, the Psalter itself."[21] In a further manifestation of his innovativeness and assertiveness, the Alexis Master appropriates the margin for a painstaking explanation of his Beatus David, lest we miss its significance: "a unique case," Pächt affirms, "of a medieval artist describing and interpreting his own work."[22]

Nor is this the sum total of the Alexis Master's providing both image and exegesis: above the *B*[eatus Vir] is a small drawing of two fighting knights, and, in order that we understand that this represents "bellum spiritualiter" rather than "corporaliter," a thorough commentary, begun on the preceding page, glosses this scene. Such a commentary would be especially appropriate, as Pächt remarks,[23] for monks who must relentlessly wage an intense struggle against the inner forces of evil, which the margin commentary takes pains

50

to point out: "de illo bello et divina hereditate mediantur die ac nocte boni claustrales. . . ." ('day and night do good monks meditate about that war and [their] divine inheritance.').

Now, appropriately, is laid before us the heavy 'armor of the Lord,' the Psalms, in Jerome's Gallican version, along with the Canticles, non-Davidic Psalms, as it were. The Psalms are prefixed by historiated initials, replete with illustrations of David and of Christ;[24] they were executed, not by the Alexis Master, but by the "artist of the initials."[25]

The last two pages of the Psalter are again devoted to full-page miniatures, also painted by the artist of the initials, according to Francis Wormald. The first depicts David as a musician, the second, the Martyrdom of St. Alban. Wormald finds the position of these two miniatures in the Psalter "remarkable" and judges it "highly probable that they were intended originally to come before the Psalter." He deduces that the introduction of the forty full-page miniatures and of the Life of St. Alexis would have occasioned their being relegated to the end of the Psalter.[26]

Indeed, the presence of the Old French Life, together with that of a free-standing series of full-page miniatures in the Psalter, has long caused wonder and speculation among students of both medieval art and literature. What might have prompted the conceiver of this volume to include within the 'canon' of the standard psalter such disparate elements as a 'pleasing song' and a veritable picture book? For the framer of the St. Albans Psalter presents an innovation which is nothing short of startling: a unique combination of art, literature and music (the Psalms). His addition of a pictorial cycle, though it had certain timid precedents, would be a fountainhead, as we have seen; subsequent psalters would routinely incorporate such an element. His introduction of a vernacular text into a devotional/liturgical book is more singular. Might not there be a master plan which would give meaning to this revolutionary procedure? Surely the mind and the imagination responsible for so bold a venture and for so careful an execution would first have envisaged the ensemble, scanning its structure, its media and their effect and purpose. I would propose that such a mind and such an eye 'dared frame' a *careful* symmetry.

51

According to my understanding, the St. Albans Master, designer of the Psalter, conceived it as a triptych whose opening 'panel' would show a forty-page pictorial series, whose center would present an ambi-media image in the "cançun" of St. Alexis, and whose third 'panel' would consist of the Psalms and Canticles. In such a schema, the Calendar and Computistical Tables, at the beginning of the Psalter, and the Creeds, Litany and Prayers, which follow the Psalms, would provide a framework of secular time and of the *secula seculorum* respectively. The three main elements of the Psalter —I. the pictorial cycle, II. the Old French poem, III. the Psalms— would partake of one another by "reciprocal illumination," all the while preserving their individual identity —a *Beata Trinitas, tria juncta in uno.* To find the *Pater* in the Psalms of King David, the *Filius* in the 'christological' cycle and the *Spiritus* working out the will of God in the *Alexis* of this world would perhaps be excessive. But to perceive a ternary design for the Psalter is eminently plausible: such a concept would allow for a terrestrial image of the celestial Trinity.

Such a reference would of course be in keeping with the all-pervading medieval understanding of the God-ordained value of numbers, by which the universe had been created, as St. Augustine had enounced:

> ...Plato Deum magna auctoritate commendat mundum numeris fabricantem. Et apud nos Deo dictum legitur: Omnia in mensura et numero et pondere disposuisti.

> (For Plato emphasizes that God created the world by the use of numbers. And we have the authority of Scripture, where God is thus addressed: Thou has set all things in order by measure, and number, and weight.)
> *De Civitate Dei*, XL, 30

In accordance with this understanding, numbers had a mystical significance, by dint of participating in the imagination and creation of God.

Allusion to this symbolism is most ingeniously and consummately executed, without doubt, in the *Divine Comedy*, whose creator planned the whole structure according to symbolic numbers, beginning with the sacrosanct three, symbol of the Holy Trinity, by which the concept would be effected in *terza rima.*[27] Within the *Alexis* itself, aside from its 'tri-partite' host, the St. Albans Psalter, scholars have perceived a numerically oriented structure as well. Anna Granville Hatcher decoded systematic number patterns in her "Mathematical Demonstration"; Eleanor Bulatkin detected the "powers of five" throughout the poem's composition; James Atkinson has inventoried twelve triplet sequences as "a modest but intimate part of the poem's structure."[28]

Nor is numerology limited to the composition of a literary text: legend credits Charlemagne with founding an abbey for every letter of the alphabet (22);[29] and, of special relevance to book design, a twelfth-century Syrian manuscript included 24 full-page miniatures in correspondence with the 24 letters of the Syriac alphabet.[30]

A reference to the Trinity by means of a tri-partite design for a book would be especially fitting. By means of such a concept's being there made manifest, things invisible might be made discernible through the visible, as St. Augustine had decreed: "Invisibilia enim ipsius, a creatura mundi, per ea quae facta sunt intellecta conspiciuntur." ([Things] of the invisible [world] itself are perceived by a creature of the world through those things which, having been made visible, are understood.) (*Epis. ad Rom.* 1:20).

Indeed, that the mind of God is implicit in a 'book' partakes of an old tradition, as Curtius has well noted in characterizing Christianity as "a religion of the Holy book."[31] At least as far back as St. Augustine, Creation itself was seen as a book, the Book of God's Works, which accords with another, the Book of His Word, the Scriptures: "In principio verbum" thus implies "in principio Creator/Auctor." There was seen, as well, a third book, the Book of Memory, which tells of History, either personal or universal.[32] Like its model, the Bible, the Book of History is eschatological: from the beginning, it thinks from the end. And, as Jeffrey describes it, this book is itself tri-partite: "history was seen as unfolding, like a triptych or the pages of a book, in a pre-determined narrative."[33]

Under such an aura, the making of a book could not fail to suggest an imitation of the Creator, an "*imitatio mentis et manus Dei.*" Such a reference is frequent in medieval iconography, as seen in a twelfth-century Missal of Limoges (Paris B.N. MS. lat. 9438) which Jeffrey offers as an example. Herein, Christ in Majesty is enthroned within a mandorla inscribing two circles, the eternal and the temporal worlds. He holds a book, which is understood both as the Book of Life and the Book of his Gospel, translated by the four Evangelists who appear in the corners, their own books in hand.[34] A similar understanding is invited in the St. Albans Psalter's scene of the Annunciation, where the Virgin holds her book, and, most especially, in its Beatus David, who holds his book open so that we may read of his authorship.[35] Moreover, a full fifty-three of the St. Albans Psalm initials, two of the Canticles, the *Te Deum*, the *Magnificat*, the Nicene and the Athanesian Creeds, and three Collects all include books in their illustrations.

But the image of the book is not limited to scriptural models, as is shown elsewhere by another example, "St. Augustine vs. Felicianus," in which three books are offered to our eyes.[36] The nimbed St. Augustine is regally positioned on a *faldestol*; against his knee rests a thick and handsome book on which rests the Doctor's hand with two fingers upheld toward his supreme authority, the haloed Christ above. Christ himself holds a book and duplicates the gesture of St. Augustine. Thus, as Jeffrey affirms, does St. Augustine "make the case for authority on the grounds that his own words inhere in the higher truth of the Word, the uncreated Logos incarnated in Christ and translated in His book."[37] By contrast, alongside the imposing St. Augustine there stands a small and insignificant figure: *unhappy* Felicianus, who foolishly points to himself as his only authority for the measly book which he holds.

Especially in a Benedictine scriptorium, as was St. Albans, would the making of a book most surely be counted as an *Opus Dei.* And in view of the understanding that God had created his Book (of Works) by measure and by number, such a *modus operandi* would be especially appropriate in producing a Book of God's Words, the St. Albans Psalter, into which would be incorporated excerpts from the Book of History —the Life of Alexis and the pictorial *exempla*.

That there are forty pictures in the opening segment surely reflects the understanding of numbers as symbolic and of their allegorical use in this Psalter.[38] The number forty would, thereby, be associated with the forty days of the Flood and with the Israelites' forty years of wandering in the desert. Both of these events would be seen by medieval exegists as prefiguring Christ's forty days in the wilderness prior to the beginning of his ministry, as is commemorated by the Quadragesima. Thus is the number forty, per se, symbolic of a preparation. As such, it is altogether fitting and proper that forty pictures should precede the Life of Alexis, *imitator Christi.*

Moreover, this series of forty miniatures comprises three subject groups: (I) Adam and Eve; (II) Jesus Christ; (III) St. Thomas, St. Martin, the Ascension, Pentecost, David. Groups I and III may be seen as the outer panels of yet another conceptual triptych whose central image is Christ in his *mortal* life, i.e., from his birth through the resurrection. (And, thus, not including the Annunciation nor the post-Resurrection scenes.) Indeed, their own outermost pictures portray the two prime *praefigurae Christi*, the First Adam and the royal progenitor, David. Most significantly, the scenes in the center segment, II, total thirty-three, a number which must surely be understood as representing the number of years Christ spent on earth.[39] Conspicuously —and astonishingly— missing from these christological scenes is that one most central to *Christkunst* whether on Evangelary cover, above the altar, or on decorated page: the Crucifixion.[40] Might not this scene have been expressly omitted not only to conform to the number thirty-three —for some other scene could surely have been left out— but in order to provide more fitting an analogy with that Life for which the pictorial cycle prepares the way: that of Alexis? His martyrdom was not by human hands, but his life was spent in suffering, his death was expiatory, and his after-life, as a Confessor saint, is intercessory: all of these are functions of Jesus Christ as well. At first blush, it might seem blasphemous to use Jesus Christ as the 'Forerunner' of a mere mortal. But, considering that Christ is the *model* for every *imitator Christi*, what could be more appropriate than to show the pattern for the life of Alexis? It is, indeed, the 'exception' that proves the rule, and as such, it is so novel a treatment as would seem consistent with the spirit of the framer of this innovative Psalter.

In view of the symbolism of the Book in medieval art and thought, and of the reference to this symbolism within its very pages, the St. Albans Psalter would seem then to be the 'Book of Works' of a 'creator' who had imagined and realized a well-ordered creation.[41] His Book of Works encases both his Master's Book of Words, the Psalms, and his own handiworks, images of the Adams made in God's image, from the First to the Second and on to a latter-day Second Adam, St. Alexis. All of them provide an insight both into the divine imagination and purpose and into our own individual and human experience, to wit:

> Omnis mundi creatura,
> Quasi liber et pictura
> Nobis est, et speculum.
> Nostræ vitae, nostræ mortis,
> Nostri status, nostræ sortis
> fidele signaculum.
> > *(magistri alani rhythmus*
> > *alter..., PL* CCD, 419.*)*

> (All the creatures of the world
> Are, like a book and picture,
> A looking glass for us.
> Our life and our death,
> Our present state, our passing on
> Faithfully are signified.)
> > Alain de Lille

So is the Old Adam reconciled to God by the New. Both of them, "faithfully signified" in the forty-page pictorial cycle of the St. Albans Psalter, are further represented by the Old Man and the New Man in the person of Alexis. And through him can we, the hearers and beholders, live an *imitatio Christi* vicariously —as did the woman at St. Albans who took his name: Christina.[42]

NOTES - CHAPTER III

1 The **L** manuscript, the *Alexis* of the St. Albans Psalter, is generally granted primacy by linguistic and literary scholars who assign to it a date of ca. 1120, with the dating of the Psalter partly in view. The **S** manuscript is judged to date from the twelfth century; the Vatican ms., **V**, is placed at mid-twelfth century; the **A**, toward the end of the twelfth century; the **P**, in the thirteenth. See C. Storey, ed., *La Vie de Saint Alexis* (Geneva: Droz, 1968), pp. 28-29.

2 The Church of St. Godehard has been most gracious in putting its priceless treasure at my disposal, beginning with my first 'pilgrimage' in 1971 and continuing on through my ensuing ones. I offer my deepest thanks to Pastor Theiler, to Bruder Wolpers, to Herr Winzel, and to the other members of Alexis's new 'family' in Hildesheim.

3 So called by T. S. R. Boase, *English Art, 1100-1216*. (Vol. 3 of *The Oxford History of English Art*. Oxford: Clarendon Press, 1953), p. 102. Adolph Goldschmidt, *Der Albanipsalter in Hildesheim und seine Beziehung zur symbolischen Kirchensculptur des XII. Jahrhunderts* (Berlin, 1895).

4 Otto Pächt, C. R. Dodwell, Francis Wormald, *The St. Albans Psalter (Albani Psalter)* (London: the Warburg Institute, 1960). This edition of the Albani Psalter constitutes a veritable *florilegium* of the Middle Ages.

5 An "inhabited scroll" aims at decorating the page in toto, in a complex ornamental design; it may be compared to a "carpet page" in this respect. The inhabited scroll was characteristic of Norman illustration, which had no place for proper picture books. Pictorial narrative, on the other hand, aims at telling a story by featuring illustrative scenes; it is especially associated with medieval English art. I have gleaned this information from Otto Pächt, *The Rise of Pictorial Narrative in Twelfth-Century England* (Oxford: Clarendon Press, 1962), pp. 21 ss.

6 Pächt, *The Rise of Pictorial Narrative* ..., p. 13. See also pp. 21 ss.

7 There is, of course, a long tradition of illustrated manuscripts, from those of Vergil onward. Among liturgical books, the Gospels —e.g. the Lindisfarne, the Echternach— were especially favored with this addition. The Missal of Robert of Jumièges (Rouen, Bibl. mun. Y 6) is an eleventh-century English example of this practice, though its pictures, unlike those of the St. Albans Psalter, are not colored. For an overview of the illustrated book's line of descent, from Carolingian examples to Anglo-Saxon and Romanesque manuscripts, see C. R. Dodwell, *The Canterbury School of Illumination* (Cambridge: Univ. Press, 1954). See also David Diringer, *The Illuminated Book* (London: Praeger, 1967); J.-B. Sylvestre, *Universal Paleography*, ed. Sir F. Madden (London, 1850); N. R. Ker, *Medieval Libraries of Great Britain*, 2nd ed. (London: Roy. Hist. Soc., 1964), for precedents to the St. Albans Psalter.

8 The St. Louis Psalter, Paris, Bibl. nat., Ms. lat 10525; the Psalter of Blanche de Castille, Paris, Bibl. Ars. Ms. 1186; the Fécamp Psalter, The Hague, Royal Lib., Ms. 76. F. 13.

9 John Harthan, *The Book of Hours* (London/New York: Park Lane, 1982), p. 11.

10 As well as non-English ones, of course. See Note 7 *supra*.

11 The Utrecht Psalter: Utrecht, Univ. Lib., Script. eccl. 484. See E. T. de Wald, *The Illustrations of the Utrecht Psalter* (Princeton: Princeton Univ. Press, 1932) and Suzy Dufrenne, *Les Illustrations du Psautier d'Utrecht* (Paris: Ophrys, 1978).

12 The Utrecht Psalter's copies: The Harley Psalter (London, Brit. Mus., Harley 603); The Eadwine (or Canterbury) Psalter (Cambridge, Trin. Col., No. R. 17. 1).

58

Facsimile ed., M. R. James, *The Canterbury Psalter* (London: 1935); "The Great Psalter of Paris" (my nomenclature, to avoid confusion with Paris B.N. gr. 139, known as "the Paris Psalter"), Paris, Bibl. nat. lat. 8846. Editions: Benjamin Thorpe, *Libri Psalmorum Versio Antiqua Latina* (Oxford, 1935); J. W. Bright and R. L. Ramsay, *Liber Psalmorum: The West Saxon Psalms* (Boston and London, 1907), a prose version of the first fifty psalms; George Krapp, *The Paris Psalter and the Metres of Boethius* (*Anglo-Saxon Poetic Records*, v. 5, New York, 1932), the remaining psalms, in verse. For the Old French interlinear gloss of the Psalms in this Psalter, see M. Francisque Michel, *Le Livre des Psaumes, ancienne traduction française, publiée d'après les manuscrits de Cambridge et de Paris* (Collection, *Documents inédits*, Paris, 1876).

13 This Psalter is dated as mid-eleventh century. See A. P. Campbell, ed., *The Tiberius Psalter* (Ottawa: Univ. of Ottawa Press, 1974); Francis Wormald, ed., *An English Eleventh-Century Psalter with Pictures* (London: Walpole Society XXXVIII, 1960-62), and his *English Drawings of the Tenth and Eleventh Centuries* (London: Faber and Faber, 1952).

14 Campbell provides plates of three of these illustrations. See also T. S. R. Boase, pp. 219-20.

15 The following is a very general description. For a more precise one, please refer to the summary which I have prepared from Wormald's "Description of the Manuscript," Appendix I. It should be noted that this Description's *cumencer, cancan, raison, nun* should be *cumencet, cancun, raisun, num.*

16 Such an assessment is evidenced by, and in, the works of the eminent St. Albans art scholars, A. Goldschmidt (1895) and its Warburg editors (1960). See, as well, Margaret Rickert, *Painting in Britain in the Middle Ages* (London, 1954; Baltimore: Penguin, 1954), p. 78 ss., and T. S. R. Boase, pp. 101-02.

59

¹⁷ Boase notes coloring as one of the elements distinguishing Norman (= post-Conquest) painting from Saxon: "Changes are equally distinct with regard to the colouring, where brighter shades of a more primary character were substituted for the delicate, gentle, blended tones so dear to the Saxon artists; brilliant reds, greens, and blues were thus in particular favour in place of the pinks, greyish-greens, or violet-blues so often found in Saxon work." (p. 221). He cites the St. Albans Psalter as typical of the Norman style. In his description of the "Albani Psalter," he defines its coloring more exactly, in speaking of the Alexis Master: "The artist of these scenes [the 40-page cycle] is the dominant personality of the book and a man of remarkable gift, though much of his work, painted in rich but sombre colours, olive green, dark brown, greyish blue, and a somewhat livid purple, is of a harsh and forbidding nature." (p. 105). To my eye, the colors do, indeed, appear more somber than brilliant.

¹⁸ See Appendix II-a. The first scene shows Alexis handing over to his bride a large (bracelet-sized) ring and holding out his sword, whose streamers she grasps. A small and graceful bird above points its beak close to the face (ear?) of Alexis. The titulus for this scene is: *Beatus alesis/puer electus.* (Blessed Alexis/chosen youth.) The second scene depicts Alexis heading out of the open door; his wife, standing within, holds a hand to her jaw. The titulus for this scene: *O sponsa beata/semper gemebunda.* (Oh blessed wife, endlessly sighing). These two scenes are set within an architectural frieze. The third scene is outdoors: Alexis is standing in the boat and paying "*sum pris*" to the boatman. From the sail, a large hand (*Manus Dei*, no doubt) is emerging, and pointing to Alexis. The boat is seaborne: three fishes swim beneath. The titulus: *Ecce benedictus alexis receptus in nave.* (Behold blessed Alexis, received into the ship) At the top of the page, above the three scenes, is the following titulus:

Ultima pudice donantur munera sponse.
Anulus & remge verborum finis & ave.

(Finally, [parting] gifts are offered chastely to the bride. A ring and a swordbelt, with the words "Farewell!" and "Hail!") [cf. the "Vale atque Ave" of Catullus to his dead brother (101).]

This pictorial 'frontispiece' to the *Alexis* is composed, as Pächt notes (p. 121), as a horizontal frieze in the continuous style of narration. The miniature is unique according to Pächt (pp. 139-40) in that it represents the beginning of Alexis's wanderings, rather than the end, as is usually depicted. Pächt sees this choice as appropriate in view of the life of Christina, who effected a similar rejection of marriage and flight from home. We shall consider this choice in the final chapter of this book.

In contrast to these scenes, the preponderantly common iconography of Alexis is the scene of "le Pauvre sous l'escalier." See L. Réau, e.g.: "Il est représenté en *mendiant* avec un *bourdon* de pèlerin, couché sous un escalier ... Son attribut le plus caractéristique, après l'escalier, est la *lettre* qu'il serre dans ses mains raidies par la mort." [Emphasis Réau's] (He is shown as a *beggar*, couched beneath a staircase, with a pilgrim's *bell*... His most characteristic emblem, second [only] to the staircase, is the *letter* which he clutches in his hands, stiffened by death.) (*Iconographie de l'art chrétien*, T. III, *Iconographie des Saints*. Paris, 1958.)

The notable exceptions to the traditional iconography of Alexis —*le Pauvre sous l'escalier*— are:

1. The eleventh-century fresco painting in the church of San Clemente in Rome, which shows: a group of horsemen greeting the trembling pilgrim; a figure deep in thought or prayer; a wind-bent tree; St. Alexis, in death, with the Pope; his father and wife weeping, following their discovery of the dead pilgrim's identity.

61

2. The **S** version of the *Alexis* (B.N. ms. fr. 12471): this is a twelfth-century interpolated redaction, and of a markedly romanticized nature. The miniature prefacing the poem (f. 51 verso) depicts the marriage of Alexis. He and his bride are in the center, his father and his mother are flanking them.

¹⁹ This Gregorian letter was, rather, addressed to Serenus, Bishop of Marseille (Lib. XI, Ep. XIII: See L. M. Hartmann, *Mon. Germ. Hist.* 1889, "*Gregorii I Registrum Epistolarum* " Tom. II, p. 269 ss.). H. Lausberg proposes ("Zum altfranzösischen Alexislied," *Archiv für das Studium der neueren Sprachen*, 194 (1957), p. 165) that the *Alexis* scribe would have taken his citation from Burchard of Worms' *Decreta* (III. Cap. XXXVI, *De pictura*), where the substitution of Secundinus for Serenus had already occurred. I agree with Pächt that the word "inclusus", attached to the name of Secundinus, would be especially appropriate for Christina, a recluse, for whom the St. Albans Psalter appears to have been designed. It would be equally appropriate for Roger the Hermit, her mentor, or, to some degree, for all members of the monastic community.

The Gregorian letter was apparently written, according to Pächt (p. 137), by the scribe-illuminator to whom are also due the Old French translation of the letter, the Prologue to the *Alexis*, the *Alexis* miniatures, and the forty full-page picture cycle which begins the Psalter: the Alexis Master. By reason of his literary/linguistic contributions —the Prologue and the Gregorian letter translation— Pächt proposes that a comparison of their language with that of the *Alexis* itself might reveal that they all knew a common author: the Alexis Master, who would be the author of the *original* Old French *Alexis*, that of the St. Albans Psalter. This is the task to which I set myself earlier; therein I concluded that the language of the Prologue is newer and more natively Anglo-Norman than that of the Poem, and that they issue from different authors. I also deduced that the Gregorian translation is notable for its high incidence of archaisms alongside neologisms in phonology and morphology; this is accepted as an Anglo-Norman characteristic. I found that archaisms are more marked in the Gregorian translation than in the Prologue, and proposed that this is perhaps due to the writer's being bound to his Latin text for the Gregorian translation, whereas the Prologue is a 'thorough-composed' work.

I shall propose in the work at hand that the Gregorian letter should be seen as a defense of the vernacular *Alexis*, as well as of the forty pages of pictures: both of them provide 'images' for instruction, in media accessible to the less erudite. Cf. the dictum of Albertus Magnus: "*Picturae sunt libri laicorum.*" (Pictures are the books of the laity.) (*Sermones*..., ed. F. M. Hippolyte de la Croix, Toulouse, 1883, p. 14.) It should be noted that Lausberg sees the Gregorian letter as an Epilogue ("Prosa-Nachtwort") to the *Alexis*, balancing the Prologue ("Prosa-Incipit") which introduces it. ("Das Prömium des altfrz. Alexiusliedes," *Archiv für das Studium der neueren Sprachen*, 192, p. 38, note 6.)

Here is the full text of the Gregorian letter in its original Latin and in its Old French translation as found in the St. Albans Psalter (reproduced in Appendix II-d, p. 270):

[E]cce responsu[m] sei [sic: sancti] gregorii secundino [sic] incluso ratione de pictu[r] is int[er]roganti.

Aliud est picturam adorare. aliud per picture [sic] historia[m] quid sit adorandu[m] addiscere. Nam quod legentib[us] scriptura hoc ignotis prestat [sic] pictura. q[ui]a in ipsa ignorantes vident quid sequi debeant. In ipsa legunt qui litteras nesciunt. unde & precipue gentibus

pro lectione pictura est. Quod
magnopere tu qui inter gentes
habitas adtendere debueras. ne dum
recto zelo incaute succenderis. fero-
cibus animis scandalum generares.
Frangi g [ergo?] non debuit quod
non ad adorandum in eccliis. set
[sed] ad instruendas solummodo
mentes nescientium constat collo-
catu[m] & quia in locis uenerabilis
s[anct]orum depingi historias non
sine ratione uetustas admisit. si
zelum discrecione condisses sine
dubio et ea que intendebas salubrit
obtinere & collectum gregem non
disperdere. set pocius [sed potius]
poteras congregare. ut pastoris intemeratum nomen excelleret. non
culpa disp[er]soris incumberet.

(Here is the reply of St. Gregory to Secundinus the Recluse
when he was asked for a reason for paintings.

It is one thing to adore a painting,
and it is another thing to learn
through the story of the painting
what is to be adored. For what writing exhibits to readers, this a painting exhibits to the unlearned; for in
it the unlearned see what they ought
to follow. In it the illiterate, who do
not know letters, read. For this very
reason, a picture is like a lesson for
the people. Which [thing] you, who
live among the people, ought especially to have heeded; lest, while un-
duly inflamed by righteous zeal, you
should set up a stumbling block for
those of simpler learning. Therefore, that [art] which is in the
churches, [though] not for the purpose of adoration, ought not to be

broken up, but, [rather,] [these paintings] are placed there for the sole purpose of instructing the minds of the unlearned. And, in so much as antiquity has, not without reason, commanded that venerable stories be painted in the places of the saints, even so, if you would temper your zeal with discretion, you might surely achieve the things that you envision and not scatter the assembled flock; but rather gather together the scattered one; so that the unsullied name of the Good Shepherd should prevail, rather than [that] the guilt of the Scatterer should weigh upon you.)

Here is the Old French translation of the Gregorian letter as found in the St. Albans Psalter:

[E]ste vus le respuns saint gregorie asecundin lereclus cum il demandout raison des paintures.

Altra cóse est aúrier lapainture ealtra cose est par le historie de lapainture aprendre quela cóse seit a aúrier. Kar ico que lascripture aprestet as lisanz. ico aprestet lapainture asignoranz. Kar anicele veient les ignoranz quet il deivent siúre. An ícele lisent icele ki letres ne sevent. ampur laquele cose maismement lapeinture est pur leceun as genz. Laquele cóse tu qui habites entra les genz deuses antentra. que tu nangendrasses scandale de crueles curages dementiers que tu esbraseras nient

cuintement I par dreit anvidie.

aluiet
Geres nient ne deut estra fruissiet
ico que nient ne parmaint ad
aurier en eglises. mais ad anstruire
sulement les penses desnient
savans. E ampur ico que
lancienetiet nient senz raisun
cumandat les hystories estra
depaint eshonurables lius des sainz.
se tu se feisses amvidie
pardiscrecion. senz dutanz poies
saluablemt purtenir les cóses que tu
attendeis (&) e nient deperdra la
cuileita folc. mais maisment
asemblier que le nient fraint num
depastur excellist. e nient anioust la
culpa del deperdethur.

[The word *aluiet* is inserted
interlineally in the manuscript.]

(It is one thing to adore the painting
and it is [quite] another thing to
learn through the story [in] the
painting what the thing to be adored
is. For what writing reveals to readers, that the painting reveals to the
illiterate. For in it those who do not
know letters see what they ought to
follow. And for this [very] reason,
[a] painting is like a lesson for the
people. To which [very] thing you,
who live among the people, ought to
have been attentive. Lest all the
while in your punctilious cautious-
ness you carefully refuse to accept
anything, you create a stumbling-
block ("scandale") for those of simpler minds. Scarcely nothing ought
to be destroyed in order that there
remain nothing to be adored in

churches; but [rather, let such things stay,] merely to instruct the thoughts of the unlearned. And [it is] for this [reason] that antiquity, not without reason, ordered that stories be depicted in the venerable places of the saints. If you practice your ardent zeal with discretion, doubtlessly you can perfectly well achieve the things you are attempting and [yet] in no way disperse the gathered flock. But, even, so arrange it that nothing should prevent the good name of the Shepherd to prevail, and that nothing should burden it with the guilt of the Scatterer.)

[N.B. *Scandalum*'s original meaning was "a snare, a trap." By semantic evolution, it came to denote a "stumbling block" and, finally, anything which startles or shocks.]

It will be noted that the Old French translation of this letter exhibits many of the Anglo-Norman characteristics which we have observed in the Prologue to the *Alexis*, e. g., -*u* for -*o*: *pur*; [archaic] -*a* for -*e*: *altra, culpa, estra, antendra*; incorrect gender: *le historie*; proclitic vowels: *ico, icele*; archaic forms: *historie, hystories* vs. *histoire* [influence of liturgical Latin?]. Especially noteworthy is the choice of the Anglo-Norman word *folc* [flock, folk] to gloss the Latin *gregem.*

20 Three versions of the Psalms —the Roman, the Gallican and the Hebrew— are attributed to St. Jerome, and in the following order:

1. The Roman Psalter, *Psalterium Romanum*, is the version which St. Jerome translated from the Septuagint, in all haste, at the re-

quest of St. Damas for the use of the church in Rome, ca. 383 A.D.

2. The *Psalterium Gallicanum* is a more careful revision which St. Jerome undertook between the years 387-391, and which he dedicated to Paula and to Eustochium. This was the version which was particularly adopted by the churches in Gaul, and which would remain in the Vulgate. It would seem to be the prevailing text of the Middle Ages, certainly in French psalters, and, for the main part, in English ones under French influence. It should be noted that the Harley Psalter uses the Roman version, though the Utrecht Psalter, its model, shows the Gallican.

3. The *Psalterium Hebraicum*, St. Jerome's third version, was made directly from the Hebrew text. He dedicated it to Sophronius, c. 405.

All three of these versions are found in those medieval psalters called "Triple Psalters," sometimes furnished with a *Commentario* and with an interlinear vernacular translation of both the commentary and the psalms. In 'the Great Paris Psalter,' for example, the interlinear gloss of the commentary reads as follows:

Adam nostre premer pere ne fu mie *beatus vir*, kar il alat al conseil des feluns, del serpent et de Eve, ki li firent la obedience Deu enfreindre; et il estut en la veie des peccheurs quant il se delitat en co ke li serpenz et Eve la decevent et li promistrent ke il savereit e bien et mal, et serrait cum Deus; ceo est ke il ne murreit ja. E il sist en la chaere de pestilence

68

quant il escusa sun mesfet envers
Deu....

(Adam, our first father, was not at
all a 'Blessed man,' for he walked in
the counsel of the wicked, of the serpent and of Eve, who [pl.] made him
break [his] obedience to God; and he
stood in the way of sinners when he
delighted in what the serpent and
Eve tricked him [into doing]; and
they promised him that he would
know both Good and Evil and would
be like God, that is, that he would
never die. And he sat in the seat of
pestilence when he excused his mis-
deed toward God...)

The gloss of Peter Lombard, Bishop of Paris
(d. 1160), enjoyed an immense popularity in the Middle
Ages; it is conserved in a large number of Parisian
manuscripts, especially. Here are the first words of the
Preface to this "Grande Glose":

Tot premierement encois que nos
lisiem les propheties dou Sautier
que David fist, nos convient aucune
chose defors dire.... Li titles dou
livre si est tex: Ci comence li livres
des hynnes ou des soles paroles dou
profete, de Crist. Titles est uns petiz
escriz que l'en fait de vermeillon sor
les   comencemenz   de   ces
livres....Ynne est loenge de Deu o
chancon et o metre....Saulm en
grezois sone autant come toichiers
en romantz, et de saulm fu apelez
sautiers,   uns   estrumenz   de
musique....Saumes proprement est
la melodie de cel estrument....
(Fol. 5 v⁰, B.N. lat. 8846)

69

(First of all, before we read the prophecies of the Psalter that David made, it is fitting for us to say something additional. . . The title of the book is like this: "Here beginneth the book of hymns or of the very words of the prophet, of Christ." A title is a little writing that one makes in vermillion at the beginnings of these books. . . A hymn is a praise of God with song and with meter. . . *Psalm*, in Greek, is the same as *to pluck* in Romance [i.e. Old French], and from *psalm* came the name *psaltery*, a musical instrument. . . A psalm, properly speaking], is a melody of this instrument.)

This passage is of special interest in our study of the psalter for at least three reasons: it reiterates the medieval understanding that David was a Prophet of Christ; it defines a manuscript's title as a 'rubrique' "in vermillion;" it equates a hymn with a psalm, and gives a respectable definition of *psalm* and *psalter*. Cf. Webster's definitions and etymologies:

psalm ... [From AS *psalm*, *sealm* (fr. LL.), and fr. OF. *salme*, *psaume*, fr. LL. *psalmus*, fr. Gr. *psalmos*, fr. *psallein* to pull, to play upon a stringed instrument.] A sacred song or poem.

psaltery ... [OF. *sautere*, *psalterie*, fr. L. *psalterium* ...] 1. *Music.* An ancient stringed instrument of the zither type. 2. cap. The Psalter.
(Webster's Fifth.)

For the *Grande Glose* of Peter Lombard, see L. M. Hartmann, *Albrici chronica*, a. 1156. *Mon. Germ., Script.,* XXXIII, p. 843; P. Meyer, *Rapport, Archives des Missions* (1871), p. 84, p. 89; S. Berger, *La Bible française au Moyen Age* (Paris, 1884).

21 Pächt, *The St. Albans Psalter*, p. 149.

22 Pächt, p. 149.

23 Pächt, p. 149.

24 S. Dufrenne, *Les Illustrations du Psautier d'Utrecht,* (Paris: Ophrys, 1978), provides a useful summary of how medieval psalters were illustrated, in three main groups, as follows:

> 1. Psalters in which a series of scenes from the life of David, of Christ, or of the Story of Salvation precedes the text of the Psalms. These become numerous beginning with the eleventh century; they are an outgrowth of earlier psalters furnished with a portrait of David, usually as a musician (e.g. the "Vespasian" Psalter), sometimes facing a portrait of Christ (e.g., the Psalter of the monastery of Notre-Dame de Soissons), sometimes accompanied with a portrait of the translator or of the king who commissioned the manuscript (e.g., the Psalter of Charles the Bald, B.N. lat. 1152).

> Western manuscripts which include a christological cycle to introduce the psalms include: the St. Albans Psalter (Hildesheim, St. Godehard's); the Psalter of Queen

Melisend (of Jerusalem —but her Psalter is, of course, of Western nature.) (London, B.M., Egerton 1139); the Ingeborg Psalter (Chantilly, Musée Condé, lat. 1695).

2. Psalters containing pictures to mark the division of the Psalms into groups of 3 (numerological divisions?), of 5 (Hebrew division), of 8 (liturgical division), and, finally, of 10 (a combination of the tripartite and of the ferial division). The division into groups of 3, 5, and 8 correspond to long-established speculation on the symbolic nature of numbers in reference to the Psalms, as commented by St. Augustine.

3. Psalters in which all (or most) of the Psalms are accompanied by illustrations throughout. (The Utrecht Psalter is the classic example of this third category.) This regularized to a figured decoration of the initials of the Psalms, a tradition followed throughout the Middle Ages, and typified by the celebrated St. Albans Psalter.

See as well: S. Berger, *Les Manuels pour l'illustration du psautier au XIII*e *siècle* (Paris, 1938) (Extr. des *Mémoires de la Société nationale des Antiquaires de France*, LVII); J. J. Tikkanen, *Die Psalterillustration im Mittelalter* (Helsingfors, 1895-1900. Soest repr.: Davaco, 1975); H. Buchthal, *Miniature Painting in the Latin Kingdom of Jerusalem* (Oxford: Clarendon, 1957) [for Queen Melisend's Psalter, especially].

[25] Dodwell distinguishes two hands in the initials, but finds that "the relationship between the two is sufficiently close for them to be treated as one for the purposes of analysis." *The St. Albans Psalter*, p. 199.

[26] *The St. Albans Psalter*, p. 9.

[27] In addition to the use of 3 in the *terza rima*, the reader will recall the 3 *canticas* of the *Commedia, Inferno, Purgatorio* and *Paradiso*, each comprising 33 cantos; their total of 99 is augmented by 1 *canto* of Prologue to yield the perfect 100. Inferno's occupants are in the 3 groups of the Incontinent, the Violent and the Fraudulent. In *Purgatorio*, it is rather the number 7 which is exploited, via the Terraces/Vices, and expanded to the perfect 10 via Ante- Purgatory's 2 levels and the Garden of Eden. And 9 (3, thrice) is certainly the number of the realm of the Angels, and of Beatrice, for whom "this number was her very self." (*Vita nuova*, XXX, 26-27.)

[28] Anna Granville Hatcher, "The Old French *Alexis* Poem: A Mathematical Demonstration," *Traditio*, VIII (1952), pp. 111-58.

Eleanor Bulatkin, "The Arithmetical Structure of the Old French *Vie de Saint Alexis*," *PMLA*, LXXIV (1959), pp. 495-502.

James C. Atkinson, "Triplet Sequences in the *Vie de Saint Alexis*," *Romance Notes*, XI, 2 (1969), pp. 414-19.

See also E. R. Curtius, "Zur Interpretation des Alexiusliedes," *Z.R.Ph.*, LVI (1934), pp. 85-93.

[29] Joseph Bédier, *Les Légendes épiques* (Paris: Champion, 1926).

[30] There are only eight of these remaining today. See H. Omont, "Peintures d'un Evangéliaire Syriaque du

XIIe ou du XIIIe siècle," *Monuments et Mémoires*, Fondation Piot, XIX (Paris, 1911), pp. 201- 10.

31 Ernst Robert Curtius, *European Literature and the Latin Middle Ages*, tr. Trask (Princeton: Princeton Univ. Press, 1953), pp. 310-15.

32 The metaphor of the Book of Memory is "a figure that controls the whole form of the *Vita nuova*," according to Charles Singleton (ed. *The Divine Comedy, Inferno*, Princeton: Princeton Univ. Press, 1970, p. 24, Commentary). See also Singleton, *An Essay on the Vita Nuova*, Cambridge, Mass.: Harvard Univ. Press, 1949. This metaphor is inherent, as well, in the Invocation in the *Inferno* II, 8: "*o mente che scrivesti cio ch'io vidi*," (O memory that wrote down what I saw. - tr. Singleton.) and in the Paradiso XXIII, 54: ". . . *mai non si stingue del libro che 'l preterito rassegna*." (. . . it can never be blotted from the book that records the past. - tr. Sinclair.)

See Charles S. Singleton, *Dante Studies I: Commedia, Elements of Structure* (Cambridge: Harvard Univ. Press, 1954).

It was Alfred G. Engstrom who called these examples from Dante to my attention.

33 David Jeffrey, ed., *By Things Seen* (Ottawa: Univ. of Ottawa Press, 1978), pp. 6-7.

34 See Appendix III-b for a reproduction of this illustration. Curtius (*Eur. Lit.*, p. 310) shows the antiquity of this tradition: "Christianity was a religion of the Holy Book. Christ is the only god whom antique art represents with a book-scroll." He refers readers to T. Birt, *Die Buchrolle in der Kunst* (1907) and to T. Michels, *Oriens christianus* (1932). After citing numerous Biblical examples of the metaphorical use of the book, Curtius concludes: "These selected passages show how magnificent the religious metaphorics of the book can be, in contrast to the purely literary form of it with which we had previ-

ously become familiar.... It is characteristic of the Middle Ages in the West that the two so different worlds not only come into contact but also intersect and interpenetrate one another —as do Church and school, piety and learning, symbolism and grammar."

[35] The Annunciation is the third picture in the 40-page christological cycle, p. 19; the Beatus Vir opens the Psalms, p. 72.

[36] This illustration is provided by Jeffrey, p. 15, Plate III, and it is herein included in Appendix III. Cf. a similar illustration in *Evangiles de la Sainte Chapelle*, Paris, B.N. lat. 8841, fol. 1, v⁰.

[37] Jeffrey, p. 11.

[38] The symbolism of numbers for medieval Christianity is of course a vast subject, reaching back to St. Augustine who, many times, set his seal of approval on numbers, 'most holy and full of mysteries.' (*Quaest. in Gen.* i. 152). His view of numbers as transcendent would be shared by Macrobius and by Isidore of Seville:

> Haec est igitur communis numerorum omnium plentudo, quod cogitationi a nobis ad superos meanti occurit prima perfectio incorporalitatis in numeris.
> Macrobius, *Commentarii in somnium scipionis*, I.5,4. ed. Jacobus Willis (Leipzig: Teubner Verlagesellschaft, 1970.)

> (But this attribute of perfection is common to all numbers, for in the progress of our thought from our own plane to that of the gods, they present the first example of perfect abstraction.)
> tr. William H. Stahl

> Ratio numerorum condemnenda
> non est. In multis enim sanctarum
> scripturarum locis quantum
> mysterium habent elucet. Non enim
> frustra in laudibis Dei dictum est
> (Sap. 11,21); "Omnia in mensura et
> numero et pondere fecisti."
>
> Isidore of Seville,
Etymol. III, iv.

(The science of numbers is not to be despised. [For] in many passages of Holy Scripture is it brought to light how much mystery they contain. For it is not said in vain in the praises of God: "Thou hast made all things according to measure and number and weight.")

Isidore of Seville devoted a large part of his *Etymologiae* to the *Liber numerorum* (*PL* LXXXII, col. 73-728), in which he cites the qualities and the mystical significance of every number from 1 to 15, and of the chief ones from 16 to 60. On the strength of such a veneration for numbers, the allegorizing of church architecture, appointments and liturgy would reach its full expression among such twelfth- century exegists as Honorius of Augustodunum (d. ca. 1125) and Jean Beleth (d. ca. 1165), as Jungmann shows:

> Often enough, besides the picture which presents itself, the number of repetitions offered a solution. Thus the triple silence in the Mass proper ... represents the three days our Lord rested in the tomb. The five-fold turning of the priest toward the people refers to the five appearances of our Lord after the Resurrection. Similarly the number of crosses made over the *oblata* received by

preference a numerological meaning. The three crosses after the *Te igitur* typify the three times our Lord was mocked before the high priests and Herod and Pilate, the five crosses in the *Unde et memores* typify the five wounds, and so forth.

(*The Mass of the Roman Rite*,
I, pp. 108-09)

A typical mystical interpretation of numbers is that of Honorius Augustodunensis in explaining the varying lengths of sojourn in Purgatory.

(He affirms that only the souls of the perfect go to heaven immediately after death. For the most part, the just make a sojourn in Purgatory; certain ones are liberated on the seventh day, others, on the thirtieth day, others, after a year, others stay there yet longer.)

- Cur magis aguntur hi dies?

- Tria et quatuor fiunt septem; per tria fides Trinitatis, per quatuor homo, qui constat ex quatuor elementis, intelligitur. Anima etiam habet tres vires, quae est rationalis, irascibilis, concupiscibilis, et omne tempus septem diebus volvitur. Agitur igitur septimus dies, ut quidquid anima in tribus viribus suis per quatuor qualitates corporis in fide Trinitatis in septem diebus hujus temporis contra septiformem Spiritum, quem in baptismo suscepit, peccavit relaxetur. Triginta per tria et decem surgunt; per tria nova lex propter fidem

Trinitatis, per decum vetus lex propter decalogum intelligitur. Triginta etiam diebus omnis mensis labitur. Agitur itaque tricesimus, ut quidquid homo in mensibus in nova vel veteri lege deliquit deleatur. Annus est Christus, ut dicitur: "Annum acceptabilem Domino." Menses sunt duodecim apostoli, ut dicitur: "Benedices coronae anni benignitatis tuae." Solis cursus post annum, lunae redit post mensem. Agitur igitur anniversarius, ut quidquid contra solem justitiae, Christum, et lunam, ejus Ecclesiam, et doctrinam apostolorum, qui sunt menses boni anni, egit remittatur.

Elucidarium, L. III.
ed. Lefevre, *L'Elucidarium et les Lucidaires* (Paris, 1954),
p. 445

(- Why these precise delays?

- Three and four make seven. Three represents faith in the Trinity; four, man, composed of the four elements. The soul has three powers: the rational, the irascible and the lustful; and all of time rotates in the space of seven days. The seventh day, then, is so spent in order that all may be effaced which the soul has committed, in these three powers, by the four qualities of the body, in faith in the Trinity, during this period of seven days, against the heptaform Holy Spirit, received by the soul at baptism. Thirty is born of three times ten. Three signifies the New Law, because of faith in the Trinity. Ten, the Old Law, because of the Decalogue. In thirty days, the whole month rolls by. That is why the thirtieth day is so spent, in order that all that man has transgressed, from month to month, against the New and the Old Law, may be effaced. The year is Christ, according to what is written: "The acceptable year of the Lord." The months are the twelve apostles, according to what is written: "Thou crownest the year with thy goodness." The sun renews its course in a year; the moon in a month. The interval of a year is thus chosen in order that all that which has been done against the sun of justice, Christ, the moon, his Church, and the doctrine of his disciples may be pardoned.)

Georges Duby, ed., *L'Europe au Moyen Age* (Paris: A. Colin, 1969), Vol. II, pp. 343-44.

39 This was the number traditionally accepted as the life span of Christ; so did St. Augustine see it as fitting that he himself should be baptized in his thirty-third year of life (*Confessions*, Book IX). By reference to this understanding, the year 1033 (once 1000 had passed) was approached with the expectation that it would see the end of this world: one thousand years after the death of Christ. (See Raoul Glaber, *Histories*, IV, 6.)

Aside from its association with Christ's life span, *33* is numerologically significant in that it is two *3*'s, thereby expressing the *two* natures, the human and the divine, of the *Second* Person of the *Trinity*. It is, however, at variance with the number which is seen as expressing Christ's life span in the *Alexis*: 34 years of *Imitatio*. Bulatkin, in endorsing this association, attributes the use of 34 rather than 33 to the medieval abhorrence of fractions: Christ actually lived 33 1/3 years by dint of the time between Christmas and Easter. (Bulatkin, p. 498). I am not convinced that so sacrosanct a number as 33 would have been so cavalierly discarded for 34 because of a dislike of fractions. I suspect that it is rather a matter of a poet's wanting parallelism, and of *needing* it in order to accommodate both the Life of the Eastern Mar Riscia and that of the Western St. John the Calybite: hence, two periods, of seventeen years each. This in itself blithely ignores the time which Alexis spent in Lalice ("*Co ne sai jo cum longes i converset.*" l. 85) before beginning his program in earnest in Alsis.

Of course, thirty-four years is not Alexis' total biological life span, but rather the years seen as constituting his spiritual life. Even so, like Jesus, who "increased in wisdom and in stature and in favor with God and man," Alexis would seem to have early been spiritually minded: on his wedding night, he fears that sin might make him *lose* God.

Should we not perhaps see *three* periods of *seventeen* years each suggested? Alexis might well have been seventeen when he was married. So would there be seventeen years as the son of Eufemien, seventeen as the Man of God (the scope of the Eastern legend), and seventeen as the quasi-Agnus Dei, the suffering Saint. Three would seem an infinitely more likely number for symbolic allusion than thirty-four.

And seventeen itself has much to commend it: the One of Unity alongside the highly revered Seven (Days of Creation, gifts of the Holy Spirit, Virtues, Liberal Arts, Planets, liturgical modes, musical 'tones' which govern the spheres, etc.).

Indeed, is it purely by coincidence that Alexis' Feastday is all but invariably (I am aware of only one exception) on a 17th? While the Saint died on the 10th (of the 7th month!), and though the day of *death* (or martyrdom) is the usual day of commemoration, Alexis is honored on the 17th, the day of his *burial*. (The People would not part from his body for 7 days.)

It is nothing short of uncanny that the number 17 should be always chosen for St. Alexis, though the month may vary: whether in the Eastern liturgy (March 17) or in the new Roman calendar (February 17), his feastday is invariably the seventeenth. And, of significance to the proposal of this monograph: the Feast day of St. Lazarus is on the 17th.

[40] I have examined this gathering carefully to see if a page might have been detached, and I found no evidence of this: the foliation is intact at this 'crucial' point in the pictured life of Christ. Pächt discusses how remarkable is this lack of a Crucifixion scene, both 'narratively' and stylistically, as follows:

> An unusual, and for Western art even unique, feature of the cycle is, however, the omission of the scene of the Crucifixion, the central theme in the drama of Salvation, whose position here is apparently taken by the scene of the Deposition from the Cross. In a pictorial cycle such as that of the St. Albans Psalter, devised to illustrate the theme of redemption, the representation of the tree of paradise introduced in the beginning would seem to require as its indispensable counterpart the picture of the Tree of Life in its most telling aspect, i.e., Christ crucified or the scene of the Crucifixion. The omission of the latter in this context is, therefore, the more surprising....
>
> (*St Alb. Ps.*, p. 50)

Pächt notes that the Byzantine iconographic tradition, and through it, certain South Italian twelfth-century bronze doors, juxtapose the Deposition and the Anastasis to represent Death and the Resurrection. But, he concludes, "[no] narrative cycle, ... whether Eastern or Western, has so far come to my knowledge in which the Deposition replaces the Crucifixion." (p. 50)

81

[41] Throughout this chapter, there has been constant reference to numbers and to their allegorical interpretation: for a useful survey of how neo-Platonism, Pythagorianism, astrology, and mysticism furnished a rich lode for the mining of the Fathers and, thence, of their medieval grandsons, see Vincent Hopper's *Medieval Number Symbolism* (New York: Columbia Univ. Press, 1933). Other useful references: Caroline Eckhardt, *Essays in the Numerical Analysis of Medieval Literature* (Lewisburg: Bucknell Univ. Press, 1979); Basil Christopher Butler, *Number Symbolism* (New York: Barnes & Noble, 1970); and R. Delort, *Introduction aux sciences auxiliares de l'histoire* (Paris: A. Colin, 1969), pp. 33- 35 and 269-71.

[42] Her secular name had been Theodora: "Ipsa vero nomen sortita Theodoram in baptismate. novissime pro Theodora nomen sibi Christinam accepit ex necessitate." *The Life of Christina of Markyate*, C. H. Talbot, ed., (Oxford: Clarendon Press, 1959), p. 34. (Indeed she had been given the name Theodora at baptism. Finally, as needs be, she took unto herself the name Christina, in place of Theodora.)

CHAPTER IV

ST. ALBANS ABBEY

St. Albans Abbey, birthplace of the celebrated Psalter, is located at the site of the martyrdom of St. Alban, the first English martyr (3rd c. A.D.).[1] A church had existed there since the time of Bede (673-735); the abbey was founded not long after (ca. 794) by King Offa of Mercia. Following the turmoil of the ninth and tenth centuries, the abbey was refounded (ca. 969) and the first of its Norman abbots, Paul of Caen, spent his rule rebuilding the monastic buildings and the abbey church. By the twelfth century, the prestige and éclat of this abbey were second to none. St. Albans was accorded its preëminence among all the abbeys in England not only because of its famous and influential scriptorium —the scriptoria of Bury St. Edmonds and of Winchester were both in its debt, for example— but for all aspects of its life.[2] Dom Knowles assesses its importance as follows:

> St. Albans, which claimed and vindicated for itself the premier plan among all the black monk houses of England, may be regarded with some justice as the house which showed the fullest combination of all the characteristics of its order. In its liturgical observance, in the splendour of its architecture and decoration, in its encouragement of learning and the arts within and without its own body, it holds a place above all others in the twelfth century, and during at least the first half of that period it was a centre of fervent spiritual life.[3]

It is especially noteworthy that the rise in the renown of St. Albans was a post-Conquest development, and that it came about with the ascendancy of *Norman* abbots. It was, indeed, due to such Normans as Abbot Richard (1097) and Abbot Geoffrey (1119) that the abbey so surged and burgeoned: the *anima* of Bec itself would seem to infuse every aspect of St. Albans' life and being.[4]

The accomplishment of two such prestigious feats as we have seen manifest in the St. Albans Psalter —the prime example of English pictorial narrative and the earliest manuscript of a major Old French literary work— is quite characteristic of the dynamism and fecundity associated with the twelfth-century Abbey of St. Albans. There, the energy of its scribes and artists, its abbots and theologians was ideally situated to spark individually, to kindle reciprocally and to blaze collectively.

It is therefore not surprising that the earliest record of a medieval dramatic performance should be associated with St. Albans: its Abbot Geoffrey is credited with staging the *Ludus Catharinae*, a miracle play.[5] The circumstances of this performance are of interest not only per se, but also because of their bearing on St. Albans Abbey, the Albani Psalter, Christina of Markyate, and, perhaps, on the Old French Life of St. Alexis.

As a layman, Geoffrey, member of a distinguished family of Maine,[6] had been summoned by the Norman Abbot Richard to serve as *Magister* of the town school in St. Albans. He arrived too late, and found that the post had been given to someone else. Undaunted, Geoffrey went to nearby Dunstable and set up a school on his own. There he organized the performance of a play that he himself had written while still in Maine: "quendam ludum de Sancta Katharina, quem 'Miracula' vulgariter appellamus." (a certain play about Saint Katherine, which we call a 'Miracle' [play] in common parlance.) For costumes he borrowed copes and albs from St. Albans Abbey.[7] It must have been a full-scale production, with staging and costuming all the more important since the play, especially if it were in Latin, was for a lay audience. A greater spectacle was to occur on the following night: Geoffrey's house caught fire, and St. Albans' copes, along with the schoolmaster's own books, were destroyed. So remorseful was Magister Geoffrey that he entered the Abbey as a monk, offering himself as 'a burnt offering to God': ". . . seipsum reddidit in holocaustum Deo, assumens habitum religionis in Domo Sancti Albani." (. . . he offered himself up as a holocaust to God, donning the habit of a monk in the House of St. Alban.) Geoffrey would eventually become Abbot of St. Albans. In that office, he established the Feast day of St. Catherine in the Abbey's calendar —and he was especially attentive to the making of copes.

During Geoffrey's abbacy, a certain Roger, monk of St. Albans, left the abbey to become a hermit on the Dunstable road. He was joined by five other brothers who also chose to live according to St. Benedict's description of the anchoritic life.[8] Into their woodland hermitage would come for refuge Christina of Huntingdon, daughter of a wealthy and prominent family.[9] Much against her will, Christina had been married by her family to one Beffred, whose property adjoined their own. Having made a childhood vow of perpetual chastity, Christina resisted stubbornly the consummating of the marriage despite the opposition of her husband, her parents and their ecclesiastical allies.[10] In a tenacious determination to remain a *sponsa intacta*, Christina finally contrived to escape her secular family, first secreting herself among a group of anchorites and finally placing herself under the guidance of Roger the Hermit. There she remained for four years, enclosed in a cell next to Roger's, and nurtured with his spiritual guidance and instruction. Upon his death, Christina fell heiress to the hermitage, and there received, in her turn, companions in the anchoritic life.

As a resident of this St. Albans cell, Christina became known to Abbot Geoffrey, who, though originally skeptical of her sincerity, came to admire her deeply and to rely completely on her guidance in all things. He would, finally, undertake no action, whether practical or spiritual, without first seeking out his 'dear friend' for advice.[11] In time, Geoffrey founded the Priory of Markyate for Christina and her companions; she became its first prioress, "prima priorissa de bosco."[12]

It was during the rule of Abbot Geoffrey (1119-46) that there flourished Roger the Hermit, Christina of Markyate and Sigar, hermit of Northaw, all of whom were highly reputed for their piety.[13] And it was also during Geoffrey's abbacy that the St. Albans Psalter was produced. With this cast of characters and in a setting which had close ties with Monte Cassino, site of an Alexis cult, Pächt has more than ample support for his suggestion that St. Albans might well be the birthplace of the original Old French version of the *Alexis*. So vibrant an atmosphere was then prevailing at St. Albans that it could easily have been the site of yet another 'first.'

Especially noteworthy is the presence of Abbot Geoffrey, whose mother tongue was "le français de France", whose innovative bent and whose hagiographical interest are evidenced by his theatrical venture, and, above all, who was the close friend and benefactor of Christina, *sponsa intacta*. And it is in the Psalter presumably made for Christina that is found the story of Alexis, scion of a noble family, and the fleeing *Sponsus*, *par excellence*. A retelling of that story, as told in the Old French *Life of St. Alexis*, will show how appropriate it would be for Christina.

There lived in Rome, in the good old days, a rich and powerful nobleman named Eufemien. Yearning for a son, Eufemien and his wife pray tirelessly for this favor, and pledge that such a child would be pledged to God. Their prayers are answered: God grants them a son. At his baptism, the child is named Alexis; he is tenderly nurtured, and is given an education fitting him to serve in the Emperor's retinue. Wishing to assure the continuation of his lineage, Eufemien arranges for the marriage of his son to a well-born maiden.

Alexis, so far a paragon of filial obedience, submits docilely enough to the wedding ceremony and to his father's admonition to enter the bridal chamber. Once inside, however, the sight of the marriage bed apparently recalls him to an all-eclipsing duty to his heavenly father. Thereupon, he commends his bride to a spiritual union with the supreme Bridegroom, hands over to her a ring and his sword-belt, and flees the house and its earthly bonds. He rushes out to a ship lying in port and engages the boatman to bear him away.

Guided by divine purpose, the ship lands at Lalice, where Alexis begins a life of thralldom to his heavenly lord. After some time, he leaves Lalice for Alsis (Edessa), site of a miraculous image made in honor of the Virgin. In this city, Alexis divests himself of all his earthly possessions, distributing them among the poor, and assumes the life of a beggar. Of the alms he receives, he keeps only enough to hold body and soul together, dispensing the surplus among his fellow paupers.

In Rome, meanwhile, the parents and the wife of Alexis lament his absence, and Eufemien sends out his best servants in search of his missing son. They encounter him in Alsis, but so changed is his appearance that they do not know him. Alexis, while receiving their alms, praises God that his identity is concealed and that he is now subservient to his servants.

After seventeen years, Alexis's sojourn is abruptly ended when the Image in the church miraculously summons "the man of God": the supernatural Voice must speak three times before the humble almsman is identified as "l'ume Deu." Again Alexis flees the honor and homage of this world, counting them as encumbrances. Again he boards a ship and sets sail for Tarsus, but heavenly intervention causes his landing instead at the port close to Rome.

Fearing that his family will recognize him and burden him again with worldly impedimenta, Alexis beseeches God that his identity again be concealed. His prayer is answered: the long-lost son is unrecognized by Eufemien and his retinue upon their meeting in the street. Alexis asks shelter of Eufemien in the name of God, and for 'your son, for whom you bear such grief.' Eufemien, strangely moved, even to the point of weeping, grants this boon, and solicits a servant to attend the pilgrim.

For seventeen more years, Alexis continues his life of austerity in ignominious lodging beneath the stairs of his father's house. Christlike, he endures the reviling of his erstwhile servants, and asks that God forgive them 'by his mercy, for they know not what they do.' Of the table scraps which are his only nourishment, Alexis partakes sparingly, giving the remainder to the other poor. Gradually, the flesh becomes ever weaker as the spirit of Alexis turns more and more to God. Sensing that the time is imminent when the corruptible shall become incorruptible, Alexis requests of his servant pen, ink and parchment and records the story of his life. He conceals the document upon his body and in a continuous renunciation of the carnal, ceases more and more to speak.

As the wretched pilgrim moves closer to shuffling off his mortal coil, an awesome Voice is heard in the city: it warns that 'l'ume Deu' must be summoned to ward off the destruction of Rome. The people turn in terror to Pope Innocent and to the emperors Arcadius and Honorius. All beseech God to point out this unknown holy man by whom their salvation may be purchased. The Voice, in its third discourse, directs them to the house of Eufemien; there, at the good servant's suggestion, they find the mortal remains of *le Pauvre sous l'escalier.*

Eufemien wishes to take the parchment clutched in the hand of the dead pilgrim, but the document will not yield to him: it releases itself only to the Pope, who remits it in turn to a learned clerk. To an audience of two emperors and a pope, the three family members, and the assorted clergy and populace, the clerk reads the life story of this pauper who was once a prince —Lord Alexis.

When the parents and wife learn that this dead pilgrim is their long-mourned Alexis, each utters an impassioned lamentation. Eufemien bewails the defection of his inheritor, the mother laments the loss of her offspring. Only the wife seems somewhat perceptive of his greater significance: she ends her plaint by committing herself to the service of God.

In words which recall the angel's remonstrance at Jesus' tomb, the Pope rebukes this blind grieving, and the authorities seek to bear the body away. But the people refuse to be parted from their saviour: not even the dazzle of gold and silver, flung by the rich and powerful into the streets to divert them, can part the masses from this 'celestial gem.' Pressing about his precious body, the people of Rome receive miraculous cures for their divers diseases.

At last, the body is borne away to the church of St. Boniface, where it lies in state for seven days; then, as befits a priceless jewel, it is lovingly and sumptuously encasked and embedded in the crypt of St. Boniface. The family of Alexis, the pope and emperors, the assorted clergy and the people all draw strength from the example of this son of God.

So may we, avers the poet, receive benefit from Alexis, who, now in heaven together with his wife, can make intercession for us. By his righteousness can we obtain peace and joy in this life, and eternal glory in the one to come. Thereupon, we are enjoined to unite in the *Pater Noster*.

Somber and noble as a statue at the portal of a Romanesque cathedral, the *Alexis* serves well to usher us into the sanctuary, as Gaston Paris asserts: "dans sa simplicité gracieuse et sévère. . . , il ouvre dignement l'histoire de la poésie nationale."[14] The Old French poem's literary merit is commonly attributed to its conceptual architecture and to the inherent beauty of its building material: critics agree that it embodies that proportion of structure, that unity of purpose and that fitness of expression required for aesthetic excellence.[15]

The poem was first brought to light by Wilhelm Müller, who published his transcription of the L manuscript in 1845. Ten years later, Gessner provided a new transcription, more correct than that of Müller. The first critical edition appeared in 1868, the work of Konrad Hofmann. This edition is especially noteworthy for its taking into account the Prologue to the poem and the Gregorian letter which follows it, for both of these are peculiar to the St. Albans Psalter; as such, they are of importance in understanding both the poem and the

Psalter.[16] *Et puis vint Paris:* in 1872 came the monumental edition of Gaston Paris; herein, the literary *Alexiusmeister* launched the method for the establishment of a text which would become the paragon. After having demonstrated that the language of the *Alexis* is more evolved than that of the *Eulalia* and of the Clermont poems, and more archaic than that of the *Roland*, Paris set himself to a study of the four major manuscripts —the **L**, **A**, **P**, and **S**— in an effort to ascertain what was the original Old French *Vie de St. Alexis*. On the basis of the essential similarity of three of these manuscripts —**L**, **A**, and **P**— and considering that all three are of English provenance, Paris concluded that there were manuscripts of an Old French Life in England toward the end of the eleventh century. **L** and **A**, which frequently show the same readings, would derive from one of these pre-existing manuscripts, "**a**". **P**, which shows variant readings, would issue from another, "**b**". Both of these, "**a**" and "**b**", would have ultimately issued from yet another hypothesized form of the poem, "**x**", which would, in turn, hearken back to a lost *Urtext*, "**O**," written around 1040, and probably in Normandy.[17]

Of the manuscripts extant, Paris judged the language of **L** to be the most archaic and he therefore granted primacy to this manuscript. He characterized its language as continental French with certain alterations due to an Anglo-Norman scribe. The *Ursprache* could be the dialect either of Normandy or of Ile-de-France, one and the same, Paris noted, prior to the twelfth century. One consideration, however, led Paris to favor Normandy as the place of origin: a poet, Tedbalt of Vernon, who was alive, and in Normandy, precisely at the time corresponding to the language's *Zeitstil*. In addition to being *in situ* for writing in Norman French, Tedbalt, a monk, would be personally disposed to sing of a saint, and especially of Saint Alexis: his holy body had wrought miraculous cures, such as the one bestowed upon Tedbalt himself by a *sainz cors*.

Paris' *rapprochement* of the *Alexis* poet and of Tedbalt is eloquently persuasive. Since it is not readily available, his 1872 edition being out of print, I am including this passage here for the reader's consideration.

En 1053, on rapporta à l'abbaye de
Fontenelle... les reliques de saint

91

Vulframn, ... qu'on avait promenées dans la ville de Rouen pour en éloigner la peste. Des guérisons miraculeuses eurent lieu en grand nombre au contact de ce saint corps, et parmi les personnes qui furent l'objet de ces effets de l'intercession du saint, un moine de Rouen dont la vue affaiblie retrouva son ancienne netteté, et à propos duquel il ajoute: "C'est ce Tedbalt de Vernon qui a traduit de leur latinité les vies de plusieurs saints et entre autres celle de saint Wandrille, les a refondues pour l'usage de la langue commune avec assez d'éloquence, et en a fait d'agréables chansons d'après une sorte de rhythme tintant." Il est certain qu'on ne peut rien trouver de plus concordant que les renseignements donnés ici sur ce Tedbalt et l'idée que nous pouvons faire de notre poète. Qu'il ait été chanoine, rien de plus naturel: son oeuvre, d'après le prologue qui la précède et que, pour ma part, je crois aussi ancien, était destinée à être chantée dans l'église le jour de la fête du saint, et se terminait par la récitation en commun d'un *Pater noster.* —Tedbalt traduisait des *Vies de Saints* "de leur latinité"; notre poète a suivi de fort près la légende latine de saint Alexis. —"Il les refondait pour l'usage de la langue commune avec assez d'éloquence"; les qualités de style qui distinguent notre poème sont des plus remarquables.... "Il en faisait des chansons agréables"; c'est précisément ainsi que le prologue de notre poème le désigne: "amiable chanson" —"D'après un certain tintement rhythmique (ou rhythme tintant);" il est clair que l'écrivain monastique cherche ici une périphrase pour désigner l'assonance dont se servait Tedbalt, et dont se sert l'auteur de l'*Alexis.* — Enfin il n'est pas jusqu'aux circonstances où nous apparaît le chânoine de Rouen qui me semblent favoriser cette hypothèse. N'est-ce pas bien le même homme qui célèbre dans ses vers les guérisons miraculeuses opérées par le corps de saint Alexis quand on le transporte dans l'église (str. 111-112), et qui a été demander la sienne au corps de saint Vulframm qu'on transportait dans un monastère? —En 1053, Tedbalt, qui avait composé "les vies de beaucoup de saints," et dont la vue était affaiblie depuis plusieurs années, devait avoir atteint un âge avancé, et l'activité poétique qui l'avait fait connaître remontait sans doute à plusieurs années avant le miracle: or c'est précisément la date où tout indique que notre poème a été composé. . . .

(pp. 43-45)

(In 1053, there were brought back to the Abbey of Fontanelle. . . the relics of Saint Vulframm,. . . which had been paraded about in the city of Rouen in order to banish the plague. Miraculous cures, in great number, took place upon contact with this holy body, and among the persons who were the recipients of these effects of the Saint's intercession [was] a monk of Rouen whose weakened eyesight regained its former clarity, and in reference to whom [the chronicler] adds: "This is that Tedbalt of Vernon who translated from their Latinity the Lives of several saints and among others that of

Saint Wandrille, [who] recast [these Lives] quite eloquently for use in the common tongue, and from them made pleasant songs with a sort of ringing rhythm." It is certain that one could find nothing in better agreement than the information given here on Tedbalt of Vernon and the idea that we can form of our poet. That he was a canon [seems] perfectly natural: his work, according to the prologue which precedes it and which, for my part, I consider equally [as] old, was designed to be sung in the church on the feastday of the saint, and [it] ended with the recitation in common of a *Pater Noster.* —Tedbalt used to translate *Lives of Saints* "from their Latinity;" our poet followed very closely the Latin legend of Saint Alexis. —"He recast them quite eloquently for use in the common tongue"; the stylistic qualities which distinguish our poem are of the most remarkable. . . "He made pleasant songs of them"; this is exactly how the prologue of our poem describes it: "pleasing song." — "With a certain rhythmic ringing (or ringing rhythm);" it is clear that the monastic writer is here seeking a paraphrase to describe the assonance which Tedbalt used and which the author of the *Alexis* uses. —Finally, it is not merely the circumstances in which the Rouen canon appears to us which seem to me to favor this hypothesis. Is this not indeed the same man who celebrates in his verses the miraculous cures effected by the body of Saint Alexis when it was carried into the church. . ., and who had gone to ask for his own [cure] to the body of

Saint Vulframon, which was being carried into a monastery? —In 1053, Tedbalt, who had composed "the Lives of many saints," and whose eyesight had been weakened for several years, must have reached an advanced age, and the poetic activity which had made him well-known doubtless went back to several years before the miracle: now that is precisely the date when, according to all indications, our poem was composed. . .)

Paris goes on to concede that Tedbalt's having written the *Urtext Alexis* must remain an hypothesis, neither disprovable nor provable: without strict proof, the poet must be held anonymous. Nor could one say with certainty whether the original poem was written in Ile-de-France or in Normandy; but the latter offers stronger possibilities, to wit:

. . . D'abord parce que l'activité littéraire (dont Tedbalt de Vernon offre au moins un exemple) paraît y avoir été à cette époque plus vive qu'en France, —puis parce que trois de nos manuscrits, dont les deux plus anciens de beaucoup, ont été écrits en Angleterre, pays qui avait naturellement avec la Normandie ses relations intellectuelles les plus fréquentes.

(p.45)

(. . . First of all because [Normandy's] literary activity (of which Tedbalt of Vernon offers at least one example) appears to have been livelier at that time than that in France, —then, because three of our manuscripts, including the two oldest by far, were written in England, a country which naturally had its most frequent intellectual contacts with Normandy.)

At any rate, for Gaston Paris there was no doubt that the original Old French Life was composed in France; it would have then been transported —in perhaps another intermediary version— to England with the Normans, and there copied by an Anglo-Norman scribe. And this *Liber generationis* of the *Alexis* has generally been accepted as 'Gospel' by its literary scholars. But the editors of the St. Albans Psalter, Pächt, Dodwell and Wormald, have arrayed impressive information calling for a re-examination of Paris's dating of the poem. Whereas Paris ascribes a date of 1040 to the **L** manuscript, the Warburg scholars deduce a somewhat later date, ca. 1123, for the St. Albans Psalter in which it is found. Whereas Paris believed, for his part, that the Prologue goes back to an hypothesized original poem ("**O**"), Pächt judges it to be original to the **L** manuscript, the creation of a St. Albans hand: that of the *Alexiusmeister.*[18]

Pächt questions, moreover, the very existence of an archetype version; as we have seen, he posits that the original Old French *Vie de Saint Alexis* may indeed be that of the **L** manuscript, composed and executed at St. Albans. In support of this hypothesis, Pächt offers highly telling evidence. There were, for example, Latin sources of the Life then available in England. There are, in addition, Italian influences obvious in the art of the Psalter. Moreover, the legend and Life of Alexis are closely associated with Rome and with Monte Cassino, site of an Alexis cult, Mother-house of all Benedictine abbeys, and possessing close connections with the Norman abbey Bec, itself linked with St. Albans. Finally, as conspicuously present at St. Albans as was Tedbalt at Vernon, there is the transplanted Frenchman, Geoffrey of Maine, who had equally good reason to write such a poem. Here is Pächt's proposal:

> If . . . there are no objections from the linguistic side to dating the French original as late as 1120 —i.e. not much earlier than the date at which it was written down at St. Albans— there would be a strong case for regarding St. Albans, towards which we have a unique

96

combination of circumstances converging at this time, as the birthplace of the Alexis poem in Old French.[19]

In view of such divergences of opinion on the part of these two masters —Gaston Paris, the grand old master of Old French philology and Otto Pächt, '*Psaltermeister*' in art history— it would seem valid to reconsider the provenance of the Old French poem. Since the 1845 discovery of the **L** manuscript, the text of the poem has been the object of assiduous linguistic and literary study. The history of the legend of St. Alexis —in Syriac, Greek, and Latin— has been carefully plotted, if on different lines, by scholars such as Amiaud and Rösler.[20] The St. Albans Psalter has now been thoroughly probed in the masterly edition of Pächt and his colleagues. However, the information yielded by their study has not yet been fully correlated with the linguistic and literary scholarship on the *Alexis*. By such a synthetic assessment, new insight may be provided into the significance of the *Alexis* as a part of the St. Albans Psalter, and into its provenance. Toward that end let us first consider the Psalter in its liturgical or devotional function at St. Albans.

[1] Of special help on St. Albans and its brother and sister houses are two works of Dom David Knowles: *The Monastic Order in England, 940-1216* (Cambridge: Cambridge Univ. Press, 1940. 2nd Ed., 1963); *Religious Orders in England*, I-III (Cambridge: Univ. Press, 1948-59). Also useful are: D. Knowles and R. N. Hadcock, *The Medieval Religious Houses of England and Wales* (2nd ed., London: Longman, 1971).

The primary source on this Abbey is the *Gesta Abbatum Monasterii Sancti Albani* (ed. H. T. Riley, Rolls Series 28), specifically that part compiled by Matthew Paris (13th century). (It is of passing interest to note that Matthew Paris was also a literary author —he probably wrote a Life of St. Alban, 1236— and an artist, noted for *his* "picture books.")

[2] Pächt et al, *The St. Albans Psalter* (London, 1960), p. 170.

[3] D. Knowles, *The Monastic Order in England*, pp. 186-7. (It will be remembered that "black monks," e.g., Benedictines, owe their name to the color of their habit.)

[4] Bec, O.S.B., near Rouen, was founded in 1041 under the abbacy of Herlouin. It became a center of monastic studies, attracting such scholars as Lanfranc and St. Anselm. Many of the post-Conquest bishops and abbots of England had earlier been monks at Bec; among them Abbot Richard of St. Albans, the immediate predecessor of Abbot Geoffrey. Bec maintained close ties with Monte Cassino, mother house of the Benedictines, which had a strong Alexis cult. Bec itself, Pächt notes (p. 135), was "the only place in western Europe other than Paderborn with a proper cult of Alexis." See as well A. A. Poirée, *Histoire de l'Abbaye de Bec* (Evreux, 1901).

[5] In view of the confusion that sometimes results from the different meanings for "miracle" in English and in French discussions of drama, let us understand that here "mystery" refers to plays of Biblical characters (e.g., the *Lazarus*), "miracle," to those of later saints (e.g., St. Denis) and of the Virgin (e.g., the 40 Coincy *Miracles*). See G. R. Coffman, *A New Theory Concerning the*

Origin of the Miracle Play (Minasha: Collegiate Press, 1914), p. 12 ss. for a discussion of these terms.

6 He is referred to variously as: Geoffrey of Maine, of Le Mans, of Gorran, of Gorham.

For his life and for his personality, see C. H. Talbot, *The Life of Christina of Markyate* (Oxford: Clarendon Press, 1959), and Knowles, *The Monastic Order in England, 940-1216* .

7 It would appear that the borrowing of these liturgical vestments, for a secular performance, was unorthodox, if we may judge from a homily in *Handlyng Synne*, which Robert Mannyng of Brunne translated from the French *Manuel des Pechiez* in 1303. Even in the fourteenth century, this was considered sacrilegious: "If a priest or a clerk lends a vestment which has been hallowed by the sacrament, he, more than others is to be blamed, for he shall have the infamy which attends sacrilege, and shall be chastised as is right." *(Robert of Brunne's "Handlyng Synne," with those parts of the Anglo-French Treatise on which it was founded, William of Wadington's "Manuel des Pechiez,"* F. J. Furnivall, ed., EETS, London, 1901, #119.) In the twelfth century, when Magister Geoffrey staged his *Ludus Katharinae*, the use of liturgical vestments for a play must have been so innovative as to be startling, if not shocking.

8 St. Benedict lists four kinds of monks, the first two of them laudable, the latter two thoroughly reprehensible. These are: Cenobites, Anchorites, Sarabaites, and the gyratory monks. The Cenobites, i.e. monks living communally, would be governed by his *Regula*. Of the second group, he says: "Second are the Anchorites [hermits] who are not neophytes. They have spent much time in the monastery testing themselves and learning to fight against the devil. They have prepared themselves in the fraternal line of battle for the single combat of the hermit. They have laid the foundation to fight, with the aid of God, against their own bodily and spiritual vices." *(Regula,* I). Despite St. Benedictine's stringent prerequisites for the anchoritic life, the woods of England were full of hermits in the twelfth century, it appears. See Rotha Mary Clay, *The Hermits and Anchorites of England* (London: Methuen, 1914), p. xviii.

9 The story of her life is found in the second volume of B.M. Cotton Tiberius E. 1, which has been edited and translated by C. H. Talbot in his *Life of Christina of Markyate*. From it is reproduced the map of the district connected with Christina in Appendix II-e.

10 One of Christina's encounters with her husband, Beffred, is so reminiscent of Alexis' wedding night as to bear a reading:

But as her parents had been outwitted in this [attempting to break down her resistance with wine and flattery], they tried something else. And at night they let her husband secretly into her bedroom in order that, if he found the maiden asleep, he might suddenly take her by surprise and overcome her. But even through that providence to which she had commended herself, she was found dressed and awake, and she welcomed the young man as if he had been her brother. And sitting on her bed with him, she strongly encouraged him to live a chaste life, putting forward the saints as examples. She recounted to him in detail the story of St. Cecilia and her husband Valerian, telling him how, at their death they were accounted worthy to receive crowns of unsullied chastity from the hands of an angel. Not only this: but both they and many others after them had followed the path of martyrdom and thus, being crowned twice by the Lord, were honoured both in heaven and on earth. 'Let us, therefore,' she exhorted him, 'follow their example, so that we may become their companions in eternal glory. Because if we suffer with them, we shall also reign with them. Do not take it amiss that I have declined your embraces. In order that your

friends may not reproach you with being rejected by me, I will go home with you; and let us live together there for some time, ostensibly as husband and wife, but in reality living chastely in the sight of the Lord....'
When the greater part of the night had passed with talk such as this, the young man eventually left the maiden.

(Talbot, p. 51)

Though Beffred apparently heeded Christina's sermon on this occasion, he was immediately thereafter persuaded by his friends that he should not be such a "spineless and useless fellow." (Talbot, p. 51). Despite his determination, Christina continually resisted his attempts, finally running away in order to preserve her virginity.

[11] Talbot, p. 9: "Christina always called the abbot 'her beloved,' whilst he on his side referred to her as his *puella.*"

[12] Christina's priory was called Holy Trinity *de Bosco*; it was in Caddington, at Markyate. So is she identified in a grant which Henry II made for her support (1155), whereby fifty shillings a year were to be paid "in corn which the king gives to Lady Christina of the Wood." Clay, p. 23. See Appendix II-e for a map of Christina's 'world.'

[13] Roger, Christina, Sigar, and Godric of Finchale are among the forest and hillside hermits and anchorites whom Clay cites (pp. 19-27, 118-21, 150-1). Sigar, who was buried in St. Albans Abbey in the same tomb as Roger, was remarkably single-minded in his asceticism, to wit: "In that richly-wooded part of Hertfordshire nightingales abounded, and their chorus disturbed the hermit's devotions. He, therefore, made supplication that they might be removed 'lest he might seem to rejoice rather in the warbling of birds than in the worship whereunto he was bound before God.' John Amundesham declares that in his own day nightingales not only never presumed to sing, but never appeared within a mile of the hermitage." Clay, p. 23.

14 Gaston Paris, ed., *La Vie de Saint Alexis* (Paris: Franck, 1872), p.vi.

15 To attempt to cite all the scholars who admire the *Alexis* would be as hopeless a task as to document the eminence accorded to the Bible. The names of three, a fitting number, will suffice, and will direct attention to many more: Gaston Paris, op. cit. et al., E. R. Curtius, "Zur Interpretation des Alexiusliedes," *ZRPh*, LVI (1934), 85-93; Anna Granville Hatcher, "The Old French *Alexis* poem: A Mathematical Demonstration," *Traditio*, VIII (1952), pp. 111-158.

16 The fact that only the **L** version shows this Prologue must surely suggest that it was written at St. Albans: the poem proper has its own Exordium, as recognized by Curtius (op. cit.), and by Heinrich Lausberg, "Das prömium (Strophen I-III) des altfrz. Alexiusliedes," *Archiv für das Studium der neueren Sprachen*, CXCII (1956), 33-58. Paris, Meunier and others see it, however, as forming a part of the 'original' poem, from the beginning. This question will be dealt with throughout this study.

17 Gaston Paris, *La Vie de Saint Alexis* (Paris, 1872). I have copied Paris' proposed genealogy of the *Alexis* from this edition, and placed it in Appendix VII.

18 Pächt, *The St. Albans Psalter*, p. 143, note 1. As Storey reminds us, "it should be noted that, according to Goldschmidt [first editor of the St. Albans Psalter], the poem would have been sung [or chanted?: *chanté*] on the occasion of the dedication of the chapel of St. Alexis at St. Albans in 1119 [performed] by Ranulf Flambard, Bishop of Durham." (Storey, p. 25)

19 Pächt, p. 143.

20 Amiaud holds that the legend originated in Syria (ca. 425), was transported to Greece (ca. 8th c.), where it was augmented with the story of St. John the Calybite, and brought to Rome (ca. 977), in this augmented form, by Archbishop Sergius of Damascus. (Arthur Amiaud, *La Légende syriaque de St. Alexis, l'homme de Dieu*, Paris: E.

Bouillon, 1889). Margarethe Rösler's discovery of a Spanish *Alexis* manuscript (ca. 925) leads her to believe that the legend existed in the West prior to the time of Sergius: she posits a Byzantine origin. From Greece and Rome, the legend would have passed to Syria, received additional material, and returned to Rome in this enriched form. (M. Rösler, *Die Fassungen des Alexius Legende mit besondere Berücksichtigung des Mittelenglischen Versionen*, Vienna/Leipzig: W. Braumüller, 1905).

CHAPTER V

THE GALLICAN LITURGY OF THE MIDDLE AGES

To trace the shaping of the Roman liturgy from catacomb to cathedral is to envisage every aspect of civilization: the rites and customs of worship during the Age of Faith, as for no other period, represent an interweaving of political, theological, artistic, societal and personal influences. For our purposes, it suffices to generalize the data of such liturgists as Jungmann, Duchesne, Martène and Netzer toward an understanding of the nature of public worship in France and England during the eleventh and twelfth centuries.[1]

With this end in mind, we can first delineate the great division which opposed the Western and the Eastern Churches and which would mark Rome as the Eternal City for occidental Christendom — but only eventually. For it was not from Rome that all of Western liturgy developed: the churches of Gaul, Spain, Ireland, Britain and northern Italy were in initial debt, rather, to "New Rome", Constantinople, for their liturgies.[2] As early as the fifth century, the celebration of the Mass in these countries gave evidence of an Eastern origin, whether in France (Gallican rites), Spain (Mozarabic), northern Italy (Ambrosian), or Ireland and Britain (a hybrid form).[3] And lacking the strong central authority that Rome provided for her adherents, the liturgy deriving from the East was open to individualization and variety from the outset.[4]

The unity of the Roman liturgy could not fail to attract advocates of a Church universal. Thus in Gaul, toward the end of the seventh century, there was developed the so-called 'Gelasian Sacramentary.' Far from being a purely Roman liturgy, this was rather a *mélange*: the sacramentary of Gelasius (Pope, 492-96), by dint of its sojourn in France, was 'revised,' 'corrected,' augmented and enriched with Gallican elements.[5] It was again the Roman ritual to which the Frankish kings aspired for a standard Churchwide liturgy. In the wake of his father, Pippin the Short, who had disseminated the Roman chant throughout his realm, Charlemagne set about to make the 'Holy' part of his Empire as uniformly Roman as was the civil. During one of his visits to Italy, he had been appalled at the liturgical diversity abounding in the churches outside of Rome. Determined to make the Roman rite prevail, he sent to Pope Hadrian a request for the Sacramentary serving Rome; the Holy Father agreed to furnish him with the one devised by his immediate predecessor, Pope Gregory, and written 'in his very hand.'[6] This book, which we can reconstruct only on the basis of an edition supplemented by Alcuin, was a specialized one, designed specifically for use in Rome, and, most probably, for the specific use of the Pope. It contained no ritual, no mass for Sundays nor for weekdays that were not feast-days, and was thus wide open to supplementation. Thus, the Roman ritual, though it would prevail throughout the West, was by no means a homogeneous entity, even within its own domain; its ultimate form would be a compilation of Roman and of local prayers and practices, incorporated into the liturgy by such 'editors' as Alcuin, Amalarius and Helisachar.[7] And even after the 'Gregorian Sacramentary' had been prescribed as the official liturgy for all the Empire, it was by no means uniformly welcomed, and nowhere did it encounter more resistance than in Gaul.

France had indeed been long notorious for her individuality. Neither the liturgical reforms of Pippin, who had imposed the Roman chant on the French clergy, nor the efforts of Charlemagne, who had sent out liturgical missionaries armed with the 'Gregorian' Sacramentary, had succeeded in standardizing the Gallican variations to the Roman norm. Even as late as the tenth century, for example, the *Gloria* and the *Credo* were still being sung in Greek in French churches; the *Kyrie* —a Greek vestige which survives, untranslated, in all the liturgies, East and West— was generously farced, that is to say, the standard text was interspersed with new elements, whether in Latin or in a vernacular idiom. Numerous divergences persisted, as well, in the prayers and in the supplements, with each church supplying according to its own needs; the Offices of Matins and of Vespers, especially, were augmented with supplementary readings.[8] Indeed, so different was the Gallican celebration of the Mass from that of Rome and so diverse were the practices among the individual churches in France as to earn the word "anarchy" for their non-conformity.[9]

With such diversity, it is not surprising to find a number of extra-liturgical texts within various service books of French and of Anglo-Norman churches and

106

abbeys. There is, as mentioned above, the addition of Latin lines (here, italicized) to the Greek *Kyrie Eleison*:

> Kyrie eleison, *Domine pater, miserere.*
> Christe eleison, *qui nos redemisti sanguine tuo.*
> Kyrie eleison, *Domine, spiritus sancte, miserere.*[10]

> (Lord, have mercy, *Lord, Father, have mercy.*
> Christ, have mercy, *who redeemed us by thy blood.*
> Lord, have mercy, *Lord, Holy Spirit,have mercy.*)

There are Psalters with an interlinear translation of the Latin into Old French, as in the Eadwine Psalter (Cambridge, Trinity College No. R. 17. 1) and its copy in Paris (B.N. Ms. lat. 8846).[11] Other French and English service books and psalters show vernacular texts augmenting the creeds, canticles, and *Pater Noster*, as in such manuscripts as Lat. 768, 778, 943, 1315 and 1670 of the Bibliothèque Nationale (Paris).[12]

Of special interest is another element with which various service books of French and English origin are supplemented: "*l'Epitre farcie de la Saint-Etienne*" ('Farced Epistle for the [Feastday of] Saint Stephen'). This is a vernacular paraphrase of the account in Acts of the stoning of Stephen, the Epistle reading for December 26, Feastday of St. Stephen. Following each portion of the Latin text, there appears a strophe in French verse paraphrasing the preceding words; this farced element is often furnished with musical notation.[13] Such farced epistles are found in the Gradual of Limoges (Limoges Bibl. munic.); in the Ordinary of Soissons; in Missals such as Paris B.N. Mss. fr. 17307 and 24870; in Psalters such as the twelfth-century Ms. lat. 238 (Paris B.N.).[14]

The oldest known example of the farced epistle of St. Stephen appears in the Missal of the Petit Séminaire of Tours (Tours, Bibl. du Petit Sém. 583). Guy de Poerck places its origin either in the church of St. Mary of Avon or else in the Abbey of Noyers; he estimates the date of its composition as ca. 1130, thus placing it among the oldest works in Old French.[15] Of especial interest for our purposes is its form: strophes (12) of five decasyllabic lines, the same form as that of the *Alexis*. And, as we shall consider more fully further along, its opening rhyme (or assonance) is the same as that which we propose is intended in the Prologue to the *Alexis*: -*un*/*um*. The opening lines of the Tours *Epître farcie de la Saint-Etienne* will demonstrate these features, as well as the arrangement of the Latin and the French texts:

> Lectio Actuum Apostolorum.

> Por amor de vos pri, saignos barun,
> Seet vos tuit, escotet la lecun
> De saint Estevre lo glorius barun,
> [5] Qui a ce jor recut sa passiun:
> [4] Escotet la par benne entenciun.

> [I have reversed these lines.]

> In diebus illis Stephanus autem plenus
> gratia et fortitudine faciebat prodigia et
> signa magna in populo.

> Seint estevres fut plains de grant bonte.
> ema tot cels qui creinent en de
> feseit miracles onon dedemede
> ascuntrat & auces atot dona sante.
> porce haierent autens liiue.[16]

> (Reading of the Acts of the Apostles).

> (For the love of God, I pray you, noble lords,
> Silence yourselves all, give heed to the Lesson
> Of Saint Stephen, the glorious noble one,
> Who did this day receive his Passion:
> Give ear to it with good attention.

> In those days Stephen, full of grace and
> power, did great wonders and signs among
> the people.

> St. Stephen was filled with great goodness.
> He loved all those who believe in God
> He performed miracles in the name of the
> Lord God

108

To the lame and the blind, to all he gave
their health.
For this did the Jews hate him so much.)

The popularity of the farced epistle of St. Stephen
is evidenced by its survival in some fifteen manuscripts
extant, as enumerated by Paul Meyer.[17] Du Méril posits
that its development represents the will of the people to
participate in worship, a role which had early been appro-
priated exclusively to themselves by the priests.[18] Lebeuf
finds it simply an attempt to explain the stories of the
martyrs to the people in their own language.[19] In any
event, the French-farced epistle flourished, and extended
its repertoire to John the Baptist, the Holy Innocents, St.
Nicholas, St. Catherine, St. Blaise and St. Thomas of
Canterbury, with 'epistles' ingeniously found to support
the farced texts.[20] Its use was characteristically French,
according to Prior Lambert of St. Vast, Arras (ca. 1194):

Lumine multiplici noctis solatia praestant
Moreque Gallorum carmina nocte
tonant.[21]

(By the manifold light of night, solace
shines forth, and, as is the custom of the
Gauls, they thunder forth songs in the
night.)

The farced epistle was apparently performed as follows: as the subdeacon went up into the lectern to read the
epistle, he was followed by one or more subdeacons or clerks
vested in copes and charged with singing, after each Latin
verse, the French strophe which gave the explanation to the
faithful.[22] Such directions are furnished by the Soissons
Ordinary, as quoted by Lebeuf: "Epistolam debent cantare
tres subdiaconi induti solemnibus indumentis: Entendez
tuit a cest sermon. . . ."[23] (Three subdeacons attired in High
Mass ceremonial vestments are to sing the Epistle: Give ye
all heed to this lesson...).

That this extraordinary practice expanded beyond
the lay congregation, indeed into a convent, is shown in a
journal entry of Eude Rigaud, Archbishop of Rouen (1248-
1269), in which he recounts that on one of his visits to

Caen, he found some of the younger sisters engaged in singing farced 'epistles':

MCCLVI.
X. KD. Novembris. Visitavimus monastarium monalium Sancte Trinitatis Cadomensis. Abbatissa tunc erat in Anglia. Ibi invenimus LXXII moniales. Una non clamat aliam. Silencium non bene servatur; iniunximus hoc emendari. Vovent tria vota in benedictionibus suis, scilicet votum obedienciae, castitatis, et paupertatis, et nichil aliud. Iuniores... in festo Innocencium, cantant lectiones suas cum farsis; hoc inhibuimus.[24]

(1256.
X. The Kalends of November. We visited the House of Nuns of the Holy Trinity of Caens. The Abbess was at that time in England. There we found seventy-two nuns. One nun [?] calls out to another. Silence is not well observed; we enjoined that this be corrected. They make three vows at their consecration, namely, the vows of obedience, of chastity, and of poverty, and no other. The younger Sisters,... on the Feastday of the Innocents, sing their Readings with farcing inserted; this [practice] we curbed.)

With such Gallic tendencies as we have seen, it is not inconceivable that the story of Alexis, like those of Saints Nicholas, Blaise, Catherine and Thomas of Canterbury, might have received a similarly colorful presentation in a Norman or an Anglo-Norman abbey church or convent on the occasion of his feastday. Nor, indeed, is it inconceivable that such a presentation would have been of a semi-representational nature, given the *mise-en-scène* of the *Etienne* Epistle: a cast of subdeacons, costumed in copes and albs, and lighting via candelabra. Such a presentation would be still embedded in the liturgy, but with exploitation of the dramatic aspects of the story: a mini-"Passion". In addition to the copes and albs for costumes, 'roles' might be assigned to different voices for

110

the direct speech (which occurs in thirty-four strophes of the *Alexis*) and for the narration.

The interweaving of narrative lines within a dramatic rendition is, in fact, a noticeable feature of the vernacular *Resurrection du Sauveur*, a later bona fide play, as may be seen in the example following. I have italicized such lines for emphasis:

PILATUS.

Levez, serganz, hastivement;
Alez tost la u celui pent:
Alez a cel crucified,
Saver u non s'il est devie.
Dunt s'en alerent dous des serganz,
Lances od sei en main portanz;
Si unt dit a Longin le ciu
Que unt trove seant en un liu-

UNUS MILITUM

Longin frere, veus-tu guainner?[25]

(PILATE)

(Rouse yourselves, servants, quickly;
Go at once there where that one is hanging:
Go to that crucified one,
To learn whether or not he is dead.

Then two of the servants went forth,
Carrying with them [their] lances in hand;
So did they say to Longinus the Blind
Whom they found sitting in a place:-

(A SOLDIER)

Brother Longinus, do you want to earn [some money)?]

The opening lines of this play, which are in the nature of a Prologue, are narrative as well:

En ceste manere recitom
La seinte resureccion.
Premierement apareillons
Tus les lius e les mansions:
Le crucifix primerement,
Et puis apres le monument.
Une jaiole i deit aver
Pur les prisons enprisoner. . . .

(In this manner let us recite
The Holy Resurrection.
First, let us prepare
All the *lieus* and the *maisons*:*
First of all, the Cross,
And then, after that, the tomb.
There must be a jail there
In order to incarcerate the prisoners.)

*(medieval theatrical terms for the conven-
tional locations of Earth, Heaven, Hell, etc.,
which remained visible throughout the
performance, in *décor simultané*.)[26]

As Karl Young and others have emphasized, the
elements of drama are inherent in the celebration of the
Mass itself: proscenium 'arch,' lighting, costumes, ges-
tures, symbolic mimesis, and, by dint of antiphonal and
responsorial voicing of 'lines,' dialogue. [27] In France, further representational treatment was utilized for the reading of the Gospel, as Du Méril shows:

Le mardi de Paques, on jouait l'office des
Pèlerins: deux simples prêtres en tunique,
portant leur chappe en travers, un bâton
noueux à la main et une bourse pendante à
la ceinture, comme des voyageurs se
rendant à Emmaus, rencontraient dans le
choeur un dignitaire en aube et en amict,
qui marchait les pieds nus, une croix sur
l'épaule droite, et ils représentaient
l'évangile du jour. Quoique le respect ne
permît pas d'y rien changer, la Passion elle-
même fut arrangée en drame; on la divisa
en parties distribuées, chacune, à un acteur
particulier, et déclamées d'une façon

différente. Un chant doux et triste marquait toutes les paroles du Christ; celles de Pilate et de Judas se criaient sur un ton aigü, qui semblait prendre à tâche d'être désagréable à l'oreille, et la partie narrative était récitée d'une voix à peine accentuée.[28]

(On Easter Monday, the service of the Pilgrims was acted out: two ordinary priests in tunics, wearing their capes sideways, with gnarled staffs in their hands and pouches hanging from the waist, like travelers headed to Emmaus, would meet in the choir a dignitary in alb and amict, who would be walking barefoot, a cross on his right shoulder; and they would act out the Gospel of the day. Although reverence does not allow changing any part of it, the Passion itself was arranged as a drama; it was divided into parts, each one assigned to a particular actor and declaimed in a different way. A sweet, sad voice marked all the words of Christ; those of Pilate and of Judas were shrieked in a piercing tone which seemed to take as its task to be irritating to the ear; and the narrative part was recited, in a voice all but monotone.)

Such a representation of the *Alexis* —the narrative part read or intoned monotonally, the direct speech sung— may be inferred from the description of the poem in its prologue: "Ici cumencet amiable cancun. . . de la vie de sum fils boneuret delquel nus avum oit *lire* e *canter*. . . ." (Here begins the pleasing song... of the Life of his blessed son, of whom we have heard, *read and sung*.) (Emphasis mine.) Such a presentation would conform to the earliest form of liturgical music-drama as described by Glynne Wickham: "It was artificial, mystical, and lyrical —in a word, operatic— rather than realistic and didactic."[29] A similar operatic nature has been remarked by Lynette Muir for the first full-scale liturgical drama, *Le Jeu d'Adam*.[30]

The precedents to the *Alexis* —the *Eulalia*, the *Passion*, the *St. Léger*— share with it a musical nature, as is twice enounced in the opening lines of *St. Léger*:

113

Domine deu devemps lauder.
et a sos sancz honor porter.
in su amor cantomps del sanz
quae por lui augrent granz aanz.
et ores temps et si est biens.
quae nos cantumps de sant lethgier.[31]

(To God our Lord must we do praise
And to His saints [our] honor bear.
In love of Him we sing of saints
Who for Him suffered great torment[s].
And time it is - and meet is so -
That we [now] sing of Saint Léger.)

Moreover, the opening lines of the *Passion*, by their *-um/
-un* assonance, are highly reminiscent of those which
open the *Alexis* Prologue: Ici cumencet amiable *cancun* e
spiritel *raisun* diceol noble *barun* Eufemien par *num*.
(Emphasis added.). The *Passion* opens as follows:

Hora vos dic vera rai*zun*.
de Jesu Christi passi*un*.[32]
                              (Emphasis added.)

(Now I tell you the true account.
of the Passion of Jesus Christ.)

The same assonance opens *La Resurrection du Sauveur*, as
we have seen:

En ceste manere recit*om*
La seinte resurecci*on.*

Similarly, the earliest form extant of the farced epistle,
the Tours *Etienne*, employs the same *-un* assonance (or
rhyme):

Por amor de vos pri saignos bar*un.*
Seet vos tuit escotet la lec*un.*
de saint estevre lo glorius bar*un.*
[5] Qui a ce jor recut sa pasi*un.*
[4] Escotet la par bene entenci*un.*[33]

In view of such an impressing array of precedents, it would seem incontestable that the *Alexis* Prologue, with its conspicuous series of words ending in -*un* and in -*é*, is intended to rhyme, and that it utilizes the characteristically Anglo-Norman tail-rhyme.[34] Like the *Alexis* poem, it is written in prose form in the manuscript: it is for us to arrange such texts in verse form, with some guidance furnished by the scribe's punctuation.[35] Like Konrad Hofmann,[36] I 'hear' rhythm and rhyme in the Prologue, and music, as well: an 'operatic' delivery in which *recitatives* would occur within the other lines, themselves sung melodically. In my 'arrangement' below, accent marks indicate stressed syllables, asterisks and italics indicate *recitative.*

Ici cuméncet amiáble cancún
E spír'tel raisún di cel nóble barún
Eufémien par núm.

É de la vie de sum fílz boneurét
Del quél nus avúm oït líre e cantér.
Par l'(e) divíne volentét.

Il desírrable icel sul fílz angendrat.

Aprés le naisánce co fut émfes
de déu methíme amét.
é de pére e de mére
nurrít par gránt certét.
                    (Ms.: par grant certet nurrit.)

La sue juvente fut honeste e spiritel.

Par l'amístet del súv'rain piétet
la sue spúse juvéne cumándat
al spús vif de véritét

Ki est un sul faiture e regnet an trinitiet.

Icésta historie est ámiáble gráce
E súverain consuláciun a cascún memorie
spirítél.
Les quéls vivent púrement sulúnc castethét.

e dignement séï delítent es góies del ciél
ed es nóces virginéls.[37]

It is of special interest that both the Tours *Etienne*
and the *Alexis* poem are written in five-line decasyllabic
strophes: may we not deduce that this versification was in
conformity to a musical chant, as is furnished in the case
of the *Etienne*?[38] And in view of the fact that the *Alleluia*
furnished the assonance for the first two lines of the
Eulalia ("Buona pulcella fut Eulalia./Bel auret corps
bellezour anima"), it bears considering that the *Te Deum*
may have suggested the *-um/-un* assonance employed in
the *opening lines* of the *Alexis* Prologue, as well as in the
Clermont *Passion, la Seinte Resurreccion*, and the
Stephen *Epître farcie*.[39] It is true that the very subject or
'title' (understood) —*Passion, Resurrection, Actuum
Apostolorum, Chanson (de St. Alexis)*— might have indicated such an assonance, especially in view of their oral
delivery and of the need to 'bring on' the poem strikingly.
Still, it is worthy of note that it was with the *Te Deum* that
the earliest liturgical dramas *ended*, from the *Lazarus* —
both of Fleury and of Hilarius— on through Rutebeuf's
Miracle de Théophile.[40]
The singing of a Saint's Life in church, even though
it was non-Scriptural, was sanctioned by the view that
such writings were, like Holy Writ, *storia*: they furnished
worthy *exempla* to the people as well as the opportunity to
take part in an act of devotion. Indeed, as the opening
lines of the *Léger* have shown us, it is a 'duty' to sing and to
remember the Lives of the holy. Accordingly, in the final
line of the *Alexis*, and in two of its earliest versions (**L** and
V), we find the engagement of the audience solicited to recite the *Pater Noster*; this line, and only this line, indeed,
includes Latin in the **L** manuscript:

En ipse verbe sin dimes: Pater noster.[41]
AMEN.

The liturgical nature of the *Alexis* is thus
'ceremonially' vouchsafed, as has been generally recognized. It is indicated, as well, by the reference to 'this, his
feastday' some hundred lines earlier:

116

Sainz Alexis out bone volentet,
Puroec en est oi cest jurn oneuret.
(ll.541-2)

(Saint Alexis had good will,
For that reason is he honored on this day.)

And along with this liturgical setting, a pastoral/gregorian tone seems repletely emphasized as well, in the poem's **L** version.[42]

Beginning with the discovery of the saint's body, the ordinary people —"la gent menude"— are portrayed with special tenderness and approval. Unlike the high and mighty —Eufemien and the Emperors, notably— who are the most blind to Alexis's worth and to his identity, the common folk are well aware that he is a precious treasure: a Saint and their saviour. So highly do they prize his body that they will not part from it even for the gold and silver which is cast into the street by the scheming 'Dives': their treasure is the holy body, a veritable Corpus Christi:

> Unches en Rome nen out si grant ledice
> Cum out le jurn as povres ed as riches
> Pur cel saint cors qu'il unt en lur bailie:
> Co lur est vis que tengent Deu medisme;
> Trestut le pople lodet Deu e graciet.[43]
> (Strophe 108)

> (Never in Rome was there such great delight
> As on that day had both the poor and rich
> For that holy body that they have in their
>   keeping:
> It seems to them that they hold God himself;
> All the people praise God and give him thanks.)

Along with the tenderness and sympathy expressed for the simple people (*le pople*) who so ecstatically worship the body of Alexis, the poem also shows a compassion for the audience of the poem, the people of God: we, as well, are enjoined to lay hold of this holy man. It is with the benevolent authority and wisdom of a father that the poet urges us to profit from Alexis's example and from his intercession: it is a *Church* 'father' who speaks. Indeed, the last fifteen strophes of the poem (lines 111-125) evoke all

117

the stately splendor of the Church in describing the funeral procession and the burial of Alexis. Candelabra and copes are solemnly and majestically paraded:

> Ad ancensers ad ories candelabres,
> Clers revestuz an albes ed an capes
> Metent le cors en un sarqueu de marbre.
> Alquant i cantent, li pluisur jetent lermes.
> Ja, le lur voil, de lui ne desevrassent.
>
> D'or e de gemmes fut li sarqueus parez
> Pur cel saint cors qu'il i deivent poser.
> En terrel metent par vive poëstet.
> Pluret li poples de Rome la citet:
> Suz ciel n'at home kis puisset atarder.
>
> (Strophes 117-118)

> (With censors and with golden candelabra,
> Priests arrayed in albs and in copes
> Lay the body in a sarcophagus of marble.
> There, some are singing, the more are shedding tears.
> Never, by their will, would they take leave of him.
>
> With gold and with gems was the casket adorned
> For that holy body which they must leave therein.
> Into the earth they place him by sheer force.
> Weeping are the people of Rome the city:
> There is not a one beneath the heaven[s] who can hold it back.)

Indeed, so developed is this appreciation of the worth of the people of God and of the Church's splendor in **L**'s last fifteen strophes as to make them appear an addition to the poem. By contrast, the *Alexis* of the **A** manuscript ends, convincingly enough, at Strophe 110: St. Alexis's body is in Rome, his soul is in Paradise, and the faithful here below are charged to mend their ways in order to join the Saint in heaven. By ending at this point, the **A** version comes full circle to the motif of the *siècles* — the secular world and time with which the poem opens.

"Bons fut li secles al tens ancïenur" is now echoed — and contrasted with perdurable eternity:

> Sainz alexis out bone volente.
> Pur oc est ui en cest iur honurez.
> Li cors en gist a rume la citez.
> E lanme sen est el paradis deu.
> Mult puet liez estre ki si est alose.
>
> Ki ad pechied il sen deit recorder.
> Par penitence mult bien se puet saner.
> Briefs est li siecles plus durable attendez.
> Co depreums la seinte trinitez.
> Od deu el ciel ensemble puissum regner.
>
> AMEN. AMEN.
> (Strophes 109-110)

(Saint Alexis had good will.
For this is he honored on this day.
His body lies in the city of Rome.
And his soul in the Paradise of God.
He who is so placed can be exceeding glad.

He who has sinned should this [well] remember:
By penitence can he make himself whole.
Brief is this life, await [that one] more lasting.
So let us beseech the Holy Trinity.
With God in heaven together may we reign.)

It should be remarked that Strophes 109 and 110 of the **L** manuscript are almost identical to those of **A**:

> Sainz Alexis out bone volentet,
> Puroec en est oi cest jurn oneuret.
> Le cors an est an Rome la citet,
> E l'anema en est enz el paradis Deu:
> Bien poet liez estra chi si est aluez.
>
> Ki ad pechet bien s'en pot recorder,
> Par penitence s'en pot tres bien salver.
> Bries est cist secles, plus durable atendeiz.
> Co preiums Deu, la sainte trinitet,
> Qu'o Deu ansemble poissum el ciel regner.

(Saint Alexis had good will,
For this is he honored on this day.
His body is in the city of Rome,
And his soul is in the Paradise of God:
He who is so placed can be exceeding glad.

He who has sinned can this well remember:
By penitence can he well be saved.
Brief is this life, await [that one] more lasting.
So let us beseech God, the Holy Trinity,
That together with God we may in heaven reign.)

But then, most anticlimactically, **L** starts off again, laboriously enumerating the various afflictions cured by the holy body of the Saint:

Surz ne avogles ne contraiz ne leprus
Ne muz ne orbs ne nuls palazinus,
Ensur tut ne nuls langerus,
Nuls n'en i at ki n'alget malendus,
Cel n'en n'i at kin report sa dolur.

N'i vint amferm de nul' amfermetet,
Quant il l'apelet, sempres nen ait sanctet.
Alquant i vunt, aquant se funt porter.
Si veirs miracles lur ad Deus mustret:
Ki vint plurant, cantant l'en fait raler.
                                                (Str. 111, 112)

(Neither deaf nor blind nor lame nor leper
Nor mute nor sightless nor any paralytic,
Nor one afflicted in any way whatever,
There is not a single one who comes suffering,
Not one, who carries back his pain with him.

There came no infirm, of any infirmity,
Who, when he called on him, straightway was not cured.

Some come there, others have themselves
carried.
Such true miracles did God show to them:
Who came weeping, singing goes away.)

Following this detailed description of the virtues and the
miracles of the holy body, there is an account of its
'Deposition' and its lying in state at St. Boniface ("un'
eglise mult bele"); a lavish description of the sarcophagus
and of the funeral ceremony; a *résumé* of the remaining
earthly days of Alexis's family members, and of their re-
union in heaven. All of these elements are surely of a
"human interest" nature; the pathos of the suffering in-
valid and of the bereaved family would have obvious
popular appeal, as would the *visualization* —whether dramatized or imagined— of the burial scene:

> Ad ancensers, ad ories candelabres,
> Clers revestuz an albes ed an capes
> Metent le cors en un sarqueu de marbre.
> Alquant i cantent, li pluisur jetent lermes.
> Ia, le lur voil, de lui ne desevrassent.
>
> D'or e de gemmes fut li sarqueus parez
> Pur cel saint cors qu'il i deivent poser.
> En terrel metent par vive poestet.
> Pluret li poples de Rome la citet:
> Suz ciel n'at home kis puisset atarder.
>
> (Str. 117-18)

> (With censers, with golden candelabra,
> Clerks vested in white albs and in copes
> Place the body in a sarcophagus of marble.
> Some are singing there, the more are
> shedding tears.
> Never, by their will, would they take leave
> of him.
>
> With gold and with gems was the casket
> adorned.
> For that holy body that they must place
> therein.
> Into the earth they put it by the force of
> their power.
> The people of the city of Rome weep:

There is not a man beneath the heaven[s]
who can hold it back.)

Following these elements, there comes (again) a eulogy for
Saint Alexis, and an exhortation to honor his memory: we
who are so blinded by sin should seek illumination from
this holy man, expiation for our sins, and his intercession
for our peace in this world and our glory in the next.

These fifteen final strophes of the **L** version —all
unknown to **A**— would seem, then, to be especially concerned with appealing to the *lay* people and with drawing
them into an immediate celebration of the saint's Life.
The use of the first person plural imperative (exhortatory)
and of the object pronoun *nous* (*nos, nus*) crowns this appeal:

> Aiuns, seignors, cel saint home en
> memorie,
> Si li preiuns que de toz mals nos tolget.
> En icest siecle nus acat pais e goie,
> Ed en cel altra la plus durable glorie!
> En ipse verbe sin dimes: *Pater noster.*
> Amen.
>
> (str. 125)

> (Let us hold, my lords, this holy man in
> memory,
> So let us pray him that he rid us of all sins.
> That he purchase for us, in this world, peace
> and joy,
> And in the other, the most enduring glory!
> On that word itself, so let us say: *Pater
> noster.*)

Indeed, the Old French secularization of the Latin Life
might be noted as its most salient feature: the Alexis of
the Latin *Vita* is at home in the monastery, the locus of silence, of solitude, and of a placid view of death as "last of
life, for which the first was made," and by which the eternal life will begin. In the Old French Life, however, the
death which would be *Joie* for the ascetic monk has become the *Dol* of the laity.[44] Other human and romantic
elements are also developed more fully in the Old French
poem: the wedding night; the long lamentations of each of
the family members; their own post-Vita 'Lives.' In addi-

tion, as so impressed Peter Damien,[45] there are the paradoxes so strikingly contrasted in the Old French Life that they could not fail to appeal to Everyman: the 'recluse' who stations himself, not in a hermitage or a desert, but, always, in a *city* (Laodicea, Edessa, Rome); the 'solitary' who seats himself in public: if among the poor, he is, even so, conspicuous at the portals of the church; the self-made orphan who takes up lodging at his family's door; the pauper who was rightful heir to the fortune of a noble count; the nameless stranger who, before dying, takes infinite pains to write his own Life in order that he may be identified.

In the light of what seems to be a careful effort to win *public* appeal, it would seem likely that the **L** version of the *Alexis* was specifically designed with a church performance in mind, a performance especially emphasizing the authority and the magnificence of the Church, and especially involving the *lay folk* in singing the praise of one who led a *chaste* and a holy life. Once again, we find ourselves with a set of circumstances which would conform with those of the Abbot Geoffrey: a 'spectacular' performance, for the laity, in a celebrated Abbey church under the rule of one who had taken the vows of poverty, chastity and obedience. In such a setting, and with such a set of circumstances prevailing, provocative questions arise: was the *Alexis* sung simply as a free-standing 'Gallic addition' to the Matins of his feastday? Or may it not, rather, have been employed to 'farce' a suitable scriptural reading, as were the Lives of Saint Stephen, St. Nicholas, St. Blaise, and St. Thomas of Canterbury? Indeed, the typical *exordia* of the *Epîtres farcies* and of one twelfth-century version of *La Vie de S. Alexis* (the **S** manuscript) are esentially the same, as their opening lines will show:

Signour et dames, entendés un sermon...
(*La Vie de S. Alexis*, Paris,
B.N. ms. lat. 12471, f 51v⁰.)

(Lords and ladies, hear [now] a sermon...)

Por amor de vos pri, saignos barun,
Seet vos tuit, escotet la lecun...
(*Epître farcie de la Saint-Etienne*,
Tours, Bibliothèque du
Petit Séminaire 583).

(For the love of God, I pray you, noble lords,
Silence yourselves all, give heed to the
Lesson...)

Moreover, the *Epître farcie de Saint Estiene* of one
manuscript ends, most significantly, with this *explicit*:

> Ci faut *la vie* saint Estiene. [emphasis mine.]
> (Here ends the *Life* of Saint Stephen.)
> (Brussels, Bibl. roy. IV, 1005, f 46.
> [formerly Phillips ma. 6664.])

In addition, the closing strophe of this "Life of Saint
Stephen" is remarkably similar to that of the *Alexis* in
inviting the audience to pray, and to beseech the saint's
intervention; here, as well, an abundant use of first person
plural pronouns and imperatives is notable:

> Or prions tuit au saint martir
> Qui vout por Damnedieu morir
> Qu'il nous puist sauver et garir,
> Et que si puissions nous morir,
> Que Dieus nous prenge a bone fin.
> Dites amen par grant desir,
> Qu'ensi [sic] nous en puisse avenir. Amen.

> [Ci faut la vie saint Estiene.]

> (Now let us pray to the holy martyr
> Who wishes to die for [the] Lord God
> That he may save and heal us,
> And that if we should [come to] die,
> That God may bring us to a good end.
> Say Amen [to show this] strong desire,
> That thus it may come about for us. Amen.

> [Here ends the Life of Saint Stephen.])

If, indeed, 'la Vie saint Alexis' served as 'farcing',
what would have been the appropriate scriptural text *par
excellence*? One Biblical character is immediately suggested by Alexis, "Le Pauvre sous l'escalier": Lazarus, the
Poor Man of the parable. A rereading of his story will recall its similarities with the Life of St. Alexis:

124

There was a certain rich man, which was clothed in purple and fine linen, and fared sumptuously every day: And there was a certain beggar named Lazarus, which was laid at his gate, full of sores, And desiring to be fed with the crumbs which fell from the rich man's table: moreover the dogs came and licked his sores. And it came to pass, that the beggar died, and was carried by the angels into Abraham's bosom: the rich man also died, and was buried; and in hell, he lift up his eyes, being in torments, and seeth Abraham afar off, and Lazarus in his bosom. And he cried and said, Father Abraham, have mercy on me, and send Lazarus, that he may dip the tip of his finger in water, and cool my tongue; for I am tormented in this flame. But Abraham said, Son, remember that thou in thy lifetime receivedst thy good things, and likewise Lazarus evil things: but now he is comforted, and thou art tormented. . . . Then [the rich man] said, I pray thee therefore, father, that thou wouldest send him to my father's house: For I have five brethren; that he may testify unto them, lest they also come into this place of torment. . . .

(Luke 16:19-25, 27-8)

St. Lazarus was one of the most *popular* saints in the Middle Ages, making his appearance in liturgical drama, in church statuary, and through conflation with Lazarus of Bethany, in Hours' illustrations of the Office of the Dead.[46] Poor, sick, and homeless, he could not fail to win the sympathy of the people, whether by reason of their own misery or of their good fortune: "There, but for the grace of God, go I." Thereby, he would well serve to embody and to evoke two sets of medieval doublets: *piété/pitié* and *charité/chasteté*.[47]

Like Alexis, Lazarus sat miserably apart and received only the crumbs from the Rich Man's table.[48] Like Alexis, he earned his reward after death, being borne away by angels into Paradise.[49] Like Alexis, he was entreated to grant mercy and guidance to sinners still on earth. This Poor Lazarus must surely be seen as the human model and

125

praefigura of Alexis, along with his divine one, who 'took upon himself the leprosy of the world.'

And as the advocate in Abraham's bosom whose intercession was sought (if vainly) for sinning mortals, may not Lazarus be seen, indeed, as the Proto-Confessor, as St. Stephen was the Proto-Martyr? As such, the reading of his story might well furnish the *scriptura* for another farcing: that of the Life of St. Alexis.

From the catacombs to the church of St. Albans has been a long and eventful journey. Let us sum up the main stages of this liturgical pilgrimage.

We have observed that two main liturgies were represented in medieval Christianity, the Roman/African and the Byzantine/Eastern. The Roman liturgy was characterized by being more standardized, being centralized in the Holy City. The Eastern was prone to a multitude of variations, since it lacked so central an authority and reference as Rome. From this Eastern liturgy, either via Milan or Lyon, the Gallican rites evolved. And from the outset, the Gallican church exhibited a remarkably individualistic nature, as evidenced by the many additions to its liturgy and the multiple variations in its performance.

Among these variations, peculiar, it would seem, to the church in Gaul, is the *Epître farcie*, an interpolation of a rhymed story in the vernacular to gloss the Latin reading of the day. This we have found highly comparable to the *Alexis* in these respects: their common French origin, as manifest in the language; their common subject matter: the Life or Passion of a saint or martyr; the existence of the same versification in the earliest *Epître farcie* and in the *Alexis* poem; and the same assonance [*-um/-un*], perhaps reflecting the *Te Deum* of liturgy and of drama, in the Tours *Epistle* and in the Prologue to the *Alexis*.

That all of these were sung in church is axiomatic. This is borne out, moreover, by their obvious sharing of the same theme as the Clermont poems: the story of the sacrificial death of Christ or of one of his saints. Whether the Passion of Christ, or the Life of St. Leger, St. Stephen, St. Thomas of Canterbury, or St. Alexis, they all treat of the same subject matter, and they are all associated with the liturgy.

That the *Alexis* may also be associated with liturgical drama in bud is suggested by its showing the same assonance as that of *La Seinte Resureccion*, a bona fide play. This play is remarkable for its containing narrative passages within the 'script.' I have proposed that the *Alexis* —which also contains both narrative and spoken lines— may have been performed in a similar way: as a dramaticized musical reading. Its Old French 'script' would have either expanded or farced a pericope[50] of the Poor Lazarus parable and the Lazarus of Bethany resurrection story. We have seen that the Reading of the Gospel on Easter Sunday was distributed among readers: this is at once suggestive of role playing. So may the *Alexis* have been delivered in the church, as a 'recitative' with individual 'arias.'

The visual features of the *Alexis* have been explored by Lausberg in his schema of twenty-five tableaux for the poem; its dramatic nature has been noted by Patrick Vincent.[51] It would seem eminently valid to explore how the *Alexis* may have been performed within the church: it may well have served as a bridge between sacred liturgy and drama.

[1] L. Duchesne, *Origines du culte chrétien* (Paris, 1898). J. Jungmann, *The Mass of the Roman Rite* (*Missarum Sollemnia*), tr. F. Brunner, 2 vols. (New York: Benziger, 1950). E. Martene, *De antiquis Ecclesiae ritibus*, 2nd edit., 4 vols. (Antwerp, 1736-38). H. Netzer, *L'Introduction de la Messe romaine en France sous les Carolingiens* (Paris: Picart, 1910).

[2] So Jungmann divides the Mass-liturgies of the West itself into two families: the Roman-African and the Gallic. Moreover, "The Gallic liturgies themselves are further sub-divided into four chief forms: the Gallican (in a narrower sense), the Celtic, the Old Spanish or Mozarabic, and the Milanese or Ambrosian." (pp. 44- 45.) As Netzer summarizes (pp. 1-2), liturgists all agree that the Gallic (in the larger sense) liturgy derives from an Eastern base; they differ as to its point of entry. Monsignor Duchesne argues for Milan (*Origines*, p. 84, ss.); the Benedictines of Solesmes, for Rome (*Paléographie musicale*, V); Guéranger (*Institutions liturgiques*, I, p. 193) and English liturgists hold the traditional view that the Gallican liturgy came directly from the churches of Asia Minor.

[3] Jungmann characterizes the Gallican Mass, in all its various locations, as manifesting a leaning towards splendor and the ceremonial along with a rhetoric that was ornamental and diffuse (p. 48).

[4] See Netzer, p. 27: "... les églises des Gaules ... ressemblent à un bloc compacte que Rome n'ose attaquer et qui paraît ne manifester aucun désir ni aucun empressement de se conformer aux usages romains." (...the churches of the Gauls resemble[d] a solid block which Rome dare[d] not attack and which appear[ed] to show not the slightest desire or compunction to conform to Roman practices.)

[5] V. Leroquais, *Les Sacramentaires et les missels manuscrits des bibliothèques publiques en France* (Paris,

1924), xiv. See also H. A. Wilson, *The Gelasian Sacramentary* (Oxford, 1894).

6 Charlemagne's letter no longer exists, but Hadrian's reply does; it is dated at between 784 and 791. In it, the Pope states that he is sending Saint Gregory's Sacramentary by Abbot John of Ravenna. At the top of the manuscript: "... Incipit liber sacramentorum de circulo anni exposito, a sancto Gregorio papa romano edito ...." (Here begins the Book of Sacraments for the whole course of the year, as set forth by Saint Gregory, the Pope, and sent forth from Rome.) In spite of this title, it was not a Gregorian Sacramentary pure and simple: it contains elements posterior to his death, including the Mass itself instituted in St. Gregory's honor. (This is a paraphrase of the summary made by Leroquais, p. xv.)

7 Jungmann, pp. 75-76.

8 A. Clerval, "Préface" to Netzer, *L'Introduction de la Messe romaine en France*, p. v, summarizes the numerous examples therein provided.

9 Leroquais, *Sacramentaires*: [La liturgie gallicane], "abandonnée à elle-même, était vouée à la division et à l'anarchie." (p. xiv.) ([The Gallican liturgy], abandoned to its [own devices], was disposed to division and to anarchy.)

10 Such troping occurred, it is true, throughout the Church, but it received a special significance in Gallic territory, as Jungmann explains (p. 341). There, where trinitarianism was especially vigorous, God the Father was invoked three times, God the Son three times and God the Holy Spirit three times: but all three were in reality directed to Christ. The *Kyrie* was there intoned by three boys.

The roots for such farcing may be seen in Aetheria's journal of her pilgrimage to Jerusalem (*Aetheriae peregrinatio*, Cap. 24, ca. 390 A.D.). At the end of vespers, she says, one of the deacons read a list of petitions, and "as he spoke each of the names, a crowd of boys stood there and answered him each time, *Kyrie eleison*, as we say, Lord have mercy (*miserere Domine*); their cry is without end." (tr. Jungmann, p. 334.)

A thirteenth-century English Psalter, the Corbie Psalter (Paris, B.N. lat. 768) shows a Marian-centered farcing:

> Kyrie virginitatis amator inclite pater et creator marie elyson.
> Kyrie qui nasci natum nolens de virgine corpus elegisti marie eleyson.
> Kyrie qui septiformis dans dona...marie elyson.

> (Lord, illustrious lover of virginity, father and creator, Mary, have mercy.
> Lord, who, not disdaining to become incarnate, didst choose the body of the Virgin, Mary, have mercy.
> Lord, who, bestowing the seven-branched gifts [of the Holy Spirit]...Mary, have mercy.)

A fourteenth-century Metz manuscript (Phillips 6664, now Brussels, Bibl. roy. IV, 1005) includes a French-farced *Pater Noster* in the form of twenty-four quatrains:

> Ci commence la paternostre en françois

> *Pater noster*, vrais peres qui es sires dou monde,
> Qui tes amis jetas de la prison parfonde,
> Tu es cilz dedans qui toutes bontés habonde;
> Par toi seront sauvé li pecheour dou monde.

> *Qui es in celis*, tu qui es ens es ciex,
> Toi qui es douz et simples, humilians et piex,
> Car nous regarde, Sire, de tes glorieus ieux

131

Si nous sera avis que nous en vaudrons
miex.

(Here begins the Pater Noster in French)

(*Pater noster*, true Father who art lord of
the world,
Who cast forth thy friends from the
deepermost prison,
Thou art the One in whom all goodness
abounds;
By Thee will the sinners of the world be
saved.

Qui es in celis, Thou who art, [indeed], in
heaven,
Thou who art kind and gentle, self-
humbling and piteous,
So look on us, Lord, with thy glorious eyes;
Thus will it be shown to us that we shall
more worthy be.

The wide dissemination and attendant
popularization of this practice is evidenced by such
'farcical' farcing as the following, *inter alii*:

Credo, fet il, de mes deniers
In Deum, qu'en porrai je fere?
Ma fame est de si pute afere,
Patrem, que si je li lessoie
Et je, de cest mal garissoie,
Tost m'en embleroit la moitié...

(*I believe*, says he, -and my copper coins
In God, -what can I do with them?
My wife is such a whorish kind,
The Father, that if I left it to her,
And if I should be cured of this illness,
She would at once take half of them away...)

(*Credo à l'usurier*, cited by
Jean-Claude Aubailly, *Le Théâtre
Médiéval*, Paris, Larousse, 1975, p. 38.)

[11] See Chapter III, Note 12.

[12] B.N. lat. 778 (Tropar. /prosar. Narbonense,
12th c.) demonstrates this practice, as may be seen from
Lauer's description of the manuscript's contents.

    F. 1. Chant des généalogies et épîtres farcies
          pour Noël et Epiphanie.
    F. 9. "Kyrie" farcis, classés par tons.
    F. 24. "Gloria" farcis.
    F. 41-199[v]. Prosier, principales fêtes du
          temporal et sanctoral.
    F. 200. "Sanctus" farcis.
    F. 216. "Agnus" farcis.
    F. 217[v] et 218. "Christus vincit ... " ...

    F. 220 "O Redemptor, sume carmen ...", et
          "Kyrie" farcis.
          (Philippe Lauer, *Catalogue Général
            des manuscrits latins*. I.)

[13] L'Abbé Lebeuf, in commenting on this Gallican
custom, notes that it was the "Chant mineur-inverse"
which was employed; he finds that this chant was especially appropriate "pour une plainte." (*Traité historique et
pratique sur le chant ecclésiastique*, Paris, 1741, p. 33.) I
have copied the musical score for "*L'Epître farcie pour la
fête de saint Etienne*" from Lebeuf and included it here as
Appendix IV.

[14] This last, the Troy Psalter, B.N. lat. 238, is dated
as "fin XIIe, commencement XIIIe siècle" by Lauer. It is of
great interest, in my opinion, by reason of its preponderant Marian emphasis, its Saint Catherine page, and its
musically noted *Epître farcie de la Saint Etienne*. Its veneration of the Virgin begins with a full-page miniature (62
v[o]) depicting the Dormition and the Coronation of Our

Lady. Between the lower third of the folio, the Dormition, and the upper third, the Coronation, her Soul is represented as a tiny a-sexual body, received, in drapery, by angels. (The conventional representation of the resurrected Lazarus is, similarly, that of a tiny child, i.e., new-born innocence.) In addition, there are two full-page miniatures depicting Miracles of the Virgin which we shall encounter *chez* Gautier de Coincy (1177-1236). Folio 48, verso, shows *Teofile*, his name on a *banderole*, in supplication before the Virgin; in its second scene, the Virgin stands behind him, with one hand on his back and the other holding the Charter . The other Miracle miniature depicts Coincy's Miracle XI; this is the story of the child who was conceived "une nuit de Pasques," after a vow of continence: if she should conceive, the mother vows, the Devil shall have the child. The miniature, again in two scenes, shows a tonsured priest, hands joined, before the altar: he looks worriedly at a small boy, whom a red devil is clasping about the hips as two of his cohorts —cleft-footed, horned, beast-headed, sexed demons— gloat in triumph. The happy ending shows the Virgin standing behind the boy, one hand on his head, the other holding a book.

I have noted these miniatures because they seem important as a remarkably early manifestation of the Virgin Miracles, whether as Legend or Play.

[15] So listed, as well, among "Manuscrits du XIIe siècle en langue française" by B. Woledge and I. Short, *Romania* CVII (1981), p. 8. See also De Poerck, "Epître farcie de S. Etienne," *Revue de Linguistique Romane* (1963), p. 27.

[16] Published by Gaston Paris, *Jahrbuch für romanische und englische Literatur*, IV, pp. 311 ss.

[17] Paul Meyer, *Bulletin Historique et Philologique du Comité* (1885-87), pp. 315 ss.

[18] Edélestand Du Méril, *Poésies populaires latines du moyen âge* (Paris, 1898), p. 269.

[19] Lebeuf, p. 31.

[20] *L'Epître farcie pour la fête de saint Thomas de Cantorbéry* (B.N. Suppl. lat. 172), for instance, is headed *Lectio libri Sapientiae*. It is, rather, from the *Ecclesiasticus* of Jesus, Son of Sirach, Ch. XXXIX, as Du Méril has found (*Les Origines latines du théâtre moderne*, Paris, 1897, p. 414, note 2.)

[21] Lebeuf, p.120.

[22] Cf. the Ordinance of Eudes de Sully, Bishop of Paris, of 1198:

> Missa similiter cum ceteris Horis ordinate celebrabitur ab aliquo praedictorum, hoc addito quod Epistola cum farsia dicetur a duobus in cappis sericeis.
> (Cited by Lebeuf, pp. 118-9)

(Similarly, Mass, along with the other [liturgical] Hours, will properly be celebrated by one of the clergy, with this addition: the Epistle with [its] farce will be spoken by two [other clergymen] dressed in silk copes.)

If a priest and two subdeacons were not used, the arrangement was for a subdeacon to read the sacred text, two choirboys, the vernacular explanation. All of them stationed themselves in the jube (the gallery behind the rood screen) for this performance. Lebeuf, p. 121.

[23] Lebeuf identifies this Ordinary only as follows: "L'Ordinaire de Soissons (écrit sous l'Evêque Nevelon I au XIIe siècle.)" (The Ordinary of Soissons, written under [the bishopry of] Bishop Nevelon I, 12th century.) He adds: "Les Ordinaires de Narbonne et de Challon font aussi

mention de ces sortes d'Epîtres doubles, qu'on appeloit des *Epîtres farsies.*" (The Ordinaries of Narbonne and of Challon also make mention of these kinds of double Epistles, which were called *Farced Epistles.*)

Here is Dom Martène's text in reference to Gallic farcing:

XI.   Epistola gallice. Memini etiam me legisse in veteri Rituali ma. Ecclesiae Suessionensis, ut in festo Sancti Stephani epistola missae latina & gallice cantaretur. Eandem etiam reperi in antiquo Missali Sancti Gatiani Turonensis ab annis circiter sexcentis exarato descriptam in folio separato pro ut sequitur. LECTIO ACTUUM APOSTOLORUM. Por amor de vos pri Saignos Barun ....
De Antiqu. Eccl. Rit.,
I, I, c. 3, art. 2.

(Gallican Epistle. I remember also that I read in the old Ritual Missal of the Church of Soissons that on the feastday of Saint Stephen the Epistle of the Mass was sung in Latin and in French. Also, that the same [Farced Epistle] was found in the old Missal of Saint Gatian of Tours, which was written some six hundred years ago; the Epistle was described as follows. READING OF THE ACTS OF THE APOSTLES. For the love of God, I pray you, Lord Barons...)

It should be noted that several misreadings of Dom Martène's Latin have yielded "around the year 600". Dom Martène's *De antiqu. Eccles. Ritibus* dates from 1736-1738; the manuscript to which he refers is dated as twelfth-century: hence, it was six hundred years *old* when Dom Martène described it.

136

²⁴ *Regestrum Visitationum,* Archiepiscopi Rothomagensis. (Odo Rigaldus (or Rigaldi)). Edited by Théodose Bonnin, 1852.

²⁵ W. Foerster and E. Koschwitz, *Altfranzösisches Ubungsbuch* (Leipzig, 1921; University of Mississippi, Romance Monograph reprints, 1973), col. 213-24. Narrative lines occur throughout this play, in twelve instances, for a total count of 82 out of the play's 872 lines.

²⁶ It will be recalled that medieval staging was according to the *décor simultané,* in which all the scenes (*loci*) represented in the play were visible throughout the performance: there were no scene changes. In the earliest of these, the liturgical dramas, it was the word, the *Parole,* which was of supreme importance: *In principio Verbum.* And, since it was Holy Writ that was being enacted, it was regarded as dogma, and faithful verisimilitude was required, according to Sepet. Du Méril finds that this went to truly spectacular staging in the 16th-century *Vengance Nostre-Seigneur,* at the end of which the *Meneur de jeu* recapitulates the performance for the spectators:

Vous avez veu vierges depuceller
et femmes maries violer,
Qui leur estoit grant tribulation.

(You have seen virgins deflowered
And married women violated,
Which was a great tribulation for them.)

Similarly, the *Ludus Coventriae* heeds such verisimilitude so far as to have Adam and Eve perfectly *un*costumed:

Therfore we be now caytyvys unkynde
oure pore prevytes ffor to hede,

Summe ffygge-levys fayn wolde I fynde,
ffor to hyde oure schame.

(Therefore are we unnatural wretches
To hide our poor private parts,
Some fig leaves fain would I find
For to hide our shame.)

In the earliest beginnings, when the church was the 'theater', a simple scaffold sufficed; all the characters were seated on it and simply rose to speak their parts. Later, there were three *loci*: Paradise, to the right, the 'good' side; Earth, in the middle; Hell —later to become a gaping and sulphur-belching *Gueule d'enfer*— either to the left, or below Paradise. The Prologue to *La Seinte Resureccion* would seem to have as its purpose the instruction of the audience as to what scenes (*loci*) are meant to be represented. See Gustave Cohen, *Histoire de la mise en scène dans le théâtre religieux du moyen âge* (Paris: Champion, 1906).

27 Karl Young, *The Drama of the Medieval Church*, 2 vols. (Oxford: Clarendon Press, 1933). Edmund Chambers, *The Mediaeval Stage* (Oxford: Clarendon Press, 1903). O. B. Hardison, Jr., *Christian Rite and Christian Drama in the Middle Ages* (Baltimore: Johns Hopkins Press, 1965).

It was especially Amalarius of Gaul who caused the Mass to become, and to be seen as, the great *drama* of salvation. As Jungmann shows, "particularly after the ninth century the whole Mass was explained as a comprehensive representation of the Passion of Jesus .... In fact, the whole life of Christ, the whole history of Redemption is seen represented in the Mass. The sacred action at the altar becomes a play, in which drama and reality are intermixed most mysteriously." (177-8). Erich Auerbach applies this concept to his understanding of the *Adam* play: "Everything in the dramatic play which grew out of the liturgy during the Middle Ages is part of one —and always of the same— context: of one great drama whose beginning is God's creation of the world, whose climax is Christ's Incarnation and Passion, and whose expected conclusion will be Christ's second coming and the Last Judgment. The interval between the poles of the action are filled partly by figuration, partly by imitation, of Christ. Before his appearance there are the characters and events of the Old Testament .... After Christ's Incarnation and Passion there are the saints, intent upon following in his footsteps, and Christianity in general —Christ's promised bride— awaiting the return of the Bridegroom. In principle, this great drama contains everything that occurs in world history." (*Mimesis*, tr. W. Trask, Princeton: Princeton Univ. Press, 1974.) Likewise, such 'spectators' as Jacques Copeau, Paul Claudel, and Hugo Ball see the Mass as the supreme theater, as Ball attests: "For the Catholic there can really be no theater. The play which dominates his life and enthralls his every morning is holy Mass." (E. Hennings-Ball, *Hugo Balls Weg zu Gott*, Munich, 1931, p. 42. Cited in Jungmann, I, p. 3.)

28 Edélestand Du Méril, *Les Origines latines du théâtre moderne* (Paris, 1897), p. 47.

29 Glynne Wickham, *The Medieval Theatre* (New York: St. Martin's Press, 1974), p. 35.

30 Lynnette Muir, *Literature and Drama in the Anglo-Norman Adam* (Oxford: Clarendon Press, 1973), pp. 3-5.

31 W. Foerster and E. Koschwitz, *Altfranzösisches Ubungsbuch*, col. 77.

32 Foerster and Koschwitz, col. 59. See also the edition of Gaston Paris, *Romania*, II, p. 302.

33 Published by Gaston Paris in *Jahrbuch für romanische und englische Literatur*, IV, p. 311 ss. Gaston Paris did not fail to notice that the oldest surviving *Epître farcie* shows the same versification as the *Alexis*. He did not, however, remark the coincidence of -*un/m* in the

Alexis Prologue and in the first strophe of the Epistle farcing.

34 See John Vising, *Anglo-Norman Language and Literature* (London: Oxford Univ. Press, 1923).

35 The text of the poem, though written in prose form, begins each strophe with a capital letter; the prologue, also written in prose form, shows capitals for certain words: this may indicate a poetic intent. These words are: *Ici, Apres, Por, Ki, Icesta*. There are 'periods' after the following words: *num, canter, volentet, angendrat, amet, nurrit, spiritiel, trinitiet, spiritel, castethet, virginels.*

3 6 Konrad Hofmann, "Ein unedirtes altfranzösisches Prosastück aus der Lambspringer Handschrift." "Das altfranzösische Gedicht auf den heiligen Alexius, Kritisch bearbeitet," *Sitzungsberichte der Königl. bayer. Akad. der Wissenschaften zu München*, I (1868).

37 See Appendix VI for a rhythmic notation.

38 See Note 13 supra, and Appendix IV.

39 These are, respectively: *cancun/raisun; raizun/passiun; recitom/resureccion; barun/lecun.* It will be recalled that the *-um* of the Latin *Te Deum* 'recurs' in the Old French *lod[e]ums<laudamus*. Thus, assonance/rhyme was possible between *Deum* and first person plural forms of first conjugation verbs such as *lodums, recituns, priuns*, etc., in their Anglo-Norman forms (*-ums, uns* for *-oms, -ons*).

40 In the Hilarius *Lazarus* (B.N. suppl. lat. 1008, 12th c.), as well: "Quo finito, si factum fuerit ad Matutinas, Lazarus incipiat: Te Deum laudamus; si vero ad Vesperas; Magnificat anima mea Dominum." (Which being finished, if it shall have been done at Matins, let Lazarus begin: *Te Deum laudamus*; if, rather, at Vespers, [let him begin] *Magnificat anima mea Dominum*.) This instance is re-

markable in that only Lazarus begins the *Te Deum*. More commonly, a group begins it, as in the *Conversion de saint Paul* (Orleans, Ms. 178): "OMNES APOSTOLI incipiant: /Te Deum laudamus." (Let ALL THE APOSTLES begin: *Te Deum Laudamus*.) This was evidently the cue for the congregation to join in the singing of this canticle, as indicated by the closing lines of Bodel's *Jeu de Saint Nicolas* (B.N. fr. 25566): LI PREUDOM / A Dieu dont devons nous canter/ Huimais: *Te Deum laudamus*. (THE GOOD MAN: To God, therefore, ought we to sing forthwith: *Te Deum Laudamus*.) Examples could be multiplied: this would seem to be a refrain especially associated with the people. Indeed, is this not indicated in the pre-Reformation German hymn, probably sung, according to Jungmann, as a Credo-refrain? "*Wir glauben* all' an einem Gott" is immediately evocative of "*Nun danken alles* Gott," the great Reformation hymn.

[41] Gaston Paris uses different punctuation for his interpretation:

> En icest siecle nos achat pais e goie,
> Et en cel altre la plus durable glorie
> En ipse verbe. Si'n dimes *Pater noster.*

> (In this life may he buy us peace and joy
> And in that other, the most enduring glory
> In this word [itself]. So let us say Pater noster.)

The **V** manuscript also shows the Latin title, but the first person plural imperative (exhortative) is here replaced by the second person plural future indicative:

> & en laceleste uos achat pais glorie
> en esse uerue [*sic*] si direz pater nostre.
> (624-5)

> (And in the celestial [one] may he buy you peace [and] glory

141

On that word so shall you say [the] Pater
noster.)

The **L**'s Latin (*in ipse verbe, Pater noster*) may be
compared to the 10th-c. *Passion*'s insertion of several
Latin words in its Old French text:

> Et mult corps sant en sun exut
> Et *inter omnes* sunt vedud.
> Qui in *templum Dei* cortine pend
> Jusche la terre per mei fend.
>
> (325-8)

(And many a holy body came out of them
[the sepulchres]
And are seen *among them all.*
The curtain which hangs in the *temple of God*
Splits half in two, all the way to the floor.)

[42] Cf., for instance, the exhortative imperative as
noted just above: 'let's ...' is more benignly paternal than
'you will ....'.

[43] The miraculous powers of the holy body and of
relics are part and parcel of hagiography from its earliest
days: they furnished proof of sanctity.   Indeed, in Old
Testament 'prefiguration', Elijah, after performing a miracle, was told: "Nunc in isto cognovi quoniam vir Dei es
tu." (Now I know that you are a man of God.) (I Kings 17,
24).   The same cognomen, it will be at once remembered,
was that of Alexis, "l'ume Deu."

So highly prized were the holy remains of the
saints that the servants of the Church, from monk to
archbishop-apparent, did not stop at theft in order to effect the 'translation' of a body or of a relic to their own
loca sancta, as we well know for Sainte Foy and Marie-
Madeleine, e.g.   So Hugh, Bishop of London (d. 1200),
chewed off a piece of Mary Magdalene's arm to add to the
treasury of his church.   Likewise, Anselm, asked to au-
thenticate the bones of St. Neot during a visit to England

(shortly before he became Archbishop of Canterbury), took away a small portion of the saint for his own use, locked the bones in a case, and took the key back to Bec. (Ronald C. Finucane, *Miracles and Pilgrims. Popular Beliefs in Medieval England.* Totowa: Rowman and Littlefield, 1977.)

Such veneration, if not such theft, had been manifested by St. Augustine, upon Bishop Ambrose's discovery of two holy bodies:

Tunc mamorato antistiti tuo per visum aperuisti, quo loco laterent martyrum corpora Protasi et Gervasi, quae per tot annos incorrupta in thesauro secreti tui reconderas, unde opportune promeres ad coercendam rabiem femineam, sed regiam. Cum enim prolata et effosa digno cum honore transferrentur ad Ambrosianam basilicam, non solum quos immundi vexabant spiritus, confessis eisdem daemonibus, sanabantur, verum etiam quidam plures annos caecus civis civitatique notissimus, cum populi tumultuante laetitia causam quaesisset atque audisset, exsiluit eoque se ut duceret suum ducem rogavit. Quo perductus inpetravit admitti, ut sudario tangeret feretrum pretiosae in conspectu tuo mortis sanctorum tuorum. Quod ubi fecit atque admovit oculis, confestim aperti sunt. Inde fama discurrens, inde laudes tuae ferventes, lucentes, inde illius inimicae animus etsi ad credendi sanitatem non applicatus, a persequendi tamen furore conpressus est. Gratias tibi, Deus meus!

(Then didst Thou by a vision discover to Thy forenamed Bishop where the bodies of Gervasius and Protasius the martyrs lay hid (whom Thou hadst in Thy secret treasury stored uncorrupted so many

143

years), whence Thou mightest seasonably produce them to repress the fury of a woman, but an Empress [Justina, mother to the Emperor Valentinian]. For when they were discovered and dug up, and with due honour translated to the Ambrosian basilica, not only they who were vexed with unclean spirits (the devils confessing themselves to be so) were cured, but a certain man who had for many years been blind, a citizen well-known to that city, sprang forth desiring his guide to lead him thither. Led thither, he begged to be allowed to touch with his handkerchief the bier of the saints, whose death is precious in Thy sight. Which when he had done, and put to his eyes, they were forthwith opened. Thence did the fame spread, thence Thy praises glowed, shone; thence the mind of that enemy, though not turned to the soundness of believing, was yet turned back from her fury of persecuting. Thanks be to Thee, oh my God!)

(*Confessions*, IX. 6.
tr. E. B. Pusey.)

It was in that year (386) that Augustine became a Christian, after having witnessed these miraculous events. See also his *Letters*, 78, 309; and the *City of God*, XXII:8.

For the veneration of relics, see the classic *Origines du culte des martyrs* of Hippolyte Delehaye (Brussels: Soc. des Boll., 1933). For a similar association with the body of the king —himself something of a God/man— see Marc Bloch, *Les Rois Thaumaturges* (Paris: A. Colin, 1961) and E. Kantorwitz, *The King's Two Bodies* (Princeton: Princeton Univ. Press, 1957).

44 Cf. St. Paul's "For me to live is Christ and to die is gain" (Phil. 1.21); "So then, they that are in the flesh

cannot please God" (Rom. 8 .8), etc. The Pauline antithesis of Life/Death and of Spirit/Flesh would seem to have provided the prime monastic model: "Imitatores mei estote, sicut et ego Christi." (Be ye therefore imitators of me, even as I am of Christ.) (1 Cor. 11.1). A less transcendent image of death was envisaged by the laity, whether in its realistic or eschatological aspects. Cf. Villon's countless grim recitals, as typified in the *Ballade des pendus*: "Quant de la chair, que trop avons nourrie,/Elle est piéca devorée et pourrie,/Et nous, les os, devenons cendre et pouldre" (6-8). (As for the flesh, which we have fed too well, Already is it decayed and putrified, And we, the bones, becoming dust and ashes.)

45 *PL* CLXXII, col. 1045-1046, as noted by Ulrich Mölk, "La *Chanson de saint Alexis* et le culte du saint en France aux XIe et XIIe siècles," *Cahiers de civ. méd.* XXI (1978), p. 355.

46 Thus, the Raising of Lazarus seems to set in motion the events of Holy Week, beginning with Palm Sunday's triumphal entry, in the Clermont *Passion*:

> Anz petiz dis que cho fus fait
> Jhesus lo lazer suscitet
> Chi quatre dis en moniment
> Iagud aveie toz pudenz.,
>
> Cum co audid tota la gent
> Que Jhesus ue lo reis podenz
> Chi eps lo morz fait se revivere
> A grand honor en contraxirent.
> (ll.29-36)

> (A few days before this was done,
> Jesus raised the lazarus [=leper]
> Who, for four days, in the sepulchre
> Had lain, full shamefully.
>
> When all the people heard of this,
> That Jesus, the mighty King,

Had made even the dead live again,
They issued forth to do [Him] praise.)

Indeed, in the Greek church, the Raising of Lazarus
is one of the twelve great feasts, celebrated on the day before Palm Sunday; and in the Russian Orthodox church, it
is called "Lazarus's Saturday."

As the prefiguration of the resurrection of the dead,
Lazarus figured prominently in early Christian art: some
forty such paintings survive in the catacombs. The subjects of the catacomb paintings —Lazarus, Daniel,
Susanna, Jonah, etc.— may be reflected in the prayers of
the early Church, and in literature. Cf., for examples, the
prayers of Roland and of Dona Jimena:

> Cleimet sa culpe, si priët Deu mercit:
> "Veire paterne, ki unkes ne mentis,
> Seint Lazaron de mort resurrexis,
> E Daniël des leons guaresis ....
> > (ll. 2383-6, *La Chanson de
> > Roland*, ed. Bédier)

> (He owns his guilt, so prays he God's mercy:
> "Father of Truth, who has never lied,
> Thou who raised Saint Lazarus from the
> dead,
> And guarded Daniel from the lions...")

> "Ya señor glorioso, padre que en çielo estase ...
> salvest a Jonás, quando cayó en la mare
> salvest a Daniel con sus leones en la mala cárçel,
> salvest dentro en Roma a señor san Sebastián,
> salvest a santa Susanna del falso criminal; ...
> resuçitest a Lázaro, ca fo tu voluntad ...."
> > (*Cantar de Mio Cid*, ll.330;
> > 339-41; 346, ed. Menéndes Pidal.)

> ("Hail, Glorious Lord, Father who reigns in
> heaven...
> Thou didst save Jonas, when he fell into the
> sea;

146

Thou didst save Daniel among the lions in
that foul prison;
Thou didst save Lord Saint Sebastian in
Rome itself;
Thou didst save Saint Susanna from the
false witnesses;...
Thou didst resurrect Lazarus, for it was thy
will...")

Among the many iconographical examples of
Lazarus, as cited by Gertrud Schiller (*Iconography of
Christian Art*, Vol. I, p. 182 ss.), are mosaics in Ravenna
(Sant' Apollinare Nuovo) and Constantinople (Church of
the Apostles); the so-called Gospels of Otto III, a tenth-cen-
tury Reichenau manuscript; pyxes in Paris and in the
Hessisches Landesmuseum (both fifth-century); the bronze
column (A.D. 1015-22) in Hildesheim (St. Michael's).
Especially well-known statuary includes capitals at St.-
Benoît-sur-Loire, at Vézelay, at Vienne, at Moissac, and
those of St.-Denis, where both the Poor Lazarus and the
Resurrected Lazarus are represented.

47 See Lucy Tinsley, *French Expressions of
Spirituality and Devotion* (Washington: Catholic Univ. of
Amer. Press, 1953) for a discussion of how *pietatem* would
give, first, *pietet* to denote God's merciful love and paternal concern for humanity; a reciprocal feeling on the part
of his children would yield **pitiet*.
   The semantic richness of these doublets allowed
Dante to use them effectively in the *Commedia*; when, for
example, the poet weeps at the sight of the horribly disfig-
ured soothsayers, Vergil rebukes him with this *jeu de
mots*: "Qui vive la pietà quand' è ben morta." (*Inferno XX,
28*) ("Here piety lives when pity is quite dead.") I am grateful to Alfred G. Engstrom for calling this to my attention.

   For a discussion of *charité/chasteté*, see Karl D.
Uitti, "The Old French *Vie de St. Alexis*: Myth, Paradigm,
Meaning," *Romance Philology*, XX (1966), p. 273.

147

⁴⁸ This motif appears in the Latin Vita as well;
when Alexis returns to Rome, he beseeches Euphemian:

> Serve Dei, respice in me et fac mecum
> misericordiam, quia pauper sum et
> peregrinus, et jube me suscipi in domo tua,
> ut pascar de micis mensae tuae ....
> > *(De Vita S. Alexii,*
> > B.H.L. 286.)

> (Servant of God, look upon me and show
> mercy to me, who am a pauper and a pil-
> grim; and grant that I may be received into
> thy house, that I may feed on the crumbs of
> thy table...)

The Dives/Lazarus image is further apparent in the
Vita's "*vir ... nobilis* Euphemianus nomine *dives* 'valde,' "
as noted by Lausberg, op. cit., p. 41.

⁴⁹ L. Grodecki, Florentine Mutherich, Jean
Taralon and F. Wormald, in their *Siècle de l'an mil* (Paris:
Gallimard, 1973) provide an excellent example of this
scene in their reproduction of the illustration in the Codex
Aureus Epernacensis, executed before 1039; this is Plate
171 in their book. I have duplicated this illustration in
order that the reader may have a visual reminder of the
Luke parable, and may especially remark the representation of Lazarus as a baby in Abraham's bosom, a convention discussed in Note 14, supra. See Appendix V.

⁵⁰ I use the word *pericope* in its liturgical sense: the
choice of selected Biblical passages appropriate to a feastday or to a subject. This differs from the service of the
early Church, when the various books of the Bible were
read straight through, a *lectio continua.* An altered system of readings developed in the early Middle Ages; it was
especially practiced in monastic churches, according to
Jungmann (p. 401). He finds: "What is not a little surprising is that this system of pericopes, although extended to
two or three days a week, nowhere gives any signs of any

continued series of lessons, not to mention a *lectio continua.* The pericope is chosen very freely, with no regard for previous or succeeding passages. For feastdays, those of our Lord and of the saints, the thought of the feast naturally dictated the choice of both Epistle and Gospel." (pp. 401-2.)

See as well Northrop Frye, *The Great Code* (San Diego: Harvest/HBJ, 1982), pp. 215-6, for the use of *pericope* in yet another context.

[51] H. Lausberg, p. 36. P. R. Vincent, "The Dramatic Aspect of the O.F. *Vie de St. Alexis,*" *Studies in Philology,* LX (1963).

CHAPTER VI

LAZARUS: PROTO-ALEXIS

The lamentations of the father, mother and wife upon discovering that the dead pilgrim under the stairs is their beloved Alexis have long been regarded as one of the most remarkable features of the Old French poem.[1] Eufemien, ever the noble count of Rome and *pater familias*, bewails the loss of his scion and inheritor (ll. 386-420). The spouse laments the beautiful young man who now must rot in the grave: her hopes now dashed and her earthly joy impossible, she will finish her life in serving God (ll. 468- 495). But the grieving of the mother is singularly wild and vehement: hers is the primal rage of the animal mother who sees the fruit of her womb cut down.[2] Of the nine strophes (ll. 421- 465) recounting her mourning, two and a half are devoted to describing her physical disarray and her frenzied actions:

De la dolur qu'en demenat li pedra
Grant fut la noise, si l'antendit la medre:
La vint curant cum femme forsenede
Batant ses palmes, criant, eschevelede:
Vit mort sum fils, a terre chet pasmede.

Chi dunt li vit sun grant dol demener
Sum piz debatre e sun cors dejeter,
Ses crins derumpre e sen vis maiseler,
Sun mort amfant detraire ed acoler,
Mult fust il dur ki n'estoüst plurer.

Trait ses chevels e debat sa peitrine,
A grant duel met la sue carn medisme. . . .

Plurent si oil e si jetet granz criz;
Sempres regret [et]. . . .

(ll.421-32;436-7)

(Of the lament that the father exerted
The noise was great, [and] so the mother heard:
There she came running like a woman demented,
Beating her palms, shrieking, disheveled;

151

She saw her son dead, to the ground she
falls senseless.

Whoever then saw her keening her deep sorrow,
Beating her chest and hurling herself about,
Pulling her hair and clawing her face,
Snatching up her dead child and folding
him to her neck,
Had to be hard of heart, were he not forced
to weep.

She tears out her hair and pommels her chest,
This her own flesh she puts to cruel pain. . .

Her eyes stream tears, she hurls out piercing
cries;
Grieves without pause. . .)

But aside from her physical expressions of grief, it
is the mother's verbal lamentations which predominate
in this *planctus*, in seven strophes (87-93), and which
make the Old French *Alexis* remarkable. For they add a
personalized expression of raw anguish to the stereotypi-
cal breast-beating and hair-yanking encountered earlier
in the Old French poem, and in the Latin *Vita* as well. In
the space of these seven strophes, the thronging people, the
Pope and the Emperors, Alexis' father and his spouse, all,
fade out, quasi-cinematographically, for a close-up scene
of the mother and her son —an animated *Pietà*. The
'script' for six of these strophes (87-92) is a *dialogue
manqué*, for the interlocutor's impassioned questions and
accusations are 'answered', poignantly, by the silence of
the dead. The language itself bespeaks maternal intimacy
in its being centered on '*moi/toi*', in twenty-six
occurrences and especially in its persistent use of the
familiar *tu*, and in its caressing vocatives, insistently
repeated: "*filz*," "*bel filz*," "*Cher Fiz*,' "*Filz Alexis*" (twice)
(strophes 87-91).

Moreover, a full six strophes of this *planctus* are
addressed *directly* to Alexis, and in his three life-stages of
dead pilgrim, stalwart youth, precious baby. This chrono-
logical reversal is, itself, mnemotically valid, and dra-
matically striking. The mother sees the corpse of the
wretched beggar: she begrudgingly recognizes him as her
son; she recalls him as she last saw him, in his prime;

152

these *personae* that the mother appeals, by name; in this one-voice 'dialogue' the silence of a triune *persona* speaks louder than words. Even so, the passionate words as well as the frenzied actions of the mother are rooted in the elemental shock of seeing dead the flesh of her flesh. The primal counterposing of birth and death is extended —and intensified— by including the prenatal and the post-mortem Alexis:

> 'E filz,' dist ele, 'cum m'oüs enhadithe!
> E jo, dolente, cum par fui avoglie!
> Net cunuisseie plus qu'unches net vedisse.'
>
> . . . 'Mar te portai, bels filz!
> E de ta medra que n'aveies mercit?
> Pur quem vedeies desirrer a murir,
> Ço'st granz merveile que pietét ne t'en prist.
>
> A! lasse, mezre[3], cum oi fort aventure!
> Or vei jo morte tute ma porteüre.
> Ma lunga atente a grant duel est venude.
> Pur quei[t] portai, dolente, malfeüde?
> Ço'st granz merveile que li mens quors tant
> duret.
>
> Filz Alexis, mult oüs dur curage,
> Cum avilas tut tun gentil linage!
> Set a mei sole vels une feiz parlasses,
> Ta lasse medre, si la [re]confortasses,
> Ki si'st dolente. Cher fiz, bor i alasses!
>
> Filz Alexis, de la tue carn tendra!
> A quel dolur deduit as ta juventa!
> Pur quem fuïs? Jat portai en men ventre,
> E Deus le set que tute sui dolente;
> Ja mais n'erc lede pur home ne pur femme.
>
> Ainz quet vedisse, [sin] fui mult desirruse;
> Ainz que ned fusses, sin fui mult angussuse;
> Quant jo[t] vid ned, sin fui lede e goiuse.
> Or te vei mort, tute en sui doleruse.
> Ço peiset mei que ma fins tant demoret.'
> (ll.432-435; 437-460)

('O son,' says she, 'how much thou hated me!
And I, in grief, how was I purblinded!
I no more knew thee than if I'd never seen
thee.'

. . .'Evil the day I bore thee, dear son!
And why hadst thou no mercy for thy
mother?
So didst thou see me yearning so to die,
Great wonder 'tis that pity did not move
thee.

Alas, [mezre,] what [evil] news I hear! [mezre: at issue.]
Now see I dead all of my progeny.
My long wait has come to grievous sorrow,
And I -sad, downcast-, why did I carry thee?
Great wonder 'tis that my heart last so [long].

Son Alexis, full hard a heart hadst thou;
How hast thou debased all thy noble line!
Hadst thou, to me alone, but one time spoken,
Thou wouldst have thus consoled thy poor mother,
Who is disconsolate. Dear son, well might
thou have so done!

Son Alexis, [oh for] thy tender flesh!
To what distress didst thou traduce thy youth!
Why fledst thou me? I bore thee in my belly,
And God [well] knows that I am deep
downcast,
[Nor] never shall be glad, for woman nor for
man. [text: man. . .woman.]

[Long] ere I saw thee, therefor was I desirous;
Ere thou wert born, thereof was I anxious;
When I saw thee born, then was I glad and
joyous.
Now I see thee dead, and I am desolate.
It grieves me sore that my end tarries so.'

Within this plaint of the mother, there occurs a
word which has long perplexed linguistic scholars. This
word, a *hapax legomenon*, occurs in line 441: *mezre*.
Gaston Paris declares: "J'ai longtemps hésité sur le sens du
mot *mezre*."[4] ('I have hesitated for a long time on the

meaning of the word *mezre*.') He assigns to it the probable meaning of "malheureuse." Müller and Suchier judge that *mezre* is an Anglo-Norman form, for "mother."[5] Now while *malheureuse* would supply a plausible meaning, though only if "que je suis" is understood by ellipsis, the fact remains that the text shows *mezre* in this one line and not *malfeüde*, which does occur three lines later when the mother clearly *is* describing herself. And, an Anglo-Norman scribe notwithstanding, the text shows seventeen appearances of *medra/- e*: a meaning of "mother" for *mezre* seems therefore out of the question. Let us assume that the poet chose *mezre*, and that the scribe recorded it accordingly.

I would propose a specific and completely different meaning for this *hapax*. Such a meaning has the advantage of being perfectly defensible phonologically. And semantically, it would offer a whole new understanding for the Old French *Alexis*.

I propose that this word represents an early form of the Old French word deriving from the Arabic *mezora*,'leprosy,' becoming *mez're* by the long-established process of syncope.[6] Its survival is seen in the Old French *mesel* and *mezellerie*, the term par excellence for the leper and his haven.[7] Semantically the word *mezre* would have merged with Latin *misellus* "poor, wretched": the semantic association of leprosy with misery is a natural one. Indeed, Paris himself notes that *mesel*, 'the Old French diminutive from *misellus*, had a special application to lepers':

> *Mezre* est un απαξ λεγόμενον. Le diminutif *mesel*
> a généralement le sens spécial de 'lépreux.'[8]
> (*Mezre* is an *hapax legomenon*. The diminutive
> *mesel* usually has the special meaning of
> 'leper.')

By the obvious association of leprosy with misery, the sentiment of compassion was engendered; the specific use of *mesel* indeed carried with it the special connotation of sympathy and pity, as Paul Rémy observes:

> Le mot *mésel*, aujourd'hui vieilli, a le sens
> étymologique de pauvret, chétif, malade
> (*misellus*, diminutif de *miser*); appliqué au

155

lépreux, il évoque une appréciation charitable, celle qui inspira les grands exemples hagiographiques, les Conciles, et les Congrégations.[9]

(The word *mesel, now archaic, has the etymological connotation of pitiful, puny, sick (*misellus, diminutive of *miser); applied to the leper, it evokes a charitable connotation, that which inspired the great hagiographical examples, the Councils, the Congregations.)

The use of *mezre* in our text could, then, be understood as signifying both the disease of leprosy —physical or metaphorical— and the affective response of the mother of Alexis in her heartbroken recognition of the miserable, wretched pilgrim as her son. The reading of this line (441) with *mezre* as a vocative is exquisitely pathetic: 'Alas, poor (leprous) wretch!' makes perfectly good sense —and it has the words to justify it. It also conforms to a pattern whereby the mother addresses her son by identifying his very persona as *Dear Son* or as *Poor Leper*. The reading 'Alas, miserable. . .' requires interpolating 'woman that I am.' The reading 'Alas, mother . . .' hardly seems plausible for the mother to utter of herself.[10]

With no other instance of the word *mezre* in Old French, unfortunately, we have no means of verifying that its etymon is *mezora* (perhaps + *misellus*). But we do have numerous examples of the use of *mesel* in medieval texts, both French and English, to denote the leper,[11] and of *mezelleries* —along with *ladreries, leproseries, maladreries, corderies, magdelaines*— to designate their hospices.[12] Of these, Europe knew 19,000, and France, 2,000, by Matthew Paris's reckoning, following the Crusades.[13]

By that time, the disease had reached pandemic proportions in western Europe: it has been called "the greatest disease of mediaeval Christendom."[14] Long prevalent in the East, its early establishment in Persia is noted by Herodotus. By the first century B.C., leprosy was well ensconced in Greece and Italy; Pliny attributes it to Pompey's return from Syria.[15] The disease appeared early, as well, in the Roman colonies of Spain, Gaul and

Britain, where it was seen as having arrived with the conquerers.[16] By the eighth century it was especially prevalent in the south of France and in Spain via contact with the Jews, long prey to leprosy, and with the Saracens, then populating the Midi. Dreaded as "le mal suprême" (the supreme malady), it was unsparing in its choice of victims: "Ki n'espargne ne roi ne conte."[17] (Which spareth neither king nor count.) The blight of Europe during the Crusades by "le mal d'Acre" occasioned the founding of leper houses by religious communities and by every considerable town. And, significantly , one of the most noteworthy of these was at Saint Albans: there, the leper hospital of Saint Julian was founded in 1146 by none other than Abbot Geoffrey, the man whose name attaches to the *Ludus Catharinae*, to Christina of Markyate, and to the Saint Albans Psalter. Later, we shall consider Abbot Geoffrey's providing for lepers at St. Julian's.[18]

Leprosy's impartiality in its choice of victims is shown by its association with such prestigious names as Constantine, St. Louis and Louis XI, along with the nameless and legion poor.[19] Its wholesale assault on every segment of society is further reflected in the foundation of the *Ordre St-Lazare* in Jerusalem in 1119. Taking the name of Lazarus, patron saint of leprosy, this order recruited its members from "*gentilshommes lépreux,*" whose original mission was to care for their fellow victims.[20]

In addition to leprosy's actual manifestation, the Middle Ages knew and hearkened to a long-existing convention on *le mal St- Lazare,* as has been effectively documented by Saul Brody:[21] so entrenched was leprosy-consciousness that it served as an 'elastic' diagnosis embracing a host of other physical diseases such as psoriasis, edema, syphilis, cancer, in addition to its allegorical usage.

The Bible, prime textbook of the Middle Ages, offered a rich lode of leper lore in Old Testament stories involving Abraham, Moses, Miriam, Uzziah, Naaman, Job and David.[22] It is especially the book of Leviticus which offers specific references to the disease, including minute rituals of purification for the leper. This Book of Laws has as its cardinal purpose the distinguishing between the clean and the unclean, the holy and the unholy, as Brody shows.[23] By extension of the idea that leprosy is unclean and therefore unholy, the disease early came to be seen as one of moral impurity: it was a foul and loathsome malady whose very source was sin, and sin continued to manifest itself as a morbid symptom in the lasciviousness of the leper. Doctors would attest to "les grands désirs vénériens [des lépreux]" ('the strong lustful desires [of lepers]') and employed the name "satyriasis" for leprosy, "à cause de la rougeur des joues et de la propension irrésistible et honteuse aux rapports sexuels" ('because of the redness of [lepers'] cheeks and [their] irresistible and shameful propensity for sexual relations.').[24] It is this understanding that underlies the *Tristan* episode in which the leper Ivain proposes that King Marc can punish Iseut more brutally by giving her over to the lepers than by burning her to death:

> Veez, j'ai ci conpaignons cent;
> Yseut nos done, s'ert conmune;
> Paior fin dame n'ot mais une.
> Sire, en nos a si grant ardor
> Soz ciel n'a dame qui un jor
> Peust soufrir nostre convers. . . .[25]

> (See, I have a hundred companions here;
> Give us Iseut: she will belong to us all.
> Never did a woman have a worse end.
> My lord, in us there is such a hot flame
> That there is no woman under the sun
> Who could for one day endure our attentions.)

But along with the image of leprosy as a shameful disease, there prevailed a contradictory idea, especially propagated by the Church: leprosy was a special mark of divine favor, a "sacred malady" bestowed upon those whom God most loved. Brody cites St. Gregory of Nazijanzus (ca. 325-390) to show that the disease was early associated with saintliness:

> We should above all be especially pitiful toward those afflicted with the Sacred Malady. . . .[26]

Indeed, Jesus himself was associated with leprosy; in accordance with the prophecy of Isaiah, he had taken upon himself the sins of the world, and its leprosy:

> Vere languores nostros ipse tulit et dolores nostros ipse portavit, et nos putavimus eum quasi leprosum et percussum a Deo et humiliatum.
>
> (Isaiah 53:4)[27]

> (Surely he himself hath borne our griefs and he himself hath carried our sorrows; and we counted him as a leper and stricken by God and humiliated.)

The several cases of Jesus' healing of lepers amplified this association and contributed to an "*aura merveilleuse*" surrounding leprosy. This "aura" pervades as well the popular legends of Jesus' childhood wherein lepers are healed upon being doused with the bath water of the Christ child.[28]

The idea that "whom the Lord loveth, him he chasteneth," was above all inherent in the story of the Christ-type Job, whom the Middle Ages considered a leper, and in the parable of the 'leprous' Lazarus whom "God loved more than others."[29] Rémy assesses the influence of the New Testament miracles and of the Job and Lazarus figures as follows:

> Ces miracles, ajoutés à la *Résurrection de Lazare*, si importante dans la littérature et l'iconographie chrétienne, sont renforcés par un apologue de l'*Ancien Testament* qui, comme celui de Job, a rang de cliché au moyen âge: la *Parabole du mauvais riche* (épisode souvent confondu avec la résurrection de Lazare).[30]

> (These miracles, added to the *Resurrection of Lazarus*, so important in literature and Christian iconography, are reinforced by an apologue [to] the *Old Testament* which, like that of Job, rates as a cliché of the Middle Ages: The *Parable of the Evil Rich*

Man [an episode often confused with the resurrection of Lazarus]).

Thus the theme of leprosy appears frequently in medieval literature, and it often includes a righteous person chosen by God to bear this infirmity. Among the better-known French examples are *Sainte Foy d'Agen*, *la Vie de Sainte Enimie*, *Guillaume de la Barre*, the *Congés* of Jean Bodel and of Baude Fastoul, *Amis et Amiles*, and the *Tristan* of Béroul. The last of these demonstrates the ambivalence of leprosy in its episode involving the noble Tristan, who 'takes upon himself' the garb of the 'leper' in order to 'save' Iseut. Having disguised himself as a leper, Tristan offers to carry Iseut across a stream, and thus permits the Queen to swear with impunity that no man but her husband, Marc, and "this leper" has ever lain between her legs.[31] Leprosy strikes both the just and the unjust in one of the Miracles de Notre-Dame: the Empress of Rome is abandoned to die by her husband's servants who had been ordered to slay her for her 'infidelity;' her innocence moves the Virgin to come down to her aid, and to supply her with herbs that can immediately heal any leper who has made a full confession. With these herbs, the Empress cures all the lepers in the "comtés (counties) de Celanne, de Malepel et de Fondi." The news of these cures reaches Rome, where the Emperor's brother is rotting with leprosy; it is his lies which had caused the downfall of the Empress. When he finally makes a full confession, including his attempted seduction of the Empress and his false accusation of her, he is at once restored to health.[32]

The "aura merveilleuse" of leprosy is notable in other pious tales, such as the following:

> . . . a monk named Martyrius comes upon a leper who cannot walk. The monk carries the leper to the monastery; as Martyrius approaches the monastery, the abbot sees that his monk is carrying Christ.

> . . . a certain pious Count Theobald cared for a leper who lived in a hut outside the village of Sezenna. Unknown to Theobald, the leper died; however, when the count went to visit the leper, he found him in the hut as usual. Later, after learning that the leper

had been dead for some time, the count returned to the hut and was greeted by an air
of sweetness-a sign given by the Lord to
show how pleasing he considers works of
piety.[33]

Among Saints' Lives involving leprosy, the best-
known is surely Flaubert's masterful retelling of *La
Légende de Saint Julien l'Hospitalier*, a legend represented
in a famous stained glass window of the Rouen cathedral
and recounted in both the *Speculum Historiale* of Vincent
de Beauvais and the *Légende dorée* of Jacques de Voragine.
After years of doing penance for having unwittingly
murdered his father and mother, Julien settles in a hut by
a river where he will 'use out his life in serving others,'
transporting them without remuneration. On a stormy,
raging night, he hears a voice calling him, three times,
from the other side of the river; he crosses to find a
hideous leper, who shows, however, the majesty of a king.
The return crossing is supernaturally tempestuous, but
Julien prevails, for he senses that this is an order that he
must not disobey. Once in the hut, he can see his guest
more clearly: a skeleton covered with scaly pustules, his
nose replaced by a hole, his bluish lips emitting a fetid
stench. Imperiously this ghoul demands that his needs be
satisfied; Julien supplies food, drink, fire, and, at last, his
own bed. The leper continues his fractious demands: his
bones are like ice! he is going to die! Julien must undress
and cover him with his own warm body! He stretches
himself out on the leper, mouth against mouth, chest
against chest:

> Alors le lépreux l'étreignit; et ses yeux
> tout à coup prirent une clarté d'étoiles; ses
> cheveux s'allongèrent comme les rais du
> soleil; le souffle de ses narines avait la
> douceur des roses; un nuage d'encens s'éleva
> du foyer, les flots chantaient. Cependant
> une abondance de délices, une joie
> surhumaine descendait comme une
> inondation dans l'âme de Julien pâmé; et
> celui dont les bras le serraient toujours
> grandissait, grandissait, touchant de sa tête
> et de ses pieds les deux murs de la cabane. Le
> toit s'envola, le firmament se déployait; -et

Julien monta vers les espaces bleus, face à
face avec Notre-Seigneur Jésus, qui
l'emportait dans le ciel.[34]

(Then the leper clasped him; and his eyes
suddenly took on a clarity like the stars';
his tresses spread out like the rays of the
sun; the breath of his nostrils had the
sweetness of roses; a cloud of incense wafted
up from the fireplace, and its vapors were
singing. Meanwhile, a wealth of rapture, a
superhuman joy descended like an engulf-
ing wave into the soul of Julien, [now] in a
swoon; and he whose arms were enfolding
him became larger, ever larger, touching
with his head and with his feet the two
walls of the hut. The roof flew away, the
firmament split in two; —and Julien as-
cended toward the ethereal blue, face to face
with our Lord Jesus, who was bearing him
up into heaven.)

But all the while emphasizing the spiritual
uniqueness and sacred aura of leprosy, the Church also re-
inforced the idea of its supreme and special loathsome-
ness, both physical and moral. The malady was used with
great frequency as the prevailing figure for sin, as in the
following lines from Robert de Brune's *Handlyng Synne*
and the accompanying *Manuel des Pechiez* of William of
Wadington:

He ðat ys yn dedly synne,
Gostely he ys a mesyl with-ynne.
(ll. 11466-11467)

(He who is in deadly sin,
Spiritually, is he a leper within.)

Chescun en péché mortel
Est un leprus espirituel.
(ll. 9892-9893)[35]

(Each one in mortal sin
Is a spiritual leper.)

Rémy provides a particularly significant anecdote,
which he characterizes as 'typical,' in which leprosy
serves as the metaphor for sin:

Quaedam pulcherrima domina quendam
sibi pulcherrimum desponsavit maritum.
Que spreto cuidam turpissimo adhesit
leproso. Ipsum soram marito legitimo
frequenter osculata est. Dicit ei maritus:
sponsa mea, quare cum leproso me presente
delicias ducis? Maritus est sponsus, sponsa
fidelis anima; leprosus diabolus, mundus,
vel peccatum.[36]

(Now a certain very beautiful lady took unto
herself a most comely husband. But,
shamefully, she attached herself to a most
repulsive leper. She kissed him frequently,
right in front of her legitimate husband.
The husband said to her: my spouse, why do
you disport yourself with a leper in my very
presence? The husband is the *Sponsus*, the
Sponsa is the faithful soul; the leper is the
Devil, the World and Sin.)

The ambivalent image of the leper as saint and
satyr is especially discernible in the *separatio
leprosorum*, a rite of confirmation in a living death. This
ritual was formally instituted in 1179 by the Third
Lateran Council and was observed, though with local
variations, throughout Europe.[37] Typically, after having
been declared a leper, the victim was subjected to a symbolic *office des morts* whereby he was declared dead to this
world, as summarized in *La Grande Encyclopédie*:

Nombre d'anciens livres ecclésiastiques en
ont conservé le rituel qui ne variait guère
d'un diocèse à l'autre; c'était après une brève
exhortation du prêtre à se montrer résigné
à la volonté de Dieu, une messe funèbre: à
genoux sous un drap mortuaire le lépreux
assistait vivant à ses obsèques, après

lesquels il était conduit processionellement à la maladerie ou dans la borde qui devait être son dernier asile. Là, nouvelle cérémonie: genouillé, le lépreux recevait sur la tête une pelletée de terre en même temps que le prêtre lui déclarait qu'il était mort au monde.[38]

(A number of ancient ecclesiastical books have preserved the ritual which scarcely varied from one diocese to another; after a brief exhortation from the priest to show himself resigned to the will of God, there was a funeral mass: on his knees, underneath a shroud, the leper, alive, attended his own funeral, after which he was led in a procession to the leper house or into the isolated hut which would be his final shelter. There, a new ceremony: kneeling, the leper received on his head a shovelful of earth as the priest declared to him that he was dead to the world.)

In one of the variations of this ritual, the leper had to stand in his symbolic grave to receive three spadefuls of earth. The standard ending to the ritual was that of the funeral Mass, as Rémy describes:

. . . Le prêtre, après avoir chanté le *Libera me* et le *De Profundis*, reconduisait le lépreux vers sa dernière demeure, en déclarant: "Sis mortuus mundo. . .vivus item Deo."[39]

(. . . The priest, after having chanted the *Libera me* and the *De Profundis*, led the leper back to his last abode, while declaring: "Be dead to this world. . . and, all the while, alive unto God.)

Thus separated from the world, the inmates of a church-affiliated leprosarium lived in accordance with the rule of St. Augustine, taking the vows of poverty, chastity and obedience, wearing the monastic habit, and leading a severely ascetic life.[40] For lepers not sequestered in a leprosarium, the *modus vivendi* varied greatly, according to the laws and sentiment of the particular time and community and upon the leper's own economic situation. Thus we encounter the full range of living conditions, from seclusion in a countryside hut, as with *Der Arme Heinrich*,[41] to conspicuous occupancy of the throne, as with Baudouin, who died leprous and sovereign, though his fingers and toes fell off in 'putrefaction.'[42] Between these extremes were the many lepers who stationed themselves in city square and church *portail* to beg alms. For the impoverished leper, this was commonly the sole means of subsistence: begging was the only occupation universally permitted by law, as well as by infirmity.[43]

Marriage rights were highly variable, as well. On the whole, the Church tended to discourage divorce from a leprous spouse, but release from marriage was sometimes permitted. Such a dispensation was made by Pope Sirice (4th C.), Pippin the Short, the Parliament of Compiègne (757) and Charlemagne, and until the Norman Conquest, leprosy constituted legal grounds for divorce in England.[44] When separation was not formally authorized, it was sometimes understood as the natural right of the spouse whose partner had become "dead to the world" by ecclesiastical ritual or legal decree; thus, the Compiègne decree permitted a leper to free his healthy spouse to remarry. More often, however, it was held that man and wife remained one flesh, indissoluble, even if one of them became leprous, as stated by Pope Alexander III in a letter to the Archbishop of Canterbury:

> We commend that you should not delay in strongly persuading wives to follow husbands and husbands to follow wives who have contracted leprosy and to care for them with conjugal love. But if they cannot be persuaded to do this you should strictly order them to observe continence whilst either of them is alive. And if they refuse to accept your order, you should excommunicate them.[45]

Similar ambiguity prevailed in the (male) leper's property and inheritance rights. Generally he was permitted to retain what he owned, using it to purchase placement in a leper house, but as an anomalous person: "dead to [this] world," he was denied the right to inherit.

In summary, the medieval leper was subjected to the widest extremes in his society's reaction to one stricken with the "Sacred Malady." He might be cast as satyr or saint, pariah or priest, depending on his community's understanding of the leprosy mystique. In any event, he was seen as a living corpse. Other lepers were his only true *semblables*; though he remained in this world, he was not of it, for the other world was the assigned habitat *des Aussätzigen* (of the leper —the one seated outside).

These are, indeed, the very paradoxes which constitute the whole ethos of the *Alexis*. They are so starkly contrasting as to form a whole series of binary oppositions, to wit: life vs. death; the spiritual vs. the carnal; health/holiness vs. infirmity/sin; inestimable spiritual riches vs. total material poverty; the company of God and his angels vs. isolation from human society; advancement toward eternal life vs. declining toward physical death; the celestial world, eternal and invisible, vs. the terrestrial world, temporal and illusory. With these similarities between the leper's lot and image and those of Alexis, it would appear incontestable that Alexis, latter-day Saint Lazarus and *imitator Christi*, might well have been seen as a leper who took it on himself to 'bear our infirmities' and 'carry our sorrows,' - "*quasi leprosum.*"

Aside from the allegorical significance of leprosy, there existed a somewhat confused understanding of the physical disease per se. The most telling sign was seen to be a change in the skin; the color might change from normal tones either to redness or to ashen lividness, and the texture might be afflicted in any number of ways, ranging from sores, chancres, pits, lesions or swellings to erosion and putrefaction of the flesh. The features might become so changed as to be unrecognizable in Leonine leprosy, wherein the forehead and eyelids thickened and the nasal wings became obscured. Clouded-over eyes and huskiness, raucousness or hoarseness of voice were seen as bona fide symptoms of one type of leprosy; a host of others were leprous manifestations by medieval lights: paralysis, blindness, muteness, a putrid odor of breath and flesh, and, even, baldness. By these criteria, the 'symptoms' of Alexis' illness can well support leprosy as a diagnosis.

166

As prime symptom, there is such a change in his flesh that his father's servants do not recognize him:

> Iloc truverent danz Alexis sedant
> Mais n'a(n) conurent sum vis ne sum semblant.
>
> Si at li emfes sa tendra carn mudede,
> Nel reconurent li dui sergant sum pedre. . . .
> (ll. 114-17)

(There they found Lord Alexis sitting
But they did not recognize his face nor his appearance.

So much had the child altered (in) his tender flesh
[that] the two servants of his father did not know him.)

His features, as well as his flesh, must also have changed, for his father does not know Alexis when he comes back to Rome, nor do his mother and wife recognize him during his seventeen years of lying at their door. When his identity is made known to them after his death, both remark upon his *flesh*, the wife especially deploring how his face has changed:

> Filz Alexis, de la tue *carn* tendra!
> A quel dolur deduit as ta juventa!
> (Mother, ll. 451-52)
>
> O bele buce, *bel vis*, bele faiture,
> Cum est mudede vostra *bela figure*!
> (Spouse, ll. 481-82)

(Son Alexis, your sweet (young) *flesh*!
To such distress have you traduced your youth:

Oh lovely mouth, *lovely face*, lovely countenance, How your *beautiful face* is changed!)

As would be natural for a leper, Alexis seats himself among the poor in Alsis, receiving alms like these his 'brothers':

> Quant sun aver lur ad tot departit,
> Entra les povres se sist danz Alexis.
>
> (ll. 96-7)

> Nel reconurent li dui sergant sum pedre;
> A lui medisme unt l'almosne dunethe;
> Il la receut cume li altre frere,
> Nel reconurent, sempres s'en returnerent.
>
> (ll. 117-20)

> (When he had shared out to them all his belongings,
> Lord Alexis seated himself among the poor.
>
> Nor did the two servants of his father recognize him;
> They gave alms to him, to [Alexis] himself;
> He received them like the other brothers,
> They knew him not, straightway they turned away.)

After seventeen years of paining his body in Alsis, where he is always seated at the door of the church —a natural *locus* for a leper— Alexis is made to come inside at the instigation of the image: 'he is worthy to enter Paradise.' All honor him, the great and the humble, and all pray that he have mercy on them. This would seem to be the appropriate ending for the first (Eastern) Life of St. Alexis. The second (Western) Life appears appended somewhat contradictorily: Alexis flees in the middle of the night to avoid this honor (already bestowed!):

> Quant il co veit quel volent onurer:
> 'Certes,' dist il, 'n'i ai mais ad ester,
> D'icest honur nem revoil ancumbrer.'
> Ensur [e] nuit s'en fuit de la ciptét:
> Dreit a Lalice revint li sons edrers.
>
> (ll. 186-90)

(When he sees that they want to honor him:
'Surely,' says he, 'never should I be here,
I do not wish to re-encumber myself with
this honor.'
Late in the night he flees from the city:
Straight to Lalice his wandering brought
him back.)

Arriving again in Rome, he has good reason to beseech his father's charity; he is completely infirm:

Eufemïen, bel sire, riches hom,
Quar me herberges pur Deu an ta maison;
Sus tun degrét me fai un grabatum
Empur tun filz dunt tu as tel dolur;
Tut soi amferm, sim pais pur sue amor.
(ll. 216-20)

(Eufemien, fine Sir, rich man,
Now shelter me, for God, in thy house;
Make me a pallet under thy stair
For the love of thy son for whom you have
such grief;
I am completely infirm, so nurture me for
love of him.)

It is noteworthy that Alexis asks to be lodged underneath the staircase: outside the quarters of the hale
and hearty. Once more, he will be "*ein Aussätziger*." His
infirmity is apparently so grave as to cause Eufemien's
immediate recognition that 'intensive care' will be necessary: the father offers to reward handsomely any custo-
dian who will take on such arduous service. A 'good and
faithful servant' —reminiscent of the sacristan in the
Eastern Life — immediately volunteers:

'E Deus', dist il, 'quer oüsse un sergant,
Kil me guardrat, jo l'en ferei franc.'
Un en i out ki sempres vint avant:
'As me,' dist il, 'kil guard pur ton cumand:

169

Pur tue amur an soferai l'ahan.'

(ll. 226-30)

(Oh God', said he, 'if I only had a servant,
Who would tend him for me, for this would I
make him free.'
There was one there who immediately came
forward:
'Here am I,' said he, 'to tend him by thy command:
For thy love I shall suffer this hardship.')

The good servant does everything for the poor pilgrim, who is apparently as helpless as a baby, or, indeed,
as a 'living corpse,' a leper. He takes him to his lodging
spot, makes his bed, and brings him his food from the
'Rich Man's' table:

Dunc le menat andreit suz le degrét:
Fait li sun lit o il pot reposer:
Tut li amanvet, quanque bosuinz li ert:
Contra [l] seinur ne s'en volt mesaler;
Par nule guise ne l'em puet hom blasmer.

(ll. 231-5)

(Then he led him straight beneath the
staircase:
He prepares for him his bed where he can
take his rest:
He provides everything for him, whatever
he had need of:
He does not want to behave badly toward
the lord;
In no way can anyone blame him for this.)

And at the end it will be the good servant who
brings the "enca e parcamin, ed . . . penne" with which the
poor pilgrim, Alexis, will write the Life within this Life.
The Poor Man spends seventeen more years *mortifying*
his body —increasingly becoming "mort au siècle"— on the
little pallet underneath the stairs. He conceals his suffering as carefully as his identity, but he cannot help its being known to his bed: did it perhaps perceive the
manifestations of leprosy via flakes of scaly skin or
globules of rotted flesh?

Iloc converset eisi dis e set anz,
Nel reconut nuls sons apartenanz
Ne n[e]üls hom ne sout les sons ahanz,
[Fors sul le lit u il ad jeü tant:
Ne puet muer ne seit aparissant.]
(ll. 271-5. ll. 274-5,
missing from **L**, are
supplied by **A** and **S**.)

(There he lived in this manner for
seventeen years,
Not one of his family recognized him
Nor did a single soul know of his
suffering(s),
Except only the bed where he had lain in
this condition:
He cannot help (change) that it be apparent
[to it].)

The servants treat him with the utmost contempt
and disgust, as would be understandable in the case of leprosy. Like the wife of Job, himself understood to suffer
from leprosy,[46] they throw their dirty water on his head:

Li serf sum pedre, ki la maisnede servent,
Lur lavadures li getent sur la teste:
Ne s'en corucet net il nes en apelet.

Tuz l'escarnissent, sil tenent pur bricun;
L'egua li getent, si moilent sun liçon. . . .
(ll. 263-7)

(The servants of his father, who attend the
household,
Throw their laundry water upon his head:
He does not become angered at this nor does
he take them to task.
All scorn him, they count him as an idiot;
They throw water on him, thus they drench
his little bed. . . .)

After thirty-four years of suffering, Alexis's body is
completely ravaged: it would appear that this was a physical malady, if an allegorical one as well:

171

Mult li angreget la sue anfermetét.
Or set il bien qued il s'en deit aler. . . .
(ll. 278-9)

Sa fin aproismet, ses cors est agravét;
De tut an tut recesset del parler.
(ll. 289-90)

(Greatly does his infirmity increase.
Now he well knows that he must go away.

His end draws nigh, his body is much worsened;
More and more he withdraws from speaking.)

But, *nota bene*, it is with the shuffling off of this mortal coil that Alexis is made truly whole and gains full sanctity: this is the first time in the poem that he is called "*sainz* Alexis."[47] And in the next line, number *333*, 'triple' 3, significantly; he goes 'directly' to Paradise:

An tant dementres cum il iloec unt sis,
Deseivret l'aneme del cors sainz Alexis;
Tut dreitement en vait en paradis   [333]
A sun seinor qu'il aveit tant servit.
(ll. 331-4)

(And during the time that they were there seated,
The soul took leave of the body of Saint Alexis;
Straightway it goes into Paradise
To his lord whom he had served so well.)
(Emphasis added.)

Now Alexis's death would seem to be premature: his mother is in fine enough fettle to come running to his body and to exercise her grief energetically in pulling her hair, beating her breast, throwing herself on the ground; his wife considers herself still nubile. But, be it noted, death at an 'early' age is consistent with the medieval view of advanced leprosy.

In conclusion, all the information we are given on Alexis's physical 'infirmity' is in conformity with the medieval understanding of the nature and the progress of leprosy: he exhibits changes in the skin, unrecognizable features, a wasting away, cessation of speech, utter enervation; and revulsion, isolation and scorn are visited upon him by those around him.

And, in addition to these clinical 'symptoms,' there are other factors in support of this diagnosis. First of all, Alexis renounces the consummation of the marriage and frees his bride to wed another, the eternal Bridegroom. Certainly this has a spiritual significance, but it also conforms to such medieval decrees as that of Compiègne, by which the leper could grant his spouse the right to remarry. In the case of St. Alexis, there would seem to be an hagiographical interpretation of civil law: historical reality and symbolic significance would provide the 'body' and 'soul' for such an interpretation as Claudius of Turin had expounded.[48]

There are a host of other symbolic truths which may well be 'incorporated' in physical facts. Alexis absents himself from his home and his family, sequesters himself from normal society, and rids himself of all his property; he thereby renounces his claims to inheritance and to his rightful occupation. He has, in essence, effected his own *separatio leprosori.*

Having detached himself from his family and his wife, to whom he ceremoniously hands over the ring and sword-belt, symbols of marital and feudal thralldom, Alexis flees: he runs not *to* but *away from*, with no apparent end in mind. Having landed in Lalice purely by the will of God, he remains there for an unspecified time before leaving for a very definite purpose: he wants to go to Alsis (Edessa), where there was a wonderful *imago.*

> D'iloc alat an Alsis la ciptét
> *Pur* une imagine dunt il oït parler,
> Qued angeles firent par cumandement Deu
> *El num la virgine* ki portat salvetét,
> Sainta Maria ki portat Damnedeu.
> (ll. 86-90)
> (Emphasis added.)

> (From there he went to the city Alsis
> *For* an image of which he had heard tell,

173

Which angels made by the command of God
In the name of the Virgin who brought salvation,
Saint Mary, who bore the Lord God.)

Now nowhere does the poem say exactly what this "imagine" was. It was made *in the name* of the Virgin but never does it say that it was a 'statue' *of* the Virgin, as modern readers sometimes infer.[49]

There was, however, a very famous image in the city of Edessa: a 'life-mask' of Jesus Christ, and a letter written with his own hand as well. Indeed, the 'life-mask' of Christ and the famous veil of St. Veronica are accounted as the only 'likenesses' of the living Jesus; to these are added the Turin shroud to furnish 'the three images not made with hands,' "les trois images achiropoètes," as Réau terms them.[50]

The legend of the Mandylion of Edessa is recounted in Voragine's *Légende dorée*; it harks back to 544 A.D., when the miraculous image was credited with warding off the onslaught of the Persians. According to the legend, King Abgar of Edessa had written to Jesus both to offer him asylum from the hostile Jews and to beseech his healing touch for his terrible disease: leprosy. Jesus replied, in writing, that he could not come: he must remain in Palestine to accomplish his mission, and would then ascend into heaven. He would, however, send one of his disciples, later, to cure Abgar. The Edessan king then sent a painter to Jerusalem to make Christ's portrait. But the divine face was so resplendent that the eyes of the artist were dazzled and he could not make its likeness. Thereupon Jesus took a panel of his cloak, and pressing it to his face, he made a perfect impression.[51] After the death of Christ, the apostles Simeon and Judas Thaddeus took the miraculous impression to Abgar: simply by touching it, he was cured of his leprosy. Consequently Abgar, his court, and the majority of his subjects, both Jews and Gentiles, became Christians. Thereby did Edessa become the 'oldest Christian kingdom in the world.'[52]

Edessa prided itself as well for its reputation as a city of healing and for its charitable provisions for the poor and infirm: hospices were established there not only for strangers, but for the sick and dying. In such an establishment, according to the Syrian legend, Alexius ended his earthly life.[53] Indeed, it was the miraculous disappearance of the body of Alexius which prompted Bishop Rabula's establishment of hospices especially dedicated to the care of the poor, of widows and orphans, and of strangers from distant shores.[54] Edessa already knew an infirmary for lepers, endowed by Bishop Nona (ca. 460); celebrated for its "healing waters," it was, fittingly, situated in the district near the Well of Job, the Old Testament leper prototype.

Although it could not boast the true Cross, the Crown of Thorns, the garments of the Virgin nor the bodies of the saints —Stephen, Timothy, Andrew, and Luke— that Constantinople offered, Edessa counted itself richly endowed in possessing the Letter of Jesus Christ and the Image of the Holy Face, along with other relics cited for their efficacy. These were carefully assembled, according to Segal, for pragmatic as well as for purely spiritual reasons:

> The Edessans collected sacred relics with the same zeal that modern museums collect Old Masters, and for much the same reasons —to stimulate the pride of the citizens in their city and to maintain the stream of visitors.[55]

For all these reasons, Edessa was deemed highly worthy of a pilgrimage, Segal maintains:

> Its shrines were the goal of pilgrims from Mesopotamia, from Persia and Syria and Asia Minor, even from the Far East and from Europe. Some came for a brief visit like the abbess Egeria of Aquitania; some came to study. . . . Others came to pray. The celebrated legend of the "man of God," Alexius, relates how a young man —writers hint that he was the son of Emperor Theodosius II— left Rome secretly on the eve of his marriage. . . . There he fulfilled all his days.[56]

Thus Alexis as a leper, either allegorical or physical, would have good reason to leave Lalice in order to make a pilgrimage to Edessa (Alsis): it had a leper hospital; it had the Healing Well of Job, the Old Testament

175

model leper; it had the unique image of Jesus Christ, which had cured King Abgar of leprosy.

Once in Edessa, Alexis seats himself among the poor beggars, "sis altres freres," and begs alms, the classic occupation for lepers. Like the founder and charter member of his own *Ordre Saint- Lazare*, he leads a life of poverty, chastity and piety, nurturing his poorer brothers from his own 'mite box.' Finally he is made to come into the church by command of the image:

> Co dist l'imagena: "Fai l'ume Deu venir. . . ."
> (l. 171)

(So spoke the image: "Have the man of God come [hither].")

Cil vait, sil quert, mais il nel set coisir.
(l. 174)

(This one goes, and he seeks him, but he cannot pick him out.)

Alexis' usual place, rather, is outside of the church, the place, indeed, of the *Aussätzigen*:

> Revint li costre al imagine el muster.
> "Certes," dist il, "Ne sai cui antercier."
> Respont l'imagine: "Co est cil qui tres l'us set. . . .
> (ll. 176-8)

(The sacristan came back to the image in the church.
"Truly," said he, "I know not whom to question."
Replies the image: "It is the one who sits there at the door.")

Upon his return to Rome, as we have noted, Alexis is unrecognized by his father, whose sympathy he evokes as a hopelessly infirm pilgrim: would Eufemien respond so mercifully if this had been an able-bodied young man? Alexis requires the ministries of a servant: such service would appear out of character for an ascete —unless he were disabled. He is bed-ridden, consistent with the medieval conception of an advanced stage of leprosy. That the servants regard him with loathing and treat him with cruelty is a typical reaction to leprosy in a society that frequently forbade lepers the use of the common water supply, made them drink downstream, required them to wear gloves and to warn others of their approach by means of a bell, forbade their habitation among the healthy, and often prohibited their entry into marketplace and church. Such segregation may well be reflected in Alexis's sequestration underneath the stairs. Most telling is the fact that Alexis is absolutely unrecognizable to those who know him best, his family and the household servants: the changes in his flesh and in his features are specifically mentioned seven times.

But after his death, there is a dramatic change: the common people —"menude, povre"— adore his dead body. They are adamant in their insistence upon their right of contact with this "gemme," now a *holy* body by whom miracles take place.

All of these factors make for the classic image of the leper-saint, the Christ figure who makes himself leprous for our transgressions. Accordingly, even though the text does not state outright that Alexis was a leper, this does not rule out that this malady was understood, and on all four levels of medieval interpretation. Significantly, there is a lack of specificity in other medieval texts in which leprosy is the haunting spectre, as Rémy remarks:

> Les célèbres *Congés* de Jean Bodel et de Baude Fastoul sont inestimables par leurs allusions historiques, mais surtout par l'atroce confession, la résignation amère de deux poètes qui se sentent "mort pour le siècle." L'un dit: "ma cars est soursamée"; l'autre avoue que ses amis l'ont supporté "moitié sain et moitié pori"; tendus vers le côté spirituel de leur affreuse destinée, ils ont pourtant négligé la peinture précise de leur mal, par pudeur, sans doute.[57]

> (The celebrated *Congés* of Jean Bodel and of Baude Fastoul are priceless for their historic allusions, but, above all, for the horrible confession, the bitter resignation of two poets who deem themselves "dead for

this world." One says: "My flesh is rotten;" the other avows that his friends endure him "half-whole and half-rotted"; bent toward the spiritual aspect of their ghastly destiny, they have, nevertheless, neglected the precise depiction of their illness, out of delicacy, no doubt.)

Similarly, as we have noted earlier, the medieval reader/hearer had no trouble in 'understanding' that Job and Lazarus had leprosy, though the word per se is mentioned in *neither* Biblical text.

Admitting the possibility that Alexis was understood to be a leper allows for a deeper structural meaning and adds a whole new perspective to his saintly and heroic program. Such an understanding would change Alexis's motivation from *askesis* to *caritas*: and such a raison d'être would surely have more bearing on the Christian *community*, the audience that the poem would seem to envisage. For askesis is, at heart, a *self*-centered renunciation of this world, and of all who and which are in it, for the sake of future and more rewarding *self*-gratification; *caritas*, however, could well embrace the compassionate giving up of identity, of selfhood and of pleasure in order to render service and to earn eternal joy and bliss for *others*. With Alexis understood as a voluntary leper, the signification shifts from interiority to alterity, from self-occupation to altruism. Such a prioritization of *caritas* may well be understood in the light of its being seen as the all-pervading virtue of medieval Christianity, as Robertson maintains.[58] Thus Alexis, like the Leper who visited St. Julian, must remain anonymous in order to allow his family the opportunity to practice pure charity: "For if ye love them which love you, what reward have ye? Do not even the heathen do the same?" By making himself "one of the least," Alexis permits his family to minister unto Christ himself.

Such an understanding, moreover, gives a fuller meaning to the poem's beginning strophe by evoking the topos of the "sin-lepered age" to explain the blanched and shriveled condition of the current world, understood accordingly:

In the time of the ancients, the world was rosy and robust, hale and holy. Now it is livid and leprous; it wastes more away each day, putrifying to its core. It has completely changed, and lost its fresh color. . .

(Bons fut li secles al tens ancïenur,
Quer feit i ert e justise ed amur;
S'i ert creance, dunt or n'i at nul prut.
Tut est müez, perdut ad sa colur,
Ja mais n'iert tel cum fut as anceisurs.)
(emphasis added)

(Good was this world in the time of the ancients,
For [then] was there faith and justice and love;
And [then] was there trust, which scarce exists today.
Everything is changed, it has lost its color;
Never will it be as it was for our ancestors.)

It is worthy of note that the word *muez* (changed) (line 4) also appears (as *mudede*) in the poem to describe the appalling change in Alexis's flesh, a change of which the poet makes much: as a physical manifestation of leprosy, it would provide the metaphor *par excellence* for a decaying world.

Continuing with the hypothesis of leprosy employed as a leitmotif allows the following paraphrase of the Life of St. Alexis:

Long ago, when the world was less corrupted, our fathers had the True Faith. During this Age of the world, there was a certain nobleman of Rome, honored and highly-esteemed in his time. It is, however, of his son that I wish to speak.

Alexis was the name of this son: he was a child after God's own heart. He had been sent to his parents, long barren, in answer to their prayers: they had promised God that if he sent them a son, they would give him to the Lord all the days of his life.

179

Now Alexis was an obedient child, honoring his parents in all things; thus he increased in wisdom and in stature and in favor with God and man.

When his father saw that he would have no other children, he resolved to perpetuate his lineage through Alexis; and so he chose for him a suitable wife, the daughter of an equally noble family. When the time came for the wedding, Alexis married the damsel in cheerful obedience to his father's wishes. But this was not according to his own purpose: his heart was set on God.

Now when the wedding festivities were over and the night had come, the young Alexis obeyed his father's command and entered into the bridal chamber. Once inside, however, the sight of the bed recalls to him his mortality by dint of its association with birth and with death: now, between them is his marriage. He looks upon his virgin bride and is aghast that carnal knowledge might cause his forgetting of his heavenly lord and his corrupting the innocence of this maiden. Filled with loathing for his 'leprous' nature, he determines to separate himself from this world —*separatio leprosorum*— before such a sin can divide him from his single-minded devotion to God and contaminate his unsullied bride. He renounces his husbandship by handing over to his wife a ring and sword-straps: the one will sign and seal that she is the bride of the Eternal Bridegroom; the other, symbol of feudal bonds, will recall to her as well the chastity belt, and the purity which it is her bounden duty to maintain.

This more sacred ceremony having superseded the previous marriage rites, Alexis rushes out. By God's will, he finds a ship in port and purchases a passage, knowing not whither. He comes to shore in Lalice, a beautiful enough city, but of no real importance in Alexis's program except as a point of departure. For here he hears of the wonderful city of Edessa and of its matchless image which had healed the leprosy of Abgar. Now he makes another voyage, not of escape, as the voyage from Rome had been, but of pilgrimage and of quest: in this holy city and before its sacred image, he may be cleansed of his leprosy of soul.

And God, in his grace, bestows upon Alexis the Sacred Malady, leprosy in its physical form, as a mark of his special favor and approbation. This permits Alexis to externalize his moral leprosy and it gives him the opportunity for purification through suffering; so he seats himself for 'good' among his true brothers, the other leper outcasts.

How joyful he is when his father's best servants come and look upon his face without recognizing him: this establishes that he is exorcising the more deadly moral leprosy as it is advancing in its physical form. After seventeen years, he has advanced to his supreme goal: he has become dead unto sin, moral leprosy, and live unto righteousness. And the Image pronounces him worthy to enter Paradise.

(Here indeed is effected a little death and resurrection for this Lazarus; it represents the fusion point of the Eastern and Western legends.)

But though the spirit is purified, the body, being inferior, must accomplish more slowly its process of wasting away. Nourished and confirmed by the pronouncement of the Image, the Man of God eschews the worldly honors of mortal men, cumbersome to his purified soul. Again he flees, heading for Tarsus, where, indeed, St.

Paul had wrestled with his own thorn in the flesh.

But God, in his infinite wisdom, brings Alexis instead to Rome. He is fraught with fear: can he withstand the pull of family ties, the human desire to rejoin his loved ones? By the grace of God, they do not know him: he has truly conquered the mortal man by taking upon himself the disguise of leprous flesh —he is a new creature in Christ. So can he show his caring love for his family by seating himself at their door: this permits their own spiritual growth through their showing charity to a nameless begger. He sees them daily, he hears their laments, but he knows that their tears are as naught in view of the joy they will know in heaven.

And when the time comes for him to leave Eufemien's house to go to his true home, he takes care to let his family know, by a letter, whom they have entertained unawares: by caring for a poor and nameless beggar, they have ministered, as it were, to Christ himself.

Now he can go to prepare a room for them in his Father's house, where they, and we, will be united in the world without end, without sin and leprosy and decay.

This seems to me to be a valid understanding of the story of Alexis as it might have been perceived by the audience of the eleventh and twelfth centuries, that is, the hearers of the Old French Life as recorded in the L manuscript.

An objection to the interpretation of Alexis as a leper may be raised on the basis of the L manuscript's Alexis miniatures, which show no spots on his face. But this scene, illustrating his taking leave of the bride, portrays Alexis before he would have taken on the physical disease: he is the fleeing bridegroom, rather than the miserable beggar under the stairs.[59] The same emphasis on

182

the bridegroom is made, indeed, in the **L** manuscript's Prologue: both it and the *Alexis* miniatures could well be due to the same hand, the *'Albanimeister'* who was creating a book for Christina of Markyate, who had fled her husband as a *sponsa intacta.* Thus, the choice of this scene to illustrate the *Alexis* may be due to a specific topical rapprochement.

In the *Marienkirche* of Rostock (site of a medieval leprosarium), there is an oil painting by Emmanuel Block (1656) entitled *"Der Arme Lazarus"* (The Poor Lazarus).[60] It portrays a man seated on the ground and surrounded by dogs who lick his wounds. The man's head is bald, his chin is bearded, his face is gentle, serene, and — unspotted! The body is clad in rags, and one hand stretches forth an alms plate in which there are a few coins. A literal representation of the Poor Lazarus, one might say. Except that in his other hand, the poor man holds a letter: did the image of Alexis superimpose itself on his own *praefigura?*

[1] The *planctus* appear in the Latin Life as well, in conformity with a long-established usage as a rhetorical form which would be continued in Ovid's *Heroides*, the *planhs* of the Provencal poets, Alanus de Insulis' *De Planctu Naturae*, and Jean de Meung's 'Plaint of Nature' in the *Roman de la Rose*. (Carl Odenkirchen, *The Life of St. Alexis*, Brookline: Classical Folio Edit., 1978, 82, furnishes these examples.) In the Latin Life, the *planctus* remain conventional —and unconvincing. In the French *Vie*, they are both humanized and mythologized. See Karl D. Uitti, *Story, Myth, and Celebration in Old French Narrative Poetry* (Princeton: Princeton University Press, 1972), pp. 3-64.

[2] The Latin Life compares her, indeed, to a lioness: "Mater vero ejus haec audiens quasi leaena rumpens rete ita scissis vestibus exiens," (Indeed, his mother, upon hearing this, [was] like a lioness tearing apart a trap and bursting out of the rent coverings.) *Acta Sanctorum, De Vita S. Alexii*, Julii, Vol. IV, pp. 251-3 (Bibliotheca Hagiographica Latina, No. 286).

[3] The meaning and significance of this word are at issue, as will be seen forthwith.

[4] Gaston Paris, *La Vie de Saint Alexis* (Paris, 1872), p. 219.

[5] See Christopher Storey, *La Vie de Saint Alexis* (Geneva: Droz, 1968), note to line 441, p. 115.

[6] Cf. DuCange, *Glossarium Mediae et Infimae Latinitatis*, Tome IV, p. 359:

> *Mesclaria*: ... Vocis etymon a Latino *misellus*, quod leprosi conditio monium miserrima sit, accersunt plures; ab Arabico *Mezora*, Lepra, deducit Thomassimus tom. 2.

> (*Mesclaria*: Etymon of the word *misellus* from Latin; because, many adduce, the condition of the leper is utterly miserable;

from the Arabic *mezora*, "leprosy,"
Thomassimus deduces [in his] Vol. 2.)

7 Both *ladre* (*ladrerie*) and *mesel* (*meselerie*) appear
in texts throughout the Middle Ages. Littré specifies that
the latter forms attach to white leprosy (*Dictionnaire de la
langue française*, Paris, 1885-89, p. 278). *Ladre*, which
survives to mean a *miser* (originally, one who lived
miserably) especially evokes the Poor Man of the Parable,
as in Villon:

C'est de Jhesus la parabolle
Touchant du Riche ensevely
En feu, non pas en couche molle,
Et du Ladre de dessus ly.
(lines 813-16, *Testament*, ed.
Longnon- Foulet, Paris, 1975, p. 38)

(It is the parable of Jesus
Concerning the Rich Man buried
In fire, not in a soft bed,
And the Leper [lit., the Lazarus] up above
him.)

8 G. Paris, p. 191.

9 Paul Rémy, "La lèpre, thème littéraire au moyen
âge," *Le Moyen Age*, LII (1946), p. 233.

10 Nor does it seem conceivable that the Holy
Mother would be addressed so informally; in the poem's
only reference to her, she is "la virgine ki portat salvatet,
Sainte Marie ...." (The Virgin who bore Salvation, Saint
Mary...) (11. 89- 90). If were being addressed, it would
more likely be as "Notre Dame," or as "Sainte Mère,"
rather than with a familiar "Mère."

11 This word survives in the English *measle(s)*, as
noted in the *Oxford English Dictionary*, Vol. VI (1933), p.
277: "That the dialectal form *measle* appears in literary
English may be due to a mistaken association of this word
with *Mesel*, leper ...."

[12] *La Grande Encyclopédie,* H. Lamirault et Cie, ed., p. 62.

[13] *Encyclopedia Britannica* (1891), Vol. XIV, p. 469. It will be remembered that Matthew Paris (1200?-1259) was the renowned chronicler of St. Albans Abbey. (*Gesta Abbatum Monasterii Sancti Albani* ed. H.T. Riley, Rolls Series 28, IV.)

[14] *Encyclopedia Britannica,* p. 469.

[15] *La Grande Encyclopédie,* Vol. 22, p. 63.

[16] Peter Richards, *The Medieval Leper and his Northern Heirs* (London, 1977), studies leprosy of the Aland Islands during the seventeenth century and the survival of European medieval traditions there. He questions this traditional view of the European advent of leprosy via Roman soldiers.

[17] *La Grande Encyclopédie,* tom. cit., p. 64.

[18] Richards uses the practices of St. Julian's as a paradigm of medieval European customs. He includes the regulations of St. Julian's, *Statuta Hospitalis de Sancto Juliano,* among his *Documents,* pp. 129-36.

[19] According to legend, Constantine is cured of leprosy by being converted to Christianity through the efforts of Pope Silvester, to whom he had been directed by Peter and Paul in a vision. This legend is recounted in Jacques de Voragine's *Legenda Aurea.* It is alluded to, as well, in the *Inferno*:

> Ma come Costantin chiese Silvestro
> d'entro Siratti a guerir della lebbra;
> cos mi chiese questi per maestro
> a guarir della sua superba febbre ....
> (XXVII, 94-97)

(But as Constantine sought out Sylvester in Soracte to cure his leprosy, so this man

Pope Boniface VIII sought me out as his
physician to cure the fever of his pride.)

tr., John D. Sinclair,
*The Divine Comedy
of Dante Alighieri*
(rev. ed. London:
John Lane, 1948),
I, 338-9

Louis IX admonishes Jean de Joinville that moral
leprosy is the ugliest of sins: the leprous soul is like the
devil. (Jean, Sire de Joinville, *Histoire de Saint Louis*, IV,
p. 27).

Louis XI, who died of apoplexy, earlier thought he
had been smitten with leprosy, for which he sought,
among other strange remedies, a cure in the blood of tur-
tles. See Thomas Basin, *Histoire des règnes de Charles VII
et de Louis XI*, ed. J. Quicherat, *Soc. Histoire de France*,
1855-59.

[20] *La Grande Encyclopédie*, vol. 22, p. 62.

[21] Saul Nathaniel Brody, *The Disease of the Soul.
Leprosy in Medieval Literature* (Ithaca: Cornell Univ.
Press, 1974). This is an excellent study of how literature
reflects the medical, theological and sociological tradition of leprosy for the Middle Ages.

[22] In the 'Great Paris Psalter' (B.N. lat. 8846), for
instance, the illustration for Psalm 37, "Psalmus David,
in rememorationem de sabbato," shows a black-spotted
David, beset by three devils. His leprosy is understood by
reference to such verses as the following:

> Putruerunt et corruptae sunt cicatrices meae,
> A facie insipientiae meae.
> Tota die contristatus ingrediebar.
> Miser factus sum et curvatus sum usque in
> finem;
> Quoniam lumbi mei impleti sum illusionibus,
> Et non est sanitas in carne mea.
> Afflictus sum, et humiliatus sum nimis;
> Rugiebam a gemitu cordis mei ....
> Cor meum conturbatum est,

Dereliquit me virtus mea,
Et lumen oculorum meorum, et ipsum non
est mecum.
Amici mei et proximi mei adversum me
appropin-quaverunt, et steterunt;
Et qui iuxta me erant, de longe steterunt ....
(Ps. 37, 6-9, 11-12)

(My wounds stink and are corrupt because
of my foolishness.
I am troubled; I am bowed down greatly; I go
mourning all the day long.
For my loins are filled with a loathsome
disease: and there is no soundness in my
flesh.
I am feeble and sore broken; I have roared
by reason of the disquietness of my heart ....
My heart panteth, my strength faileth me;
as for the light of mine eyes, it also is gone
from me.
My lovers and my friends stand aloof from
my sore; and my kinsmen stand afar off ....)
(Authorized Version)

The association of leprosy with the psalm's "*Miser
factus sum*" is immediately apparent. Also notable are the
physical signs —putrid sores, blindness, enervation,
eroded flesh— and the scorn and repugnance which they
elicit from David's family, 'friends' and neighbors. We
shall encounter all of these elements again, further along
in this chapter.

23 Brody, pp. 108-10.

24 Rémy, p. 210.

25 Béroul, *Le Roman de Tristan*, ed. Muret (rev. ed.
Paris: Champion, 1962), 11. 1192-7.

26 Brody, p. 101, cites "Oratio XIV: De pauperum
amore," 261 (*PG*, XXXV, 866).

The saintly aura of leprosy is discussed by Bédier
in reference to Ami and Amile, venerated as saints (Cf.
Vita sanctorum Amici et Amelii carissimorum.) It will be

remembered that Ami is smitten with leprosy, which can be healed by nothing other than the blood of his friend's children. Bédier comments: "Dieu frappe Ami parce qu'il l'aime, *juxta illud quod scriptum est: Omnem filium quem Deus recipit, corripit, flagellat et castigat.* C'est l'idée chrétienne. Seule elle s'accorde avec le reste de l'histoire....Il met bien en relief le caractère hagiographique de la légende." (*Les Légendes épiques*, II; Paris: Ed. Champion, 1926. p. 189, note 1.) (God strikes Ami because he loves him, "just as it is written: Every son whom God receiveth, him he reproveth, scourgeth and chasteneth." There is the Christian idea. Only it is in tune with the rest of the story. . . It very well puts into focus the hagiographic nature of the legend.)

27 Thus, one of the Regulations of St. Julian's: "Nor should [lepers] despair or murmur against God because of this, but rather praise and glorify Him, who when He was led to His death wished to be compared to the lepers. As witness of this consider the prophet Isaiah who said 'And we thought him struck down as a leper by God and humiliated '...." Richards, p. 131.

Similarly, a fourteenth-century English metrical homily refers to Christ's taking upon himself the leprosy of mankind:

> For man quaim sinne mad unhale,
> Haft noht ben bette of his bale,
> But yef Crist haued til him comen,
> And his seknes opon him nomen,
> And clensed him of leper of sinne,
> That alle mankind was fallen in.
> (*English Metrical Homilies: From Mss. of the Fourteenth Century*, ed. John Small, Edinburgh: W. Patterson, 1862)

> (For man, whom sin made unwhole,
> Would not have been relieved of his blight,
> Unless Christ had come to him,
> And taken his sickness upon Himself,
> And cleansed him of the leprosy of sin,
> That all mankind had fallen in.)

[28] See A. S. Rappoport, *Mediaeval Legends of Christ*. (New York: Charles Scribner's Sons, 1935), pp. 98-100, 102-103.

[29] Guy de Chaulic, *La Grande Chirurgie*, Ed. E. Nicaise (Paris, 1890): "... if the world loathes [the lepers], God —who loved the leprous Lazarus more than others— does not." (p. 103)

[30] Rémy, pp. 230-1.

[31]   "-Seignors," fait el, "por Deu merci,
        Saintes reliques voi ici.
        Or escoutez que je ci jure,
        De quoi le roi ci aseüre....
        Qu'entre mes cuises n'entra home,
        Fors le ladre qui fist soi some,
        Qui me porta outre les guez,
        Et li rois Marc mes esposez.
        Ces deus ost de mon soirement ...."
                    (Beroul, *Le Roman de Tristan*, ed. Muret, 128-9)

        ("My lords," says she, "as God is my witness,
        I see holy relics here.
        Now listen to what I hereby swear,
        And what I certify to the King here: ....
        That no man ever entered between my thighs
        Save the leper, who made himself a beast of burden
        Who carried me across this ford,
        And the king, Marc, my husband.
        These two I exclude from my oath...")

[32] "Un Miracle de Nostre-Dame, de l'Empereris de Romme," in *Théâtre français au moyen âge* , L.-J.-N. Monmerqué and Francisque Michel (Paris, 1885), pp. 365-416, from Manuscript 7208 .4. B (Paris, B.N.).

This miracle also appears in a manuscript of the Arsenal (Paris, Ars. Manus. 3516, 283 B.F. f. 133, ss.): "De la sainte empereris qui garissoit les lieprous." ("Of the holy Empress who cured lepers.")

33 Brody, p. 104. In these stories, parallels with the Syrian and the Greek legends of St. Alexis may be remarked: the hut, the unnamed *misérable*, the pious man's care of him, the mysterious and miraculous circumstances of the death. The odor of sweetness emanating from the body, a hagiographical commonplace, occurs as well in the Latin Life, both in the version usually accepted as the source for the Old French Life, and in the Latin text employed in the *Gesta Romanorum*.

34 Gustave Flaubert, *Trois Contes: Un Coeur simple; La Légende de Saint Julien, l'hospitalier; Hérodias*, Edit. Suffel, Paris (1965), pp. 130-31.

35 Robert Mannyng of Brunne, *Robert of Brunne's "Handlyng Synne," A.D. 1303, with Those Parts of the Anglo-French Treatise on which It was Founded, William of Wadington's "Manuel des Pechiez,"* ed. Frederick J. Furnivall, EETS, O.S., nos. 119, 123 (London, 1901), p. 357.

36 Rémy, pp. 238-9. He credits this citation to J. Klapper, *Exempla aus Handschriften des Mittelalters (Sammlung mittellateinischer Texte, hgg. von Alfons Hilka)*, Heidelberg, 1911, p. 72, no. 99.

37 Brody, p. 64.

38 *La Grande Encyclopédie*, Vol. 22, p. 63.

39 Rémy, pp. 236-37.

40 Brody, p. 76.

41 Hartmann von Aue, *Der Arme Heinrich*, hgg. durch die Brüder Grimm (Berlin, 1815). Rémy (pp. 217-18) provides the following summary of the German tale:

... Un chevalier devenu subitement lépreux consulte tous les médecins de Montpelier et de Salerne, jusqu'au jour où l'un d'eux lui conseille de chercher une jeune fille saine et prête au sacrifice: seul le sang de son coeur pourra sauver Henri. Une victime s'offre, mais quand tout est prêt pour l'holocauste, le sentiment humain du chevalier se redresse; il est récompensé et miraculeusement guéri; tout se termine par un mariage.

(A knight, suddenly become leprous, consults all the physicians of Montpelier and of Salerno, until, one day, one of them advises him to seek a young girl [who is] healthy and ready for sacrifice: only the blood of her heart will be able to save Heinrich. A victim offers herself, but when everything is ready for the holocaust, the human [kindness] of the knight is aroused; he is rewarded and miraculously cured; it all ends by a marriage.)

The popular belief that human blood, especially that of little children or of virgins, could effect a cure for leprosy is an ancient one. It figures in the story of *Amis et Amiles*, and in the legend of Constantine as recounted by Jacques de Voragine, as cited by Rémy (pp. 221-1):

Constantin s'étant mis à persécuter les chrétiens, Silvestre sortit de Rome et se retira avec son clergé sur une montagne voisine (le mont Soracte). Mais voici que Constantin lui-même, en châtiment de sa persécution, fut atteint d'une lèpre incurable. Les prêtres des idoles lui conseillèrent alors de faire égorger, aux portes de la ville, trois mille enfants, et de se baigner dans leur sang, tout chaud. Devant la douleur des mères, Constantin préfère voir triompher la pitié: "Mieux vaut pour moi mourir et conserver la vie à ces innocents que de recouvrer, par leur mort, une vie souillée de cruauté"; guidé par saint Pierre et saint Paul, Constantin suit alors les conseils de Silvestre; il guérira en se plongeant trois fois dans une source,

symbole du baptême dans le Jourdain. De
là le fameux et faux "acte de donation au
pape Silvestre."

(*La Légende dorée*, trad. du
latin par T. De Wyzewa,
Paris, 1902, p. 66)

([Since] Constantine [had] set himself to
persecuting the Christians, Silvester left
Rome and retired with his clergy to a
nearby mountain (Mount Soracte). But, lo
and behold, Constantine himself, as pun-
ishment for his persecuting, was smitten
with incurable leprosy. The priests of the
[pagan] idols advised him, then, to have
three thousand children strangled, at the
city gates, and to bathe in their still-warm
blood. Faced with the grief of the mothers,
Constantine prefers to see pity triumph:
'Better for me to die and to preserve the life
of these innocents than to regain, by their
death, a life besmirched with cruelty;'
guided by Saint Peter and Saint Paul,
Constantine, then, follows the advice of
Silvester: he will be cured by dipping himself three times in a spring, symbol of baptism in the Jordan. From this [story de-
rives] the famous and false "Act of
Donation to the Pope Sylvester.')

The belief in the efficacy of human blood as a cure
for leprosy is attested in numerous medieval documents,
as exemplified by the following, selected from Rémy (221
ss.): Michael Scot, astrologer to Frederick II and denizen
of the Maleboge in Dante's *Inferno* (XX, 116-117), recommended in his *Phisionomia* an immersion in the blood of
little children for a cure from leprosy (cited in L.
Thorndike, *History of Magic and Experimental Science*,
London, 1923, II, pp. 331-2); Louis IX was advised by his
Jewish physician to bathe in the blood of two children to
be healed of his leprosy (Boutarel, "Le sang dans la vieille
médecine," *Pro Medico*, 1931, p. 31); Richard the Lion-
hearted, to whom tradition imputes leprosy, was advised,
again, by a Jew, to submerge himself in the blood of a new-
born baby to be cured (Hoffmann-Krayer, *Marbachs*

Volksbücher, Leipzig, 1841, p. 22); a Ferrara text (1587) shows the same suggestion made, once more, by Jewish doctors, to the wife of the Duke of Florence (Hoffmann-Krayer, ibid., I, col. 835).

As to the recommendation of the blood-bath by Jews, is there perhaps an analogy with the blood of Jesus Christ, by whom all mankind is cured of the 'leprosy' of sin? The blood of this Innocent, the Lamb of God, was spilled by "Jews," as is abundantly emphasized in Christian exegesis, and reflected, thereby, in medieval art and literature.

[42] *La Grande Encyclopédie*, vol. 22, p. 62: "Le roi Baudouin IV mourut lépreux en 1185 sur le trône de Jérusalem, bien que les extrémités de ses membres tombassent en putréfaction; le comte Raoul de Vermandois, au XIIe siècle, Robert Bruce au siècle suivant, vécurent et moururent lépreux sans avoir été jamais déchus de leur dignité."

(King Baudouin IV died a leper in 1185, [still] on the throne of Jerusalem, although the extremities of his limbs fell [off] in putrefaction; Count Raoul of Vermandois, in the 12th century, Robert Bruce in the following century, lived and died leprous without ever having been stripped of their dignity.)

[43] Brody, p. 79.

[44] Brody, p. 84.

[45] Richards, p. 62.

[46] Louis Réau, indeed, in his commentary on the iconography of Alexis, interprets this detail as a 'borrowing' from that of Job.

Par suite d'une contamination avec l'iconographie de Job sur son fumier, Alexis est parfois bafoué par une servante qui verse sur sa tête un seau d'eau sale.

(As the result of a contamination with the iconography of Job on his dungheap, Alexis is sometimes jeered by a servant woman who pours a bucketful of dirty water on his head.)

Iconographie de l'art chrétien, T. Second. III, *Les Saints.*

As we know, this detail is clearly stated in the Old French poem, l. 264 and l. 267:

Lur lavadures li getent sur la teste.

L'egua li getent, si moilent sun licon.

Again, we note a detail that demonstrates the apparent conflation of Alexis via Job.

Perhaps it is the femaleness of the spiteful servant ["Une servante"] which was borrowed , rather, *from* Job: the reputed shrewishness of this *sponsa* did much to develop the patience of Job. Thus: "il était invoqué, à cause de sa patience conjugale, par les maris affligés d'une épouse acariâtre." (he was invoked, because of his conjugal patience, by husbands [cursed] with a nagging wife.) (Réau, *Iconographie ...,* Tome Second, *I, Ancien Testament,* p. 312).

[47] Contrary to what Odenkirchen finds: "When the pope now takes hold of the letter, Saint Alexius relinquishes it to him." ["This is the first time that Alexius is called 'Saint' Alexius in the present version."] (Odenkirchen, p. 81. Note 104.) Odenkirchen is referring to line 371; Alexis is, however, first called 'sainz Alexis' here in line 332.

[48] As remarked in Chapter II, Claudius of Turin found: "The letter appears as flesh; but the spiritual sense within is known as divinity." *In Libros Informationum Littarae et Spiritus super Leviticum Praefatio, PL*(1844 ed.), CIV. 615-7.

[49] e.g., Christopher Storey: "Ce train de vie tranquille continue pendant dix-sept ans jusqu' à ce qu'un beau jour l'image de la Vierge dont la renommée avait

seventeen years, until, one fine day, the image of the Virgin, whose fame had attracted the young man in the first place, begins to speak.)

[50] Louis Réau, *Iconographie de l'art chrétien*, T. second, *Iconographie de la Bible*. *Nouveau Testament* (Paris, 1957), pp. 17- 18.

[51] Réau, p. 17.

This legend is reminiscent of the one attaching to the Image of Lucca, as recounted by Bédier, *Les Légendes épiques*, II, 223:

> Après l'ascension du Christ, Nicodème voulut sculpter de mémoire l'image de son maître, tel qu'il l'avait vu sur la croix. Déjà il avait taillé dans le bois la croix et le buste et il s'efforçait de se rappeler les traits du Sauveur, quand il s'endormait: à son réveil, la sainte tête était sculptée. Sur un ordre céleste, il jeta le crucifix à la mer, et les flots le déposèrent au port de Luni; il fut transféré de là à Lucques, toute voisine.

> (After the Ascension of Christ, Nicodemus wanted to sculpt the image of his master, such as he had seen him on the cross, from memory. He had already carved the cross and the bust into the wood, and he was trying to remember the features of the Saviour, when he fell asleep: on his awaking, the holy head was sculpted. On an order from heaven, he cast the crucifix into the sea, and the waves deposited it in the port of Luni; from there, it was transferred to Lucca, hard closeby.)

[52] M. Delcor, *Compte rendu* of H. J. W. Drijvers, *Cults and Beliefs at Edessa* (Leyde, 1980), in *Bulletin de littérature ecclésiastique*, LXXXIII (1982), pp. 40-1.

[53] J. B. Segal, *Edessa The Blessed City* (Oxford: the Clarendon Press, 1970), p. 148.

54 Segal, p. 173.

55 Segal, p. 173.

56 Segal, p. 167. Obviously, this refers to the Eastern legend.

57 Rémy, p. 196.

58 See D. W. Robertson, Jr., *Essays in Medieval Culture* (Princeton: Princeton Univ. Press, 1980), for the importance of *caritas* in the Middle Ages. Robertson notes that charity was seen as the source of all the virtues, and that a fundamental tension between *caritas* and *cupiditas* must be understood throughout medieval literature.

59 This iconography will be discussed more fully in the following chapter.

60 This painting is not, as the reader will appreciate, one of the World's Great Masterpieces of Religious Art: I happened upon it, purely by chance, in Rostock and have yet to find it acknowledged by any art historian.

CHAPTER VII

CONCLUSION

In considering why the *Alexis* was included in the St. Albans Psalter, this investigation has ranged wide and it has envisaged some provocative possibilities. Let us examine and evaluate our findings, both as separate parts and in their *mise ensemble*: thereby may considerations both practical and esthetic combine toward a holistic understanding, which may, in turn, shed light on the constituent parts.

We have seen that the medieval psalter, as a book of liturgy, of private devotion, of instruction, and of "magic" was indispensable for monk or merchant, abecedarian or abbess. We have seen as well that the medieval eye perceived the book as a symbol of God's two Books, the Book of Works and the Book of Words. By such an understanding did the psalter, *par excellence*, signify both of these Books.

By reason of its own beauty, as well as of its sacred Truth, the St. Albans Psalter would seem to refer to this code: indeed, we have remarked a number of its illustrations that are self-referential in depicting the authority and the power of the Book.

Our investigation has included a consideration of medieval numerology, according to which numbers were understood to inform all of Creation: by them was the Universe brought into being, according to scriptural account, and by them is it sustained through the 'mathematical' Music of the Spheres.[1] The creation of the Book of Works 'by the number' would seem to be the model inherent in the making of any medieval book, but especially in a book containing God's Words, i.e., the St. Albans Psalter. Its inclusion of His images, both human and divine, and in both word and picture, would relate the St. Albans Psalter as well to that third volume, the Book of Memory: temporal history, as viewed from an eschatological perspective.

On such authority, the St. Albans Psalter was designed, I have proposed, by and with reference to a well-understood sub-code according to which "creation" and "book" would at once connote the use of numbers, as ordained by the Creator.

According to this ethos, the St. Albans Psalter would represent a reference to three, the sacrosanct number of the Trinity, in comprising three essential parts: the pictorial cycle, the *Alexis* and the Psalms. In addition, the *Alexis* itself may also refer to the *Beata Trinitas* in presenting the *Son* of Eufemien (*Filius*), the Man of *God* (*Pater*), and the holy *Saint* (*Spiritus Sanctus*) in the sanctified Alexis. The poem's triplet sequences would reaffirm this doctrine, so dear to the Gallican Church,[2] and to St. Albans, as is indicated by the *Dedicatio ecclesie sancte trinitatis* added to the Calendar of its famous Psalter. Indeed, in the Prologue to the *Alexis*, which occurs only in the St. Albans Psalter, this tenet of the faith is so vigorously affirmed as to seem a paraphrase of the *Credo in unum Deum:* "Qui est un sul faitur et regnet an trinitiet." (Who is one sole creator and reigns in trinity.)[3]

The carefully-wrought numerical and arithmetical structure of the *Alexis* —that of the **L** manuscript— has been convincingly demonstrated by Curtius, Hatcher, Bulatkin and others, as we have seen. In view of the numerological concept which seems also to inform the poem's 'housing,' the St. Albans Psalter, an irresistible idea suggests itself: is the numerical structure of the poem, as well, the contribution of the 'Albanimeister,' the designer of the Psalter? We shall consider this possibility later in summarizing the 'Master plan.'

The christological cycle of the St. Albans Psalter would certainly imply a numerical reference in comprising forty pictures: by medieval understanding, forty would well represent the mystical number of preparation. In addition, yet another 'trinity' —a temporal one— may be perceived in the 'unity' of the Albani pictorial cycle. The first part of the cycle would portray the time before Christ came to Earth. Accordingly, this segment includes the picture of the First Adam, and of the Annunciation to the new *Eva: Ave.* [4] The second conceptual segment portrays Christ's days on earth as the New Adam, the Son of Man: hence, thirty-three scenes of his Incarnation, beginning with the Visitation[5] and ending with the three Holy Women at the empty tomb. The final segment is composed of five scenes after the Resurrection: the triumph of the Eternal Son of God evokes the timelessness of the *secula seculorum*. The depiction herein of three adopted Sons of God —Saints Thomas and Martin who lived after Jesus Christ, and David who prefigured him— reinforces the supertemporality of the World without End, as further evoked in the two scenes of the Ascension and of Pentecost. Thereby are human *locus* and *tempus* both transcended. By such a temporal and supertemporal understanding would the pictorial portion of the St. Albans Psalter be understandable as a Book of History/Memory, the third manifestation of the book as a symbol. As such, well might it include the Alexis whose Life we are called upon to commemorate.

It must be granted that so numerological a design as is herein proposed for the St. Albans Psalter could depend upon the eye of the beholder.[6] But, having looked with a "modern" eye at a number of other medieval psalters and service books, many a medievalist ends by seeing with the 'eye of the heart,' a "medieval" eye, which properly looks beneath the veil. So Dom Leclercq has described the power of the imagination of medieval man as "exuberant," yet possessing "a vigor and a preciseness which we find it difficult to understand."[7]

That the St. Albans Psalter as we now possess it was designed for Christina of Markyate seems certain, thanks to the careful analysis of its Warburg editors: the obits of Christina's family have been added to its Calendar, along with the names of female saints, certain of whom are comparable to Christina in resisting marriage; two of the prayer illustrations would seem to have reference to Christina.[8] Later, we shall consider what may have been the 'original' St. Albans Psalter, to whom it might have belonged, and why an '*Albanimeister*' should be credited with the design and with the realization of the Psalter as it now appears.

We have noted that the presence of the *Alexis* in this Psalter is generally explained as reflecting Christina's resolve to remain as celibate as was Alexis: it is *une pièce justificative*. We have noted that if this were its sole raison d'*y* être, a female saint would have afforded a better analogy. We have further observed that 'justification' (or exoneration) would hardly have been required in the cloister. It would seem that there were, however, other very strong practical reasons, and equally compelling esthetic ones, determining the choice of St. Alexis.

First, as a Christ-type, Alexis would be eminently identifiable with the *Sponsus* to whom Christina had betrothed herself in childhood and whom she had wed in the

201

nuptial ceremony of her religious vows. On yet another allegorical level, Alexis would represent the *Sponsus* of *Ecclesia*, the community of believers; for this very reason does the bride of Alexis remain anonymous in the poem, as Uitti has demonstrated.[9] By means of this understanding, the laity, as *Sponsa* of Christ, could fully participate in the Life of Alexis, along with the religious community, for whom the *Sponsus/Sponsa* metaphor was especially appropriate.

Indeed, so immediately and universally is Christ understood to be the prime model for Alexis, that "Imitator Christi" could well serve as his emblematic surname, transcending those of "Filz Eufemien," "l'ume Deu," or, even, "Sainz" (Son of Euphemian, Man of God, Saint). In the Eastern form of his name, in fact, the Christ symbol would find itself exactly at the center: *AleXius*.[10] It would seem of vital importance to determine the nature of the Christ whom Alexis imitates.

First and foremost, it is the human Christ, the Son of Man who is evoked. As such, he is the Suffering Servant, who is 'despised and rejected, yet openeth not his mouth.' So Alexis refrains from rebuking his scorning servants, asking God's mercy on them, 'for they know not what they do':

> Tuz l'escarnissent, sil tenent pur bricun;
> L'egua li getent, si moilent sun liçon;
> Ne s'en corucet giens cil saintismes hom,
> Ainz priet Deu quet il le lur parduinst
> Par sa mercit, quer ne sevent que funt.
> (ll. 266-70)

> (All of them mock him, for they hold him
> as worth nothing;
> They throw water on him, so do they drench
> his little bed;
> At this does this most holy man not once
> get angry,
> Rather prays he God that He might pardon
> them
> By His mercy, for they know not what they
> do.)

Alexis's Model is, as well, the *Agnus Dei*, who takes upon himself the sins —the leprosy— of the world as *Leprosus mundi.* So Alexis, "mezre," seats himself as an outcast, *der arme Aussätziger,* reviled and held as less than naught, a "bricun". Finally, however, with Alexis's apotheosis, it is the *Filius Dei* who is evoked, the divine Christ who triumphed over death and the grave, who has the power to work miracles, and by whose expiation and intercession our sins are forgiven. So Alexis purchases the redemption of a city by his righteousness, so does his body effect the healing of every disease, and so may we seek his intercession before the throne of God:

> E si li preient que d'els ai[e]t mercit:
> Al son seignor il lur seit boens plaidiz.
>
> (ll. 599-600)

(And so they pray him that he have mercy on them:
That, before his lord, he may be a good advocate for them.)

> Si li preiuns que de toz mals nos tolget.
> En icest siecle nus acat pais e goie,
> Ed en cel altra la plus durable gloirie!
>
> (ll. 622-24)

(So let us pray him that he remove from us all ills.
In this life may he purchase for us peace and joy,
And in that other, the most unending glory!)

By hagiographical convention, these two natures, the human and the divine, would be understood not only for Christ, but for Alexis's human model, Saint Lazarus. The Lazarus 'known' by the people of the Middle Ages was a conflated figure: the Poor Man at Dives' door and the resuscitated Lazarus of Bethany, the 'first fruit of them that sleep.' The conflation of these two Lazaruses is an ancient one; indeed, the Poor Lazarus, the only person in Jesus' parables with a name, is suspected of having 'borrowed' it from the Lazarus of Bethany.[11] The two became 'as one flesh' for the *people* of the Middle Ages as, likewise, did Mary of Bethany, sister of Lazarus, and Mary Magdalene.[12] And it is strikingly remarkable that

Lazarus, along with Job, his Old Testament prototype, is judged to share the iconography of Alexis, *le Pauvre sous l'escalier*, as we have seen.

Indeed, it would seem natural that Alexis would be so identified with Lazarus, "*le Pauvre*," as to be understood to suffer his illness, "*le mal St.- Lazare*," the "Sacred Malady" early associated with Christ.[13] On the literal level, we have seen that the case history of Alexis's infirmity is that understood for leprosy, and that his life style as a *persona non grata* was consistent with that of a *mesel*. By such an understanding, as proposed above, the word *mezre* is well explained. Indeed, it would perfectly resolve the cruel perplexities which have so beset certain modern readers, such as why Alexis so 'coldly' abandoned his bride, and how he so 'heartlessly' placed himself anonymously on his family's threshold.[14] For if he had willingly received the "Sacred Malady" as "a gift from God," then was he obliged to live with *it*, and only with it: he has made himself a leper for the sake of Christ and for the salvation of his family. Therefore, it is *Caritas* which is the prime and motivating force: only it leads properly to an *Askesis* being undertaken —and to its being beautifully justified.

Moreover, if Alexis is understood as a latter-day Saint Lazarus, his Life would seem eminently suitable to gloss the parable of St. Lazarus, just as the Lives of Saints Blaise, Nicholas, and Thomas of Canterbury served to farce 'Epistles.' Although we have no other examples of a farced Gospel reading per se,[15] the ubiquitous variations and the unorthodox additions which we have seen for the Gallican liturgy would seem to allow amply for such a liberty. And in view of the fact that St. Stephen is the Proto-Martyr and that his is the earliest farced Epistle extant, it would seem highly likely that a Proto-Confessor would be required as well: who better than St. Lazarus could be seen in this role? What vernacular poem better than the *Alexis* could serve to farce this reading?[16] By such an *oeuvre* might the Church most effectively instruct the faithful in the 'twin' virtues of *Caritas/Castitas* and *Pietas/*Pitias*: by dint of perfect love (*Caritas*) do the Sponsa and Sponsus retain their chastity (*Castitas*) and eschew all temporal unions; by dint of his unfailing care of his children (*Pietas*) does the Father, the 'Supreme Piety' of the Prologue, pour out his mercy (*Pitias*) upon them through the 'anointed one.' In both sets of these doublets, there is an overlapping of concepts; in both sets, both imitation and reciprocity are enjoined: the mutual love and devotion of Father and children —the *people*— are implicit. And we have observed that the **L** version of the *Alexis* appears to have been composed with the express purpose of appealing to the people, for whom the use of the vernacular had been so long prescribed.[17]

That the **L** version of the *Alexis* was expressly designed for liturgical use is evidenced by its apparent addition of fifteen final 'ecclesiastical' strophes, by its textual reference to 'this his feastday' ("Puroec en est oi cest jurn oneuret," 542), and by its final line's exhortation to recite the *Pater Noster*. A presentation of the *Alexis* within the church would seem to invite the full exploitation of the dramatic nature long-associated with the church and its liturgy. And we well know that the Gallican church was especially noted for its dramatic propensity, to reach its fullest expression, indeed, in furnishing the stage for the first bona fide liturgical drama, the *Adam*.[18] We have seen, as well, that the *Epître farcie* was long noted as a particularly Gallic phenomenon. For its performances in French churches, more 'staging' would seem to have been added to the already dramatic constants of the church 'theater' in that the subdeacons were 'costumed,' they effected the equivalent of a stage entrance, and their 'script' was presented in 'dialogue,' certainly between the Latin and the French readers and possibly among the French readers as well.

With the passing of time and the crossing of a channel, an even more dramatic presentation is well possible, and especially in the milieu in which the **L** *Alexis* would see the light. St. Albans, whose *éclat* and assertiveness, we have seen, were remarkable, would have enjoyed both the Gallican traditions of its Norman rulers and the 'frontier' freedom of twelfth-century England, where the customs and the language of the Conqueror would be accommodated to the particular needs and nature of the Anglo-Saxons. Under such conditions, the likelihood of liturgical adaptations would be indeed strong, for the Church would need to instruct and to convince a people whose native tongue was far-removed from Latin. For them, "Hoc est meum corpus" would be just so much "hocus pocus," the Magdalena would become simply "maudlin," a person *non compos mentis* would turn into a "nincompoop," and the *Pater Noster* —with which, notably, the *Alexis* is 'sanctified'— might well be the sole pure Latin of which the people were capable. The popular knowledge of the *Pater Noster* is evidenced by its frequency in the Lay Folks' Mass Book and by its widespread use in 'de-hexification,' its incantation being prescribed to detect and to cancel the evil spells of witches. Surely there could be no more likely an environment for a dramatic presentation of a saint's Life in the vernacular than the Abbey church of St. Albans, which, as a Benedictine house, set its own rules and practices. An appeal to the eye, as well as to the ear, would make the presentation of an *exemplum* —St. Alexis— doubly effective. And St. Albans' Abbot Geoffrey, whose theatrical bent had already been displayed in his early staging of a saint's Life, would be superbly capable of expressing his dramatic flair in presenting the Old French *Alexis* innovatively, as in an *Epître farcie*, wherein parts, if not roles, might be distributed, as in the Gospel Reading on Easter Sunday.

We have remarked that the earliest surviving *Epître farcie*, the Tours *St. Stephen*, is in the same versification and form as the *Alexis*: strophes of five decasyllabic lines. We have seen that the same assonance is used to open both this *Epître farcie* and *La Seinte Resureccion*. And we find that the Prologue to the *Alexis*, unique to the **L** manuscript, begins with a sentence containing four words with this same ending in -*un/m*: it was surely meant to rhyme, as Hofmann, as well, has judged. In addition, if my arrangement of the passage as poetry is accepted, its opening comprises two decasyllabic lines and an Anglo-Norman tail rhyme. A comparison of these three passages will show that they all share the same assonance/rhyme, and that the *Alexis* Prologue and the Tours *Etienne* would seem to share the same meter as well.

> En ceste manere recitom
> La seinte resureccion.
> Premierement apareillons
> Tous les lius e les mansions.
> > (*La Seinte Resurreccion*)

> Por amor de vos pri saignos barun.
> Seet vos tuit escotet la lecun.

206

De saint estevre lo glorius barun.
(5) Qui a ce ior recut sa pasiun.
(4) Escotet la par bene entenciun.
(Epître farcie pour la fête de saint Etienne)

Ici cumencet amiable cancun
E spiritel raisun di ceol noble barun
Eufemien par num.
(Prologue, *La Vie de St. Alexis*)

We have noted that this -*um*/n assonance could reflect some association with the *Te Deum* so prominent in both liturgy and in the earliest specimens of liturgical drama.

According to the traditional view of theater historians, medieval drama represents an evolution: from pure liturgy —itself quasi-drama— to farced liturgy to free-standing extraliturgical drama. From the *Eulalia* which troped the *Alleluia* of the Gradual, to the Lives which farced the 'Epistles,' to the Passions which represented the supreme drama of the liturgy, and, eventually to the farce 'pure' and free, an organic flow appears obvious.

This evolution involves not only such theatrical concerns as costuming and staging, not only the subject matter treated, not only the quantitative expansion of the matter at hand, but, most significantly, the vehicle by which it all is carried: the language. We have seen that the earliest liturgical dramas, in Latin, knew only the briefest incursions of the vernacular: a few Old French lines in the *Lazarus* and in the *Sponsus* are this 'infant's' first words. Soon they would become so lusty and expressive as to provide a full-fledged *Adam* script to 'farce,' in a sense, the Latin Responses and Readings of the day, and thereby to make 'St. Augustine' and the Scriptures comprehensible to the people in word *and* in deed. [19]

The earlier specimens of vernacular lines within the Latin liturgical drama, the *Lazarus* and the *Sponsus*, share a feature which should surely be regarded as highly significant. In both cases, the mother tongue 'intrudes' — and often intrudes *as* a mother, e.g. the Virgin and Rachel— in order to make a *lament*, and a very human lament: thereby, there occurs a certain humanization of the divine. By dint of this humanization, we are already en route for a *laïcization* of the sacred matter, whether of liturgy or Life. And, indeed, we have seen that it is the *planctus* which constitutes one of the most striking of the differences between the Latin *Vita* and the Old French *Vie de St. Alexis*. Thereby does the *locus* and the ethos represent a point of view different from that of the cloistered cell, where self-mortification, solitude and physical death constitute the penultimate *summum bonum*. For the lay community, however, pain is 'best' to be avoided, solitude is pitiful aloneness, and death is the ultimate terror. So would the suffering, loneliness and dying of Alexis appear to the people as exquisitely pathetic: popular *Dol* replaces monastic *Goie*. By suffering along with him, in *sym*pathy, and by feeling deep pity, through *com*passion, might the people perform their own good deed of *Caritas*, that supreme of virtues for the Middle Ages. Moreover, by participating in the life/Life of St. Alexis might the people both effect their own *Imitatio* and be cleansed of their own 'leprosy.'

Indeed, a liturgical performance of the *Alexis* (**L**) would invoke a double reality: the intertextual reality of the tale and the paratextual reality of the audience's role within it. Thus, in the timeless present of this polychronistic time, the people of God, both in Rome and in England, call upon the Saint to save them. Whether in the church of St. Boniface or that of St. Albans, all the regalia of the High and Holy Feastday are called into play in honoring him.

Such a doubling of the People of God is especially appropriate for the *Alexis*. Itself a narrative intaglio within the St. Albans Psalter, the *Life* of St. Alexis encases its own miniature: his 'Life' as he wrote it, with his own hand, using the "enca e parcamin e. . . penne" fetched by his "bel frere." (281-2). And this tale within a tale might well imply the reverse procedure, availing itself of another Church and clergy and people to furnish the larger frame for the story of St. Alexis —at St. Albans. The microcosm would, thereby, reveal and explain the macrocosm.

Indeed, within such a concentric temporality, the people of St. Albans might well re-enact the people of Rome, both tacitly and orally: the Church and the clergy are clearly indicated for the formal ceremonies of celebrating the Saint's feastday, and the audience is written in textually for at least one *parole* (or *verbum!*), the *Pater Noster*. Who knows if the St. Albans congregation did not identify with the 'people of Rome' so completely as to thrice wail along with them for Alexis, either in the flesh, as a miracle-working *cors*, or as a   Saint in Paradise? Indeed, we have seen that it was the *lay* congregation which sang the Old French farcing of the Epistles, by Du Méril's reckoning.   Thus would be accomplished more fully an ambivaluation of Alexis: the 'Man of God' would signify both 'Son of Man' and 'Son of God.' Thereby could the people of God attune to his humanization, and fully value his 'deification'; thereby could the religious community identify with his spirituality, in its own avowed extra-materialism.   In serving the needs of both the lay and the religious community, the *Alexis* is at home in both secular and monastic space.

In fact, Lausberg has proposed that the appeal to the hearers in the poem's final strophe is not to "seignors," (non-clerics) but, rather, to "serors" (*soeurs*, religious sisters):

Aiuns, *serors*, cel saint home en memorie.
(l. 621)[20]

(Let us, Sisters, keep this holy man in memory.)

While such a reading may be textually inadmissible, it well may reflect a super-reality transcending the raw fact: Lausberg intuited that the *Alexis* was at home among his 'Sisters,' among them, surely, the noble Christina, *Sponsa intacta.*

But if, as would appear indubitable, the **L** *Alexis* was designed for popular cɔnsumption, within the church, in the liturgical celebration of his feastday, why should it be in Christina's Psalter?   The presence of such 'apocryphal' elements as the Old French *Alexis* and a pictorial cycle in the St. Albans Psalter may, in fact, be due to its being (re-)designed for a woman: like a child, by medieval lights, she might be granted certain indulgences. So are 'children' envisaged for picture books, such as the forty-page series in the Saint Albans Psalter. So are they understood to require a simpler language as well: hence, a saint's life in the vernacular, rather than in Latin, *lingua Dei.*

Woledge and Clive have remarked the high incidence of Anglo-Norman in *didactic* texts. I would offer that there seems to be a high incidence of *pictured* books, some of them with Anglo-Norman texts as well, which were destined for women. Among them are such illustrious Psalters as the following: the Psalters of Queen Melisende, of Blanche de Castille, of the Nuns of Shaftesbury, of Henri de Blois, the Troyes Psalter, the Ingeborg Psalter, and our text at hand, the St. Albans Psalter.

In view of a full forty pages of pictures in the Saint Albans Psalter, are we then to infer that Christina could not read? "In ipsa legunt qui litteras nesciunt"? (In this those who do not know letters [can] read.) Then why should she be furnished with a book containing literary texts, both in Old French and Latin, as well as pictures? Was her Latin a product of rote learning, via liturgical repetition and hearing, and with no comprehension of the words' meaning? Yet her own Life speaks of her constantly reading the Psalms, indubitably in Latin. Was this perhaps all the Latin she knew, and was, then, Anglo-Norman, the language of the *Alexis*, her mother tongue? But her spiritual advisor, Roger, used Anglo-Saxon to address her as his brightest star:

> Et ad virginem letare mecum, ait anglico sermone. Myn sunendaege dohter, quod latine dicitur, mea dominice diei filia. eo quod ceteris omnibus quas Christo genuerat aut nutrierat, Christinam plus amaret: quantum dominica dies reliquis septimane feriis honorabilitate preestaret."

> (And he said to the maiden in English: 'Rejoice with me, myn sunendaege dohter', that is, my Sunday daughter, because just as much as Sunday excels the other days of the week in dignity, so he loved Christina more than all the others whom he had begotten or nursed in Christ.)
>
> [C.H. Talbot, ed.,
> *The Life of Christina*
> (Oxford, 1959), p. 21]

It would appear, then, that Christina, a gentlewoman in Norman England, was trilingual: she would naturally know the language of her forebears and of her countrymen, English; she would be fluent, as well, in

French, the language of the upper class in twelfth-century England; moreover, as the daughter of a wealthy family, she would likely have been taught Latin. With these considerations in mind, should we not understand the St. Albans' Gregorian letter as a defense both of the pictures in the Psalter and of the Alexis 'song' as well? For the *Alexis* is an exceptional element in the Psalter in three ways; it is non-scriptural, it is in the vernacular, and it is unequivocally introduced as an aesthetic delight, even before its moral worth is stated: "amiable cançun" (pleasing song) precedes "spiritel raisun" (spiritual account.) With a dual interpretation of Pope Gregory's endorsement, the Old French poem can be unimpeachably acquitted: like the painted illustrations, the *Alexis* serves as an image, a true *Imago Christi*, the contemplation of which can lead the beholder beyond the written word to the one in whose image all of creation was understood to be made: In principio *Verbum*. And its presence in a book destined for a woman would be even more defensible: the proper spiritual food for 'babes in Christ' is 'pap', as St. Paul had directed. It must surely be for Christina's delectation within her cell and among her sister recluses that the *Alexis* was included in the St. Albans Psalter. And how better to enjoy it than as a dramatic reading?

We have found goodly proof, indeed, of the dramatic tendencies of nuns: there is Hrodsvitha of Gandesheim who made plays of saints' Lives, there is the Bishop Eudes' record of discovering younger sisters in the act of farcing Epistles, there is the judgment of Cohen that sisters may have acted even male roles in their miracle plays, there are the plays that Sister Katherine Bourget either wrote (composed) or 'wrote out,' there is even the concession of Sepet that, though women must wait long to act professionally, Sisters may well have performed the Easter play, given the locus of its manuscript, "dans une abbaye de religieuses."[21] What could be more likely than that women, given their 'hysterical' nature, should also be inclined to histrionics? Indeed, we have seen that it is the lamentation —*le propre à femmes!*— which furnishes our *earliest* vernacular dramatic lines, in the *Sponsus* and *Lazarus*. Moreover, the very germ of medieval drama, the St. Gall *Quem quaeritis*, presents "three women who enter, weeping, bearing spices rare." Again, both in dramatic script and in dramatic action, are we reminded of the ma-

211

jor role given to lamentations, and especially that of the mother, as in the *Alexis*. What would of course make nuns' performance of our earliest plays supremely feasible is the simple fact that they were women, and thus naturally suited to enact the very majority of the roles: with the exception of Christ (who, out of reverence, was late to receive a speaking role or a stage appearance), of Lazarus and of Daniel, the women have, essentially, "all the lines." There are the three Maries, (the Angel?), the Five Wise and the Five Foolish Virgins, Mary and Martha of Bethany, Rachel and her 'sisters', the weeping mothers of the Innocents.

With so rich a tradition of the Emoting Female, it is quite appropriate that the wife and the mother of Alexis should be given such full scope for the expression of their grief in facing his dead body: sixty lines of the text are devoted to the lamentations of these women.

Indeed, as Sepet has shown, the *planctus* of the weeping woman is of vital importance in the development of liturgical drama.[22] The Lamentation of the Virgin was early associated with the dramatic liturgy of Good Friday, whence it would naturally expand to the lamentation of the three Maries, and become juxtaposed, finally, onto the Easter liturgy. Again a process of 'farcing' is to be remarked: the 'stage was set' for Rachel's Lamentations to find words, and for the vernacular *planctus* of all the mothers (and sisters) bereft of their 'Innocents.'

The expansion of such a procedure surely informs our first bona fide Old French liturgical drama, *Le Jeu d'Adam*. The sermon *preached* was first transformed to a sermon *recited*, a *recitative* in the style of a Bach cantata, as Sepet has so happily termed it.[23] From this it was an easy step to divide the *recitative* into parts, distributed among several actors, with the original form left intact to "carry" the dialogue. In the case of the Adam play, the 'Sermo beati Augustini' would be 'preached' operatically, or better, oratorically, but with staging, costuming, dialogue and action to represent rather than simply to present the story. While the '*recitatives*' —the responses— would remain in Latin and properly liturgical, the *paroles* would most appropriately be in the vernacular, for there is *impersonation*, that crucial element which marks the division between liturgy and drama.

In the case of the *Alexis*, we would certainly have all the elements which might well lend themselves to making rudimentary theater. First of all, there is a deeply moving story whose very lines invoke the catharsis of the audience:

> Ki ad pechét bien s'en pot recorder,
> Par penitence s'en pot tres bien salver.
> Briés est cist secles, plus durable atendeiz.
> Ço preiums Deu, la sainte trinitét,
> Qu'o Deu ansemble poissum el ciel regner.
> (ll. 546-50)

> Las! malfeüz! cum esmes avoglez!
> Quer co veduns que tuit sumes desvez.
> De noz pechez sumes si ancumbrez,
> La dreite vide nus funt tresoblïer,
> Par cest saint home doüssum ralumer.

> Aiuns, seignors, cel saint home en memorie,
> Si li preiuns que de toz mals nos tolget.
> En icest siecle nus acat pais e goie,
> Ed en cel altra la plus durable glorie!
> En ipse verbe sin dimes: Pater noster.
> (ll. 616-25)

(Whoever has sinned can well remember:
By penitence can he full well be saved.
This life is short, await the one more lasting.
Thus let us pray God, the Holy Trinity,
That together with God we may in heaven reign.

Alas! Wretched creatures! How are we blinded!
For this we see: that we are all demented.
So burdened are we with our sins,
That they make us completely forget the good life.
Through this holy man must we [be] re-enlighten[ed].

Let us keep, my lords, this holy man in memory,

So let us pray him that he remove from us all
sins.
In this life may he purchase for us peace
and joy,
And in that other, the most unending glory!
In the Word Itself, then, let us say: Pater
Noster.)

Moreover, the *Alexis* is not only recitable (*recitative*) and
chantable, but it would allow for distribution of parts.
There are 199 lines of direct speech in the poem's 625;
hence, close to one third of the lines are spoken. They are
distributed among the following: Alexis; his father,
Eufemien; his mother; his wife; the Image; the Good
Servant; the Voice; the Pope; the two Emperors; the People.
The number of lines accorded to each of the roles is as
follows:

Alexis: 29 lines.
Eufemien: 40 lines. (32, final planctus)
Mother: 45 lines. (32, final planctus)
Father and Mother together: 2 lines.
Spouse: 32 lines. (28, final planctus)
Image: 7 lines.
Sacristan: 1 line.
Servant: 7 lines.
Voice: 2 lines.
Pope and Emperors (together): 16 lines.
Pope: 5 lines.
Emperors: 4 lines.
People: 7 lines. [plus the *Pater Noster*]

As for a 'theatrical' presentation of the *Alexis*, the
three essential elements —audience, performers, stage—
would already be on hand. There would likely be a 'full
house': at any rate, there would be 'standing room only,'
the medieval cathedral not yet being equipped with seating. There would be a 'repertory' cast provided by the
clergy. The situation would be theatrical per se, the
church being the proto-stage for medieval drama.
Moreover, its altar, the first stage prop, might well represent the principal *lieus* for the life of Alexis: altar per se
for the parents' praying for a child, his infant *praesepe*,
the marriage bed, his death bed, the *sepulchrum*. These
are *the* pivotal scenes in the life of Saint Alexis, suitable

214

for Lausberg's proposed division of the *Alexis* into twenty-five tableaux of five strophes each.[24]

Precedents for at least an 'Oratorio' performance of the *Alexis* may be seen in the singing of the Clermont *Passion* and *Léger*, as evidenced by the neumes (medieval musical notes) accompanying the first three lines of the *Passion* manuscript.[25] In addition, the lamentations of the Three Maries, long attached to the liturgy, were undoubtedly sung; with this scene's development into the *Quem Quaeritis*, we are well on our way to liturgical drama.

As to the justification for an *Alexis* performance, there is the long-honored directive that instruction should be made understandable to the people. From the time of the Tours decree (A.D. 813), the sermon had supposedly been delivered in the vernacular, though the Readings remained in Latin: hence, were they susceptible to farcing. We have taken note of the special need of the English people for an amplification of the Sacred Word. The reading of a pericope of the two Lazarus stories —a collation of the stories of the Poor Man, and of the resuscitated Saint of Bethany— would afford the perfect narrative backdrop for a dramatic reading of *La Vie de St. Alexis* as *Epître farcie*. How could Abbot Geoffrey, once *Magister* and *metteur en scène*, help but see this as the chosen way to instruct God's people? Though it must wait for the thirteenth century to be fully staged as a *Miracle*, the *Alexis* might thus serve as a bridge between sacred liturgy and liturgical drama.

Outside of the church, rather than being simply presented, the *Alexis* might well have been represented more fully; the refectory of the monastery or convent could well accommodate such a performance. So, in the Priory of Markyate, topical associations might be the better evoked by the casting of Geoffrey himself as Alexis and of Christina as the Bride. As such, it might well function as a *pièce de théâtre laudative* if not *justificative*, of two servants of God who had plighted their troth in "*noces virginels*": Christina and Geoffrey. Indeed, who better than Geoffrey would be analogous to the young man who left his home, his family and his country, and sailed away to do God's service in a foreign land?

As we have found time and again in exploring the unusual at St. Albans, it is the name of Geoffrey that unerringly comes to the fore. Like Paris's positing of

Tedbalt of Vernon as the author of the proto-*Alexis*, my proposing Geoffrey as its *metteur en scène* and leading actor must remain in the realm of hypothesis. But this would appear an hypothesis which would accommodate all the data. As such, I offer it gratuitously, for the consideration of fellow 'mystery' buffs: perhaps, together, we may find the 'miracle,' in assessing the following considerations. As Abbot of St. Albans, Geoffrey might well present the Alexis of popular appeal quasi-dramatically, in a liturgical setting, and for didactic purposes. As friend and *confrère* of Christina, he might well represent Alexis, chaste *Sponsus*, in a monastic setting, both for "consulaciun" and for esthetic reasons. To envisage two such totally different *loci* and rationales would require their co-existence in the text. *Ecce et voilà*: this is precisely what we have found in the **L** manuscript of the *Alexis*. Strophes I-CX are preponderantly ascetic, grave, and *private*; Strophes CXI-CXXV are patently liturgical, human and communal. Hereby might the people be instructed and moved to repentance and charity, thereby might the monastic community draw strength and comfort in living the Life of Alexis vicariously. And on a more personal level, Christina and Geoffrey, who appear closely bound to each other in a quasi-*mariage blanc*, could both commemorate, *à deux*, their chaste union and exonerate it to others, as *Sponsus* and *Sponsa*. Though the whole life-story would have been presented both in church and refectory, the participation and the character-identification of its two such audiences would have been engaged in appropriately different ways.

The St. Albans Psalter offers two pieces of evidence, unique to itself, which do indeed affirm that it is the *Sponsus/-a* aspect of the *Alexis* which is therein prioritized: the *Alexis* miniatures and the Prologue. Whereas the prevailing scene in other Alexis iconography is that of the Poor Man under the Staircase, the three miniatures illustrating the *Alexis* in the St. Albans Psalter are concerned, rather, with the bridal couple. The first of these scenes shows Alexis handing over the "renges...ed...anel"; its *titulus* reads "*Beatus Alesis/puer electus*" (Blessed Alexis/chosen youth). The second shows the bride standing alongside the door, out of which Alexis is departing. Its *titulus* is concerned with the bride: "*O sponsa beata/semper gemebunda*" (O blessed bride/always lamenting). The third scene shows Alexis in the boat, at sea; he is paying his passage to the boatman. Its caption is *"Ecce ben(e)dictus alexis/receptus in naue"* (Behold the blessed Alexis/received into the boat). At the top of the page, the following title is written in verse:

Vltima pudice donantur munera sponse.
Anulus et remge uerborum finis et aue.

(Finally parting gifts are offered chastely to the bride.
A ring and a sword-belt, with the words "Farewell" and "Hail.")

These *tituli* may represent the opening lines of Latin hymns, as has been proposed; or, according to the provocative suggestion which Wormald has made to Pächt, "it may be worth considering the possibility of some of these inscriptions being quotations from the very poem which was the main model of the French 'chanson.'"[26]

If, indeed, the *tituli* have reference to hymns, an even stronger case may be made for the presentation of the *Alexis* in Christina's Priory: in addition to her model's being featured pictorially, as the *Sponsa*, Christina would have her own Bridal Song as well. The singing of such hymns in church, as well as in the cloister, immediately suggests itself. It is the nature of the Forsaken and Forlorn Bride that we have earlier remarked as the prevailing characteristic of the *Alexis* when it became laïcized: here is how and where it might well have first caught the popular fancy.[27]

In addition to the miniatures, the Prologue, as well, (both unique to the **L** manuscript) presents Alexis only in the role of the Departing Bridegroom, whose sole act is that of commending his young Bride to the Eternal Bridegroom. The remainder of this short text stresses the value of the poem for those living purely, keeping themselves chaste in virginal marriages.

It will at once appear odd that the Prologue's portrayal of Alexis ends where his spiritual life barely begins in the Poem. Not a word is said of his thirty-four years of suffering, either in Alsis or in Rome, nor of his death, his miracles, and his burial —the stock credentials for a saint's Life.   So glaring an omission is, in fact, tantamount to ignoring —whether by not knowing or by

217

purposely avoiding— the program of Alexis as described in the poem. Most conspicuous is the fact that the Saint is completely unnamed in this introduction to his Life. Obviously, this Prologue was written expressly for (or about, or *by*) someone who had taken the vow of chastity; its *conclusio* commends the poem, and on this basis alone, to others so engaged.

Solely on the basis of its content, it would appear incontestable that this Prologue was written at St. Albans, as Pächt has judged on artistic grounds. My earlier analysis of its language as later and more Anglo-Norman than that of the poem would further affirm this judgment.

Yet Gaston Paris would attach the Prologue to the Poem *ab ovo*: "Je suis plus porté, pour ma part, à croire que ce prologue précédait déjà le texte original de notre poème..." (I am more inclined, for my part, to believe that this prologue already preceded the original text of our poem...) It would at first appear that this is impossible. But having analyzed the style as well as the form and content of the poem, I believe that both Pächt and Paris are right, though with some modification: there was *a* Prologue to the Old French *Alexis*, Part I (Strophes I-CX, **L** ms.), which the writer *revised* for his own topical purposes. Indeed Paris himself concedes such a possibility in the remainder of the immediately preceding quotation: ". . . en tout cas il devait se trouver dans le manuscrit que l'auteur de **L** a eu sous les yeux."[28] (...in any case, it must have been in the manuscript which the author of **L** had before his eyes.)

A reading of the Prologue will reveal that it is remarkably awkward, illogical, and *incorrect*. Let us examine the Prologue first in its Old French original, and then in a rawly literal translation, with commentary interspersed for each. Then we shall seek explanation for its gracelessness.

(Slashes indicate the lines in the manuscript. Asterisks indicate commentary.)

Ici cumencet* amiable cancun e* spiritel raisun	
	(1)
diceol* no/ble barun eufemien par num e de la vie	(2)
de sum filz* boneü/ret del quel nus avum oit	(3)
lire e canter. par le* divine/ volentet. il	(4)
desirrables icel sul filz* angendrat. Apres	(5)

le* naisance/ co fut emfes de deu methime amet.*   (6)
e de pere e de mere/ par grant certet nurrit.*   (7)
la sue iuvente* fut honeste e spiritel./   (8)
Par l'amistet del* surerain* pietet la sue   (9)
spuse iuvene cuman/dat al spus vif de veritet   (10)
Ki est un sul faitur* e regnet/an trinitiet.*   (11)
Icesta istorie est amiable grace e suverain/   (12)
consulaciun a cascun* memorie spiritel. Les   (13)
quels vivent/ purement sulunc* castethet. e   (14)
dignement sei* delitent/ es goies del ciel   (15)
& es noces virginels.   (16)

The more glaring abnormalities, as indicated by asterisks,
follow:

> Lack of definite article. (line 1)
> Confusion of nominative and accusative. (lines 3,5,11)
> Masculine articles, adjectives for feminine nouns.
> (lines 4,6,9,13)
> Analogical or otherwise irregular forms, typically
> Anglo-Norman. (lines 2,3,14,15: *diceol, filz,
> sulunc, sei*)

(Here begins agreeable song and spiritual discourse*   (1)
of that noble* baron Euphemian by name* and of the life
[Life?]   (2)
of his blessed son of whom [which?] we have heard   (3)
read and sung. By the divine will. He   (4)
desirable this one son engendered. After   (5)
the birth this was* child of God himself loved.   (6)
And of father and of mother by great affection nourished.   (7)
His youth was upright and spiritual.   (8)
By the friendship of the sovereign piety* his   (9)
 young wife [he] commended to the living bridegroom of
truth   (10)
Who is one sole maker and reigns in trinity.   (11)
This story is pleasing grace and sovereign   (12)
consolation to each spiritual memory. The   (13)
 which [for those who?] live purely according to chastity.
And   (14)
worthily delight themselves in the joys of heaven   (15)
and in virginal nuptials.)   (16)

Line 1, with its "cançun" and "raisun," cannot
fail to evoke the terms *Canso* and *Razo* attached

to the Provençal love lyrics.   Indeed, this Prologue itself is by nature of a *Razo*.

Line 2's "*noble* baron" and "Euphemian by name" would seem redundant, unless understood as 'poetic' in nature. But be it well noted: it is *not* "La Chanson d'Euphemian," but rather "La Vie de St. Alexis" which will follow the Prologue.

Line 4's *desirrables* for *desireux* is a hapax: Anglo-confusion?   Surely Euphemien is desir*ous* of a son, not desir*able*! The Poem proper (l. 256) shows *desirruse*, the logical adjective for this emotion.

Line 6's "this was child" (*co fut emfes*) would not appear so awkward if the "child" were not qualified, "of God himself loved" (*de Deu methime amet*). The phrase is reminiscent of the Biblical David, "whom God loved after his own heart."

The "sovereign piety" should surely be understood as an epithet for God, as Ultimate Goodness; it is not uncommon in medieval texts.[29]

Even with the most skillful editing, via interpolation of missing articles and expansion of elliptical phrases, this is still an awkward text, as may be seen by the translation of Odenkirchen:

Here begins the beloved poem and the holy history of that noble baron Euphemian by name, and of the life of his blessed son, about whom we have heard read and sung; by divine will he whose desire was so great engendered this only son. After his birth the child was loved by God himself, and brought up by his father and his mother with great affection, so that his youth was honorable and religious. Because of his friendship for the sovereign source of piety (?), he recommended his young bride to the living spouse of truth, who is the only creator and rules in the Trinity. This history is beloved grace and highest consolation to [unintelligible phrase follows] . . . those who live pure lives according to chastity, and who deservedly find delight in the joys of heaven and in marriages kept virginal.[30]

Even with this sympathetically edited text, we are confronted with a series of baffling omissions in what purports to be the Prologue to the Life of St. Alexis. The most glaring omission, as we have remarked, is surely that of his *name*. Nor is it so simple a matter as a stylistic trait, for Euphemian, his father, is most carefully named and identified. Moreover, the assertion is forcefully and primarily made that this is the very Song of Euphemian. Then comes, almost as an afterthought, the allegation that this is also about the life of his worthy son — unnamed. Yet this son is prematurely introduced: he does not yet even exist as a wish in his father's heart. This will be described only after reference is made to our having heard this *Chanson?/Vie?* read and sung. Then, by God's will, Euphemian, *kinderdurst*, engenders this only child, apparently by spontaneous regeneration (male parthenogenesis?): his wife has not yet been mentioned. Even after his birth, this only son is not given a "bel num sur la Christientet." The Prologue's story remains centered, rather, on God and the parents, with the blandest reference to their son's virtuous youth, until, suddenly, without any mention of a marriage, 'he' (only understood, in the verb "cumandat") commends his young bride to the Bridegroom. This is, indeed, the only thing 'he' actually does in the entire text. In fact, he not only lacks a name, he forever lacks a personal pronoun. Once, he is "ço"; otherwise, he is merely understood in the third person singular verb form, or cast in a passive construction: de Deu . . . amet; de pere e de mere . . . nurrit. Never, surely, has the passivity of a saint been so *under*stated as to make him amorphous: he does not, indeed, need to die in this piece, for he has never yet come to *Life*.

Having reached a rousing climax in what is surely a paraphrase of the *Credo*, the Prologue does its own 'commending' —of this story. This *envoi* is the most energetic part of the Prologue: its hero/ine(s) are obviously the flesh-and-blood saints of chastity who are reading this

221

story, fighting the battle against the world, the flesh and the devil, and glorying in their spiritual warfare.

Obviously, not only was the writer of the Prologue not on intimate terms with Alexis, the *exemplum*: he does not even know him. Indeed, he apparently hasn't even read the story he is introducing, viz. '*la Cancun d'Euphemian.*' What he has read, I feel sure, is *another* Prologue, preceding an earlier Old French *Vie de St. Alexis* (untitled, as is common in medieval manuscripts), which he sweepingly adapts to his own purposes, to wit: a 'rhymed' introduction/frontispiece which is a veiled 'dedication' to Christina.

What I surmise he had before him would have been both chronologically and logically well ordered. First, I would propose that *boneuret* represents the proper name *Boneuree*: this is the name of the wife of Euphemian in **S**, the Old French version of the *Alexis* as discussed by Hofmann in his edition of the **L** manuscript.[31] This change alone would impose a certain order within the **L** Prologue: thereby are we introduced to the parents of Alexis, Eufemien and *Boneuree*, and to the pious life *they* led, as is so emphasized, in fact, in the Latin Life. Then, in the natural order of Lives, would come their desire for a child. Their barrenness redeemed by the birth of a son, they have him baptized, with the name proper to this Life, raise him up in the way he should go, and arrange an appropriate marriage.

Here is what this twentieth-century 'Anglo-Norman' reader, your writer, conjectures as the *Urtext* for the twelfth-century Anglo- Norman scribe and author of the **L** Prologue.

> Ici comencet l'amiable chanson de ce noble de rome, eufemien. E de sa vie od sa femme boneuree, [i.e., Boneuree] desquels nos avons oït lire e chanter. Par la volontet Deu, ils, desirreux, ont un fil engendret. Apres la naissance fut l'emfes od nom alexis baptizets. E norits de grant chertet de son pere e de sa mere. La sue juvente fut honorable et spirituel. Al commend de son pere il esposat une pucelle de halt parentet. Por l'amor del soverain Pedre, la soe espose juvene il comendat al espos vif de verite.

(Qui est unus cum Patrem et regnet en la Trinitet.)[32]

(Here begins the pleasing song of that Roman nobleman, Euphemian. And of his [pious] life with his [virtuous] wife, Boneurée, of whom we have heard in story and song. By the will of God, they, desirous [of a child], engendered a son. After his birth the child was christened with the name Alexis. And he was nurtured with great tenderness by his father and mother. His youth was honorable and spiritual. By the command of his father [=Euphemian], he married a maiden of noble blood. Out of love for the sovereign Father [=God], he commended his young bride to the living bridegroom of truth. (Who is One with the Father [Creator], and reigns in the Trinity.)

The last line may have suggested itself to the writer through his familiarity with the Nicene creed: *Credo in unum Deum*, with whom he associated the *Filium/Sponsum*, 'reigning one with the Father' and the 'Spirit' 'in the Trinity.'[33] It would be a rousing finale for a Prologue.

At any rate, this is as far as our Anglo-Norman would need to read: he has now reached his *moment culminant*, the effecting of virginal marriage. From this point he builds his application of the story to St. Albans celibates, closing his opus, indeed, with the very words "noces virginels" (virginal nuptials). In summary, for the Prologue, I posit an Anglo-Norman writing a very topical résumé of the Old French work to follow, by referring either to a Proto-Prologue under his eyes or perhaps to the first folio (Strophes I-VI) of an Old French version of the poem, hastily scanned. The result would have been prose on its way to being poetry, at least by M. Jourdain's definition. The function of the Prologue would have been one or more of the following: textual frontispiece; veiled allusion and dedication (to Christine, and to her *semblable*, Geoffrey); dramatic *silete*, to invoke the silence and the attention of an audience.

The final conclusions which I draw from my study of the *Alexis* within the St. Albans Psalter are as follows.

The **L** *Alexis* was collated by a *Français de France*—and Geoffrey could well have been he— from two Old French manuscripts, represented by **L**'s Strophes I-CX, an ascetic Life, and by its Strophes CXI-CXXV, an ecclesiastical, liturgical and lay-oriented *Chanson*. The addition of the last fifteen strophes to the first of these Old French Lives may well have had the end in mind of a liturgical dramatic (but not dramatized) presentation: a dialogued performance in which visualization may have been suggested by means of a series of tableaux. These can be imagined as farcing an 'Epistle,' the Parable of the Poor Lazarus, with whom the Life of Alexis has so many parallels: indeed, the feast-day of St. Lazarus, like that of St. Alexis, is on a seventeenth (of December).[34] Such a presentation would be a great step beyond liturgy toward impersonational drama. Perhaps, within the Priory of Markyate or the Abbey of St. Albans, the step was lengthened further: outside the church sanctuary, a fuller staging could well have occurred under the direction of Abbot Geoffrey, who had, years earlier, both *written* and *staged* the *Ludus Sanctae Catharinae*. (Though naturally recorded in Latin in a chronicle, this play may, indeed, have itself been in the vernacular, as Fawtier-Jones has observed.) [35] In either event —for ecclesiastical or conventual presentation— the inclusion of the *Alexis* in Christina's Psalter would serve as *aide-mémoire*, and, perhaps, as script.

As has been abundantly proposed, the composition of the St. Albans Psalter and of the *Alexis* would appear to have been carefully designed; reference to the mystical nature of numbers seems inherent in both Psalter and Poem.

Since the Poem appears to be a collation, its noted mathematical and arithmetical design would represent a careful framing on the part of the **L** editor. Since the Poem is a very purposeful addition to the St. Albans Psalter, itself a 'collation,' it would seem logical that the larger work would but magnify the numerological rationale of the smaller one. Such an understanding would be well within the macrocosm/microcosm understanding of Creation, reaching the Middle Ages through such authorities as St. Augustine, Macrobius, St. Ambrose, and Isidore of Seville. Thus would the ultimate miniature within the St. Albans Psalter —the 'Life' of Alexis, the 'letter' written by his own hand, *within* the *Alexis*— imagine its larger host, the

poem; the *Alexis* in turn, might be understood to minia-
turize the St. Albans Book, which would in turn refer to
God's three Books, of Works, of Words, and of Memory.
Preceding this Psalter, so carefully designed for
Christina, would have been a simpler book, the basic matter onto which the order was imposed. I would propose
that the original Psalter was just that: the Psalms of
David, the Calendar in its unaugmented state, the
Canticles, Litany and Prayers. It may well have been
made for Roger, Christina's spiritual mentor: hence his
obit is "in a different . . . and earlier hand than that of the
insertions in the calendar."[36] Roger was apparently the
recluse *par excellence*, not even forsaking his cell to walk
to St. Albans each night for divine services, as his contemporary hermit, Sigar of Northaw, took care to do.
(*Gesta Abbatum*, I. 105).[37] So would he have need of a
psalter, as Talbot has judged: "The recitation of the
psalms. . . must have been his main spiritual exercise."[38]
Upon Roger's death, Christina, his "sunendaege dohter,"
(Sunday daughter) would likely have inherited his Psalter,
just as she inherited, by his express command, his cell.
Once the Psalter was Christina's, the name of her
spiritual father, Roger the Hermit, would immediately
have been added to the obits. Then the Psalter could well
have been redesigned for Christina according to her special needs and interests. It would then have received the
ternary design which I have proposed by the additions of
the Alexis and the pictorial cycle. No one could be more
likely than the Abbot Geoffrey to execute such a project: he
had the authority, the means and the temperament. And
no one would have had such motivation, as we have seen.
It was his meeting with Christina that marked the
turning-point in his career and in his character: the
strong-willed, haughty man of affairs had, through
Christina's direction and influence, become increasingly
more spiritual-minded and compassionate. Ultimately,
he did not hesitate to put the needs of the poor and lowly —
including lepers— above the material interests and the
wishes of his House. Finally, he had first undertaken the
monastic life in order to expiate: guilt had caused him to
give over his life to the service of God. His identifying with
Alexis would thus appear perfectly natural.
In all of our intermediate steps, we have found
Geoffrey as the person most likely to have effected
innovations and enterprises, whether in liturgy,

225

paradrama, scriptorium, or 'copy desk.' Since he, *Français de France*, might well have been familiar with Alexis, in legend and in Life, even before coming to St. Albans, and since this story would have been of particularly applicable to himself and to Christina, it would seem highly plausible that he introduced it, in a collated form of his making, to the St. Albans community. As former *Magister*, he might well have seen it as an effective didactic work, and have introduced it into the liturgy within the church: hence, the express addition of the final fifteen strophes, absent in the **A** manuscript, to his version of the *Alexis*. The case, then, is strong for Geoffrey's having composed the **L** *Alexis* out of pre-existing elements, though it cannot be proved. The Prologue, however, while attributed to the *Alexiusmeister*, cannot be credited to this native of Maine: its thoroughly Anglo-Norman language far removes it from the purview of Goeffrey; its fumbling poetizing, and its 'blindness' to the story of Alexis are completely incompatible with the Old French poem, in matter, style, and structure.

Since the scope of this study has been so vast, many topics have had to be treated perfunctorily in order to provide a *mise ensemble*. The corrections and additions which may be proposed by fellow-lovers of the *Alexis* in its most noble version, that of the St. Albans Psalter, will surely increase our appreciation of this Book within a Book. My own understanding of the *Alexis* itself has been both deepened and enriched by looking beneath the veil to find the spirit of *Caritas*, which so rosily fleshes out the bones of *Askesis*.

[1] For a well-documented account of this belief, see Kathi Meyer-Baer, *The Music of the Spheres and the Dance of Death* (Princeton: Princeton Univ. Press, 1970).

[2] Jungmann, in discussing the Roman Mass in France, attaches this dogma, result of the anti-Arian struggle, to changes in the very shape of the liturgy: prayers were considered, in Gaul, to be addressed to the Son, even if they "had the introductory greeting *Deus qui*." Jungmann explains that this represents a rejection of the mediation formula (praying to God the Father through the Son), and "a similar stressing of the essential equality of the three divine Persons, just as the oriental liturgies have done." He concludes that "the Gallican emphasis on the Trinity has had visible effect even on our present Ordinary of the Mass." (*The Mass of the Roman Rite Missarum Sollemnia*, I, tr. Brunner, New York: Benziger, 1950, p. 80.)

[3] Cf. the opening Article of the Niceno-Constantinopolitan symbol: Credo in unum Deum, Patrem omnipotentem, Factorem coeli et terrae, visibilium omnium et invisibilium.

The form *Factorem* in this Creed is especially noteworthy: from it might well the Prologue's author have devised his *faitur*, which he uses incorrectly instead of the nominative *faitre* which would have derived from *factor*. The line in question: "Ki est un sul faitur e regnet an trinitiet."

[4] Readers will remember the medieval delight in word-play, as in juxtaposing these names to form a palindrone.

[5] As remarked earlier, the Annunciation, since it precedes Christ's becoming Flesh, would naturally belong among the scenes of prefiguration.

[6] That is, the St. Albans Psalter in its present three gatherings, and including as its main elements: the pictorial cycle, the *Alexis*, and the Psalms. The Calendar and

Computistical Tables (A) and the Litany and Prayers (B) serve as a 'frame' for these three elements.

7 Dom Jean Leclercq, *The Love of Learning and the Desire for God* (New York: New Amer. Lib., 1966), pp. 80-1.

8 As Talbot describes them: "Furthermore, in the body of the psalter itself there are two drawings which are most revealing: one of them, which occurs between the end of the Athanasian creed and the beginning of the litany, depicts six nuns with an abbot in their midst holding up before the Blessed Trinity two books, on which are inscribed the opening invocations of the litany. These invocations are addressed separately to the Father, Son, and Holy Spirit, with the fourth and final appeal, *Sancta Trinitas unus Deus*, summing them up. This is an obvious reference to the name of the priory of Markyate, Sanctae Trinitatis de Bosco .... The other drawing ... shows a nun introducing four monks into the presence of Christ .... This is almost certainly intended to depict Christina interceding with Christ for the monks of St. Albans." *The Life of Christina of Markyate* (Oxford: Clarendon Press, 1959), p. 24.

9 Karl D. Uitti, *Story, Myth, and Celebration in Old French Narrative Poetry* (Princeton: Princeton Univ. Pr., 1972), p. 41-2.

10 The importance of a person's name - "*Nomen omen*" - would seem to be universal, whether in literature, folklore, or, as in the case of the Hebrew *Adonai*, religion. For this reason, the name of *Alexis* is of especial interest: it means "Help," deriving from the Greek *alexein*, to ward off. So, as we have seen, Alexis is sought out to ward off the destruction of Rome; his body effects the warding off (away) of diseases; and he is invoked, as a Confessor saint, to ward off our moral ills.

11 Brown, Fitzmyer, Murphy, ed., *The Jerome Biblical Commentary* (Englewood Cliffs, Prentice Hall, 1968), p. 122.

12 These two Maries were early identified as one and the same, at least as early as St. Augustine. See V.

Saxer, *Le Culte de Marie Madeleine* (Auxerre: La Société ...
de l'Yonne, 1959), Introduction.

13 As we have seen above: "Vere languores nostros
ipse tulit et dolores nostros ipse portavit, et nos putavimus
eum quasi leprosum et percussum a Deo et humiliatum."
(Isaiah 53:4). (Surely He Himself hath borne our griefs and
He Himself hath carried our sorrows, and we counted Him
as [like] a leper, and stricken and humiliated by God.)

14 Cf., for example, the diatribe of Emil Winkler:
"... Alexius hardly takes the time in the bridal chamber to
admonish her [the bride] in a Christian way .... What a
selfish asceticism! ... What a didactic, soulless asceticism!
... With unconcern Alexius beholds the suffering of the
members of his family ...." "Von der Kunst des
Alexiusdichters," *Zeitschrift für romanische Philologie*,
XLVII (1927), p. 589, tr. by Carl Odenkirchen, *The Life of
St. Alexius*, Brookline: Classical Folio Edn., 1978, p. 69.
Winkler, of course, is a hostile critic of the *Alexis*, but
more sympathetic ones as well, such as Hatcher, see more
askesis than *caritas*.

15 Jungmann, p. 418. We would argue that, aside
from the possibility of such examples having been destroyed by time or through prudence, the early appearances of vernacular Resurrection and Nativity plays, as
well as of "the Lazarus" (*Jeu du Lazare*), suggest that the
Gospels were early 'troped.' Indeed, Clement of Alexandria
had said: 'Mysteries such as divinity are entrusted to
speech, not to writing.'

16 Though St. Martin of Tours was, it is true, the
first confessor saint to be added to the litany, there does
not seem to have been a vernacular *Vita S. Martini* available at the time in question.

17 For the people, the virtues of *caritas* (charity,
compassionate love) and *pitias* (mercy) might be invoked,
to the benefit of the individual's soul, of the Christian
community, and of the Church. For the monk, *chastitas*
(chastity) and *pietas* (dutiful obedience) would be more especially valued. We have seen, above, that these words
were doublets. Tinsley, pp. 58-65.

[18] Jungmann cites two peculiarities of the Gallic tradition: the tendency toward the *dramatic*, and the predilection for long prayers. P. 77.

[19] It will be remembered that a sermon falsely attributed to St. Augustine, the *Contra Judaeos, Paganos et Arianos, Sermo de Symbolo*, is generally seen as the source for the *Ordo Prophetarum* segment of the *Jeu d'Adam*; therein prophets from the Old Testament announce the coming of the Messiah, Christ.

[20] "Zum Alexiuslied," *Archiv für das Studium der neueren Sprachen* CXCI (1955), p. 211.

[21] Marius Sepet, *Les Prophètes du Christ* (Paris, 1878), p. 65: "Les femmes n'ont pris part aux représentations dramatiques qu'à une époque beaucoup plus rapprochée de nous, si ce n'est toutefois dans les monastères où les religieuses, officiant en quelque sorte avec le clergé, pouvaient, sans enfreindre les règles liturgiques, prendre part aux offices dramatiques comme aux offices ordinaires." (Women did not take part in dramatic performances until a time much closer to our own, except in monasteries [convents], where the Sisters, officiating somewhat with the clergy, could take part in the dramatic rites, just as in the ordinary rites, without infringing the liturgical rules.)

[22] Sepet, *Origines catholiques du théâtre moderne* (Paris: P. Lethielleux, 1901), p. 22.

[23] Sepet, *Les Prophètes* ... , p. 10.

[24] "Zum Alexiuslied", *Archiv für das Studium der neueren Sprachen*, CXCI (1955), 202-213, and CXCV (1958), 141-144.

[25] For a photographic reproduction of this manuscript, see *Album*, Société des anciens textes français (Paris: Firmin-Didot, 1875), p. 3.

[26] Pächt, Wormald, Dodwell, ed. *The St. Albans Psalter*, p. 132, note 5.

27 G. Cohen, *La poésie en France au Moyen-Age* (Paris: Richard-Masse, 1952), notes "un système d'échange entre la poésie religieuse et la poésie profane." He furnishes as an example the following Ballade, of unknown authorship. Its application to the *Sponsa* of Alexis is uncanny:

> Ami, Ami,
> Trop me laissez en étranger pays.
>
> L'âme qui cherche en Dieu toute s'entente [son désir]
> Souvent se plaint, fortement se lamente
> Et son ami à l'arrive trop lente
> Va regrettant et s'en impatiente.
>
> Ami, Ami,
> Trop me laissez en étranger pays.
>
> Dieu, donnez-moi ce que mon coeur désire,
> Pour qui languis, pour qui suis au martyre—
> Jesus Christ est mon ami et mon sire,
> Le beau, le bon, plus que nul ne sait dire.
>
> Ami, Ami,
> Trop me laissez en étranger pays.
>
> Il m'appela avant que l'appelasse
> Et me requit qu'après lui m'en allasse;
> Or est bien droit que de chercher me lasse
> Et que du monde pour le trouver trépasse.
>
> Ami, Ami,
> Trop me laissez en étranger pays.
>
> (p. 19)

> (Friend, friend,
> Too long do you leave me in alien land.
>
> The soul which in God seeks all its delight
> Often laments, bitterly mourns
> [4] Waxing impatient and ever deploring
> [3] Its friend [whose] arrival [is] so long-delayed.

Friend, friend,
Too long do you leave me in alien land.

God, give to me what my heart desires,
[The one] for whom I languish, for whom I am in torment—
Jesus Christ is my friend and my master,
The fair, the good, more than anyone can
tell.

Friend, friend,
Too long do you leave me in alien land.

He called to me ere I called to him
And commanded me that after him I should set my
way;
Now is it fully right that I weary of the
search
And that I pass out of [this] world in order to find
him.

Friend, friend,
Too long do you leave me in alien land.)

[28] Gaston Paris, *La Vie de Saint Alexis* (Paris, 1872),
p. 177.

[29] See Tinsley, pp. 58-65, for a discussion of these
terms.

[30] Carl J. Odenkirchen, *The Life of St. Alexius*,
Appendix A, following p. 141.

[31] K. Hofmann, p. 88, in his introductory remarks
to his edition of the **L** *Alexis*, discusses **S**: it had been of
value in establishing certain readings, but it had gone far
beyond the purity of the older manuscript, the **L**. In his
discussion, he mentions **S**'s naming the mother
"Boneuree": this is how I came to consider that she may,
indeed, have been originally so named.

Sonst ist die Abweichung von 632 [**S**
manuscript] so gross, dass die Frau des

232

Eufemien Boneuree und ihr Vater Flourens (Acc. Flourent), und der Kaiser Otevians (Octavianus) heisst, welchem Alexius 7 Jahre als Oberkämmerling (maistre cambrelent) gedient hat.

(So completely deviated is the reading [in **S** manuscript] that the wife of Euphemian is named Boneuree, her father [is named] Flourens (*Flourent*, in the accusative case), and the Emperor is named Octavian (*Octavianus*), while Alexius has [herein] served seven years as Master Chamberlain (*maistre cambrelent*).)

It is of course possible that the reverse could have occurred: the 'common' adjective *boneuret* might have been read as a proper noun, *Boneuret*.

32 The proper nouns, *Eufemien* and *Boneuree*, are begun with minuscules, as is common in medieval manuscripts, often, even, for *Deus*.

33 See Note 2, supra.

34 But even though the feastday of St. Lazarus was December 17 in the Roman liturgy, we have seen that the Eastern Church celebrates "Lazarus Saturday" on the day before Easter. And in the *Eastern* Church, the feastday of St. Alexis is March 17, a time significantly close to, if not coincident with, the feastday of St. Lazarus. Once again, we are reminded of the preponderantly Eastern tradition of the Gallican church: so might the *Alexis* farce the Lazarus parable. French churches had long read Lives in church.

35 E. C. Fawtier-Jones, "Les vies de sainte Catherine d'Alexandre en ancien français," *Romania*, LVI (1930), 84.

36 Talbot, p. 23. See also Pächt et al., *The St. Albans Psalter*, p. 277.

[37] See also Clay, p. 83.

[38] Talbot, p. 21.

BIBLIOGRAPHY

Items are grouped according to subject and are listed according to date of publication.

I. Selected Editions of *La Vie de Saint Alexis*

Müller, Wilhelm. *La Vie de St. Alexis* in *Zeitschrift für deutsches Altertum*, V, 1845, pp. 299-318.

Hofmann, Conrad. "Das altfranzösische Gedicht auf den heiligen Alexius, kritisch bearbeit." *Sitzungsberichte der königl. bayer. Akademie der Wissenschaften*, I (1868), pp. 84-120. In addition to this critical edition of the **L** *Alexis*, Hofmann also included his transcription of the Gregorian letter which follows the poem in the St. Albans Psalter, "Ein unedirtes altfranzösisches Prosastück aus der Lambspringer Handschrift," pp. 81-83, and the Prologue which precedes it, "Prosaeinleitung des Alexis," pp. 88-89.

Paris, Gaston and Léopold Pannier, ed. *La Vie de Saint Alexis*. Paris: Libr. A. Franck, 1872. Rpt. Geneva, Slatkine, 1974. The seminal and the definitive work on the **L** ms.

Foerster, Wilhelm and E. Koschwitz. *Altfranzösisches Ubungsbuch.* Leipzig: O. R. Reisland, 1921. Rpt. University, Mississippi, Romance Monographs, Inc., 1973. Includes diplomatic editions of versions **L**, **A**, and **P**, along with the variant readings of **S** and of **M**.

Rajna, Pio. "Un nuovo testo parziale del Saint Alexis primitivo." *Archivum Romanicum*, XIII (1929), pp. 4-10. (**V**[atican] verson.)

Meunier, J.-M. *La Vie de St. Alexis*. Paris: E. Droz, 1933. Includes a study of the legend, of the versification, and of the language of the **L** version.

Storey, Christopher. *La Vie de Saint Alexis. Texte du Manuscrit de Hildesheim (L).* Geneva: Droz; Paris: Minard, 1968.

Odenkirchen, Carl J. *The Life of St. Alexius. In the Old French Version of the Hildesheim Manuscript.* Brookline, Mass. and Leyden: Classical Folia Editions, 1978.

II. History of the Legend of St. Alexis

Paris, Gaston. *Romania,* VIII (1879). A survey of the legend, pp. 163-165, precedes his edition of the 12th-century *"La Vie de Saint Alexis* en vers octosyllabiques," pp. 163-180.

Brauns, Joseph. *Uber Quelle und Erwicklung der altfr. Cançun de St. Alexis.* Kiel, 1884.

Amiaud, Arthur. *La Légende syriaque de St. Alexis, l'homme de Dieu.* Paris: E. Bouillon, 1889.

Rösler, Margarethe. *Die Fassungen des Alexius Legende mit besondere Berücksichtigung des Mittelenglischen Versionen.* Vienna and Leipzig: W. Braumüller, 1905.

Uitti, Karl D. "The Old French *Vie de Saint Alexis.* Paradigm, Legend, Meaning." *Romance Philology,* XX, No. 3 (1967), pp. 262-295. This study is expanded in Uitti's *Story, Myth, and Celebration in Old French Narrative Poetry.* Princeton Univ. Press, 1973, Chapter I, "The 'Life of Saint Alexis,'" pp. 3-64.

Stebbins, Charles. "Les Grandes versions de la légende de St. Alexis." *Revue belge de philologie, et d'histoire,* LIII (1975), 679-695.

III. The Anglo-Norman Dialect and Literature

Menger, Louis Emil. *The Anglo-Norman Dialect: a manual of its phonology and morphology, with illustrated specimens of its literature.* New York: The Columbia Univ. Press, 1904.

Vising, Johan. *Anglo-Norman Language and Literature.* London: Oxford Univ. Press, H. Milford, 1923.

Waters, Edwin George Ross. *The Anglo-Norman Voyage of St. Brendan.* Oxford: Clarendon Press, 1928.

Walberg, Emmanuel. *Quelques aspects de la littérature anglo-normande.* Paris: E. Droz, 1936.

Legge, Mary Dominica. *Anglo-Norman in the Cloisters; the Influence of the Orders upon Anglo-Norman Literature.* Edinburgh: Univ. Press, 1950.

Pope, Mildred K. *From Latin to Modern French with Especial Consideration of Anglo-Norman.* Manchester: Manchester Univ. Press, 1952.

_____. *Anglo-Norman Literature and its Background.* Oxford: Clarendon Press, 1963.

IV. Selected Studies on the *Alexis*

Eis, G. "Alexiuslied und christliche Askese." *Zeitschrift für französische Sprache und Literatur,* LIX (1935), pp. 232-236.

Curtius, Ernst R. "Zur Interpretation des Alexiusliedes." *Zeitschrift für romanische Philologie,* LVI (1936), pp. 113-137.

Gaiffier, B. de. "Intactam sponsam relinquens. A propos de la vie de S. Alexis." *Analecta Bollandiana,* LXV (1947), pp. 157-195.

Hatcher, Anna Granville. "The Old French *Alexis* Poem: A Mathematical Demonstration." *Traditio,* VIII (1952), pp. 111-158.

Auerbach, Erich. *Mimesis. The Representation of Reality in Western Literature,* trans. from the German *Dargestellte Wirklichkeit in der abendländischen Literatur* by Willard R. Trask. Princeton: Princeton Univ. Press., 1953. *Alexis* commentary in the chapter "Roland against Ganelon," pp. 111-120.

Lausberg, Heinrich. "Zum altfranzösische Alexiuslied." *Archiv für das Studium der neuren Sprachen*, CXCI (1955), 202-213; 285-320. CXCII (1956), 33-58. CXCIV (1957), 138-180. CXCV (1958), pp. 141-144.

Sckommodau, Hans. "Alexius in Liturgie, Malerei und Dichtung." *Zeitschrift für romanische Philologie*, LXXII (1956), pp. 165-194.

Fotich, Tatiana, "The Mystery of 'les renges de s'espethe' ", *Romania*, LXXIX (1958), 495-507.

Bulatkin, Eleanor. "The Arithmetical Structure of the Old French *Vie de St. Alexis*." *PMLA*, LXXIV (1959), pp. 495-502.

Sckommodau, Hans. "Das Alexiuslied: Die Datierungsfrage und das Problem der Askese." *Medium Aevum Romanicum, Festschrift für H. Rheinfelder*. Munich, 1963, pp. 298-324.

Vincent, Patrick R. "The Dramatic Aspect of the Old French *Vie de Saint Alexis*." *Studies in Philology*, LX (1963), pp. 525-541.

Sprissler, Manfred. *Das rhythmische Gedicht "Pater Deus Ingenite" (11.JH.) und das altfranzösiche Alexiuslied*. Münster/Westfalen: Aschendorffsche Verlagsbuch., 1966.

Atkinson, James C. "Triplet Sequences in the *Vie de St. Alexis*." *Romance Notes*, XI, 2 (1969), pp. 414-419.

Damien, Peter. *P.L.* CLXXII, col 1045-1046, as noted by Ulrich Mölk, "La *Chanson de saint Alexis* et le culte du saint en France aux XIe et XIIe siècles." *Cahiers de civilisation médiévale*, XXI (1978), pp. 339-355.

V. The St. Albans Psalter

Goldschmidt, Adolph. *Der Albanipsalter in Hildesheim.* Berlin: G. Siemans, 1895.

Pächt, Otto, C. R. Dodwell and Francis Wormald. *The St. Albans Psalter (Albani Psalter).* London: The Warburg Institute, 1960.

VI. Art History and Iconography

Birch, Walter de Gray. *The History of the Utrecht Psalter.* London, 1876.

Springer, Anton Heinrich. *Die psalter-illustrationem im frühem mittelalter, mit besonderer rücksicht auf den Utrechtpsalter. Ein beitrag zur geschichte der miniaturmalerei... Mit zehn tafeln in lichtdruck....* Leipzig: Hirzel, 1880.

Berger, Samuel and Paul Durrieu. "Les notes pour l'enlumineur." *Mémoires . . . de la Société nationale des Antiquaires de France.* LIII (1893).

Delisle, Leopold. "Livres d'images destinés à l'instruction des laïques." *Histoire littéraire de la France,* XXXI (1893), pp. 246-261.

Wilson, Henry A., ed. *The Missal of Robert of Jumièges.* London: Henry Bradshaw Society, 1896.

James, Montague R., ed. *The Canterbury Psalter. [A facsimile reproduction of the Psalter illuminated by Edwin of Canterbury.] With Introduction by M. R. James.* London: P. Lund, Humphries & Co., 1935.

Adams, Henry. *Mont-Saint-Michel and Chartres.* Orig. publ.: Amer. Inst. of Architects, 1913. Garden City: Doubleday and Company, 1959.

Springer, Anton Heinrich. *Handbuch der Kunstgeschichte,* Vol. 2: *Frühchristliche Kunst und mittelalter.* Leipzig: A. Kröner, 1920-21.

Mâle, Emile. *L'Art religieux du XIIe siècle en France; étude sur les origines de l'iconographie du moyen âge, illustrée de 253 gravures.* Paris: A. Colin, 1924.

_____. *L'Art religieux de la fin du moyen âge en France; étude sur l'iconographie du moyen âge et sur ses sources d'inspiration.* Paris: A. Colin, 1925.

Millar, Eric George. *La Miniature anglaise du Xe au XIIIe siècle.* Trans. M. E. Mautre. Paris/Brussels: G. van Oest, 1926.

Saunders, O. E. *English Art in the Middle Ages.* Oxford: Clarendon Press, 1932.

Wald, E. T. de, ed. *The Illuminations of the Utrecht Psalter.* Princeton: Princeton Univ. Press, 1932.

Réau, Louis. *L'Art du moyen âge.* Paris: La Renaissance du livre, 1935.

Focillon, Henri. *Art de l'occident.* Paris: A. Colin, 1938.

Ker, N. R. *Mediaeval Libraries of Great Britain.* London: the Royal Historical Society, 1941.

Wormald, Francis. "Decorated Initials in English MSS." *Archaeologia,* XCI (1941), pp. 108-135.

Réau, Louis. *Histoire de la peinture au moyen âge.* Melun: Librairie d'Argences, 1946.

Focillon, Henri. *Le peintre des miracles Notre Dame.* Paris: P. Hartmann, 1950.

Wormald, Francis, ed. *English Drawing of the Tenth and Eleventh Centuries.* London: Faber and Faber, 1952.

Boase, Thomas Sherrer Ross. *The Oxford History of English Art.* Vol. 3, *English Art. 1100-1216.* Oxford: Clarendon Press, 1953.

Dodwell, Charles Reginald. *The Canterbury School of Illumination.* Cambridge: University Press, 1954.

Rickert, Margaret. *Painting in Britain in the Middle Ages.* London, 1954. Rpt., Baltimore: Penguin Books, 1954.

Réau, Louis. *Iconographie de l'art chrétien.* Paris: Presses Universitaires de France, 1955.

Buchthal, Hugo. *Miniature Painting in the Latin Kingdom of Jerusalem.* Oxford: Clarendon Press, 1957.

Salmon, Pierre, ed. *Les 'Tituli Psalmorum' des manuscrits latins.* Paris: Ed. du Cerf, 1959.

Ker, N. R. *English Manuscripts in the Century after the Norman Conquest.* Oxford: Clarendon Press, 1960.

Wormald, Francis, ed. *An English Eleventh-Century Psalter with Pictures.* London: The Walpole Society, 1960-62.

Pächt, Otto. *The Rise of Pictorial Narrative in Twelfth-Century England.* Oxford: Clarendon Press, 1962.

Diringer, David. *The Illuminated Book.* New York: Praeger, 1967.

Labarre, A. "Livres d'heures." *Dictionnaire de spiritualité ascétique et mystique,* VIII (1968), pp. 410-431.

Schiller, Gertrud. *Iconography of Christian Art.* Trans. Janet Seligman. Greenwich, Conn.: New York Graphic Society, 1971.

Delaissé, L. M. J. "The Importance of Books of Hours for the History of the Medieval Book." *Gatherings in Honor of Dorothy Miner.* Baltimore, 1974, 203-225.

Campbell, A. P., ed. *The Tiberius Psalter.* Ottawa: Univ. of Ottawa Press, 1974.

241

Harthan, John. *The Book of Hours.* London: Thames and Hudson Ltd., 1977. Rpt. New York: Park Lane, 1982.

Dufrenne, Suzy. *Les Illustrations du Psautier d'Utrecht.* Paris: Ophrys, 1978.

Backhouse, Janet. *The Illuminated Manuscript.* Oxford: Phaidon, 1979.

Martin, Henri. *Les Joyaux de l'Arsenal.* I: "Le Psautier dit de S. Louis" (Bibl. Arsen. MS 1186 Rés.). Paris, no date.

VII. The Religious Life: Monastic and Cenobitic

A. St. Albans Abbey

Matthew Paris. (c. 1199-1259.) *Gesta Abbatum Monasterii Sancti Albani.* Ed. H. T. Riley, Rolls Series 28. London: House of the Rolls, 1867.

B. Benedictines

St. Benedict of Nursia. *Regula.* Ed. C. Cuthbert Butler, *Benedict Regula, S.* Freiburg-im-Breisgau, 1912.

Berlière, Ursmer. *L'Ascèce bénédictine, des origines à la fin du XIIe siècle.* Paris: Namur, 1927.

Butler, Cuthbert. *Benedictine Monachism.* London (Longmans Green), 1919.

Knowles, David. *The Benedictines.* London: Sheed & Ward, 1929.

St. Benedict of Nursia. *The Rule of St. Benedict.* Trans. by A. Meisel and M. del Mastro. Garden City: Image, 1975.

C. Monasticism and Monasteries.

Porée, Adolphe-André. *Histoire de l'Abbaye de Bec.* Evreux: impr. de C. Hérissey, 1901.

Berlière, Ursmer. *L'ordre monastique.* Maredsous, 1923.

Knowles, David. *Monastic Order in England, 940-1216.* Cambridge: Univ. Press, 1940; 2nd ed., 1963.

_____. *Religious Orders in England,* I-III. Cambridge: Univ. Press, 1948.

Leclercq, Jean. *L'Amour des lettres et le désir de Dieu.* Paris: Ed. du Cerf, 1957.

_____. *The Love of Learning and the Desire for God.* Trans. Catharine Misrahi. New York: Mentor Omega, 1961.

Knowles, David and R. Neville Hadcock. *Medieval Religious Houses, England and Wales.* London: Longman, 1971.

Brooke, Christopher. *Monasteries of the World. The Rise and Development of the Monastic Tradition.* London: Elek, 1974. Rpt. New York: Crescent, 1982.

D. English Nuns and Recluses

Clay, Rotha Mary. *The Hermits and Anchorites of England.* London: Methuen & Co. Ltd., 1914.

Power, Eileen Edna. *Medieval English Nunneries.* Cambridge: The University Press, 1922.

Darwin, Francis D. S. *The English Mediaeval Recluse.* London: Society for Promoting Christian Knowledge. No date. [flyleaf inscription: "Book Production War Economy Standard."]

Talbot, C. H. *The Life of Christina of Markyate. A Twelfth Century Recluse.* Ed. and trans. of "De S. Theodora, Virgine, quae et Christina dicitur.," Brit.

Mus. MS. Cotton Tiberius E. 1. Oxford: The Clarendon Press, 1959.

VIII. Liturgy, Liturgical Books and Lay-Folk

Waterland, Daniel. *A Critical History of the Athanasian Creed*. Cambridge: Univ. Press for Corn. Crownfield, 1724.

Martène, Edmond. *De antiquis ecclesiae ritibus libri.* 4 vol. 2nd edit., Antwerp, 1736-38. Rpt. Hildesheim: G. Olms, 1967.

l'Abbé Lebeuf. *Traité historique et pratique sur le chant ecclésiastique.* Paris, 1741.

Dom Ceillier. *Histoire des auteurs ecclésiastiques.* Paris, 1752.

Mabillon, Jean. *De liturgia Gallicana, libri III.* , *PL* LXXII.

Muratori, L. *Liturgia romana vetus.* 2 vol. Venice, 1748.

Rigaud, Eude. *Regestrum Visitationum, Archiepiscopi Rothomagensis, Odo Rigaldi.* Ed. Théodose Bonnin, Paris, 1852.

Migne, G-P. *Patrologiae, Cursus Completus, Series Latina.* Paris, 1865.

Guéranger, Prosper. *Institutions liturgiques.* Paris, 1878.

Le Blant, Edmond Frédéric. *Etude sur les sarcophages chrétiens antiques de la ville d'Arles.* Paris: Imprimerie nationale, 1878.

Simmons, Thomas Frederick. *The Lay-Folks Mass Book.* EETS No. 71. London: N. Trübner & Co., 1879.

Berger, Samuel. *La Bible française au moyen âge.* Paris, 1884. Rpt. Geneva: Slatkine, 1967.

Bonnard, Jean. *Les traductions de la Bible en vers français au moyen âge.* Paris, 1884. Rpt. Geneva: Slatkine, 1967.

Delisle, Léopold. *Mémoires sur d'anciens sacramentaires.* Paris, 1886.

Gautier, Léon. *Histoire de la poésie liturgique au moyen âge. Les Tropes.* Paris: V. Palmé, Alphonse Picard, 1886.

Mabillon, Jean. *Histoire de la Vulgate.* Paris, 1893. Rpt. New York: B. Franklin, n.d.; Geneva, Slatkine, 1978.

Wilson, Henry A. *The Gelasian Sacramentary.* London/New York: Oxford Univ. Press, 1894.

Du Méril, Edélestand. *Mélanges archéologiques et littéraires.* Paris, 1897. (*Epîtres farcies,* pp. 269 et seq.)

Bäumer, Suitbert. *Histoire du bréviaire.* Updated by Réginald Biron. Paris: Letouzey et Ané, 1905.

Cabrol, Fernand and Henri Leclercq. *Dictionnaire d'archéologie et de liturgie.* Paris: Letouzey et Ané, 1907-13.

Netzer, H. *L'Introduction de la Messe romaine en France sous les Carolingiens.* Paris: A. Picart & Fils, 1910.

Mearns, J. *The Canticles of the Christian Church, Eastern and Western.* Cambridge: The Univ. Press, 1914.

Guéranger, Prosper. *The Liturgical Year.* Trans. Dom Laurence Shepherd. London: Burns, Oats, & Washbourne Ltd., 1922.

Leroquais, Victor. *Les Sacramentaires et les missels manuscrits des bibliothèques publiques de France.* Paris, 1924.

245

Duchesne, L. *Les Origines du culte chrétien.* Orig. pub. 1898. Paris: Boccard, 1925.

Leroquais, Victor. *Les Livres d'heures manuscrits de la Bibliothèque nationale.* Paris: Mâcon, Protat Frères, impr., 1927.

Cabrol, Fernand. *The Books of the Latin Liturgy by the Right Reverend Abbot Cabrol, O.S.B., tr by the Benedictines of Stanbrook.* London: Sands & Co.; St. Louis, Mo.: B. Herder Book Co., 1932.

Perdrizet, P. *Le Calendrier parisien à la fin du moyen âge d'après le Bréviaire et les Livres d'Heures.* Paris: Les Belles Lettres, 1933.

Leroquais, Victor. *Les Bréviaires manuscrits des bibliothèques publiques de France.* Paris: Mâcon, Protat, 1934.

_____. *Les Pontificaux manuscrits des bibliothèques publiques de France.* Paris: Macon, Protat, 1937.

_____. *Les Psautiers, manuscrits latins des bibliothèques publiques de France.* Paris: Mâcon, Protat, 1940-41.

Jungmann, Joseph. *The Mass of the Roman Rite (Missarum Sollemnia).* Trans. F. Brunner. 2 vols. New York: Benziger, 1950.

Snaith, Norman Henry. *Hymns of the Temple.* London: SCM Press, 1951.

Botte, Bernard and Christine Morhmann. *L'Ordinaire de la Messe.* Paris: Ed. du Cerf, 1953.

Gaiffier, B. de. "La lecture des Actes des martyres dans la prière liturgique en Occident." *Analecta Bollandiana,* LXXII (1954), pp. 134-166.

Blaise, Albert. *Manuel du latin chrétien.* Strasbourg: Le Latin Chrétien, 1955.

Amiot, François. *Histoire de la Messe*. Paris: F. Brouty, J. Fayard et cie., 1956.

Sheppard, Lancelot C. *The Liturgical Books*. New York: Hawthorn Books, 1962.

Mabillon, Jean. *Traité des études monastiques*. Farnborough, Hants.: Gregg Press, 1967 (rpt. of 1736 edition).

Salmon, Pierre. *L'Office divin au moyen âge. Histoire de la bréviaire du IXe au XVIe siècle*. Paris: Ed. du Cerf, 1967.

Gy, M. "Typologie et ecclésiologie de livres liturgiques médiévaux." *La Maison-Dieu*, CXXI (1975), 72 et seq.

Schmidt, H. "Les lectures scriptuaires dans la liturgie." *Concilium*, CXII (1976), 125-243.

Sinclair, Keith V. *Prières en ancien français*. Hamden, Conn.: Archon Books, 1978.

_____. *French Devotional Texts of the Middle Ages*. Westport, Conn. and London: Greenwood Press, 1980.

Hughes, Andrew. *Medieval Manuscripts for Mass and Office: a Guide to their Organization and Terminology*. Toronto: Univ. of Toronto Press, 1982.

IX. Homilies, Sermons and Didactic Works

Gesta Romanorum. Entertaining Stories. Invented by the monks as a fire-side recreation and commonly applied in their discourses from the pulpit whence the most celebrated of our own poets and others have extracted their plots. (Oesterley considers that the book must have been compiled towards the end of the 13th c.) Trans., Charles Swan, from Henry Gran's edition, printed at Hagenau in 1508. London: George Routledge & Sons Ltd., 1824.

Gesta Romanorum. Hermann Oesterley, ed. Berlin: Weidmannsche, 1872.

Le Renclus De Moiliens. *Li Romans de Carité et Miserere.* Ed. by A.-G. Van Hamel. 2 vols. Paris: F. Vieweg, 1885.

Robert of Brunne. *Handlyng Synne.* Frederick J. Furnivall, ed.: *Robert of Brunne's "Handlyng Synne," with those parts of the Anglo-French treatise on which it was founded, William of Wadington's "Manuel des Pechiez."* EETS, 119. London: Kegan Paul, Trench Trübner & Co, Ltd., 1901.

Bardy, Gustave. "Cassiodore et la fin du monde ancienne [sic]." *Année théologique,* 6(1945), 383-425.

Jacobus de Voragine. *Legenda aurea.* Trans. T. De Wyzewa: *La Légende dorée.* Paris, 1902.

Längfors, A., ed. "Sermon de la Chastété aux Nonnains de Gautier de Coinci." *Romania,* LVI (1930), 35-44.

Owst, G. R. *Literature and Pulpit in Medieval England.* Cambridge: The Univ. Press, 1933.

William of Wadington. *Le Manuel des Péchés.* E. J. Arnould, ed. Paris: Droz, 1940.

Smalley, Beryl. *The Study of the Bible in the Middle Ages.* Oxford: Clarendon Press, 1941.

X. Medieval Drama

Paris, Gaston and U. Robert, ed. *Les Miracles de Nostre Dame par personnages, publiés d'après le manuscrit de la Bibliothèque Nationale.* Paris: Le Puy, 1876-93.

Michel, Francisque Xavier and Louis Jean Nicolas Monmerqué. *Théâtre français au moyen âge.* Paris: Firmin-Didot, 1885.

Sepet, Marius Cyrille Alphonse. *Le Drame chrétien au moyen âge*. Paris: Didier, 1878.

_____. *Origines catholiques du théâtre moderne*. Paris: Didier, 1878.

Petit de Julleville. *Histoire du théâtre en France. Les comédiens en France au moyen âge*. Paris: L. Cerf, 1885.

Du Méril, Edélestand. *Les Origines latines du théâtre moderne*. Leipzig/Paris: Welter, 1897.

Sepet, Marius Cyrille Alphonse. *Les Prophètes du Christ*. Paris: P. Lethielleux, 1901.

Chambers, Edmund Kerchever. *The Mediaeval Stage*. Oxford: The Clarendon Press, 1903.

Cohen, Gustave. *Histoire de la mise en scène dans le théâtre religieux au moyen âge*. Paris: H. Champion, 1906.

_____. *Mystères et moralités du Ms. 617 de Chantilly*. Paris: H. Champion, 1920.

Jeanroy, A. *Le théâtre religieux en France du XIe au XIIIe siècle*. Paris: Ed. de Boccard, 1924.

Young, Karl. *The Drama of the Medieval Church*. 2 vols. Oxford: The Clarendon Press, 1951.

Cohen, Gustave. *Anthologie du drame liturgique en France au Moyen Age*. Paris: Editions du Cerf, 1955.

Wickham, Glynne William Gladstone. *Early English Stages*. London: Routledge and Paul; New York: Columbia Univ. Press, 1959.

Frank, Grace. *Medieval French Drama*. Oxford: The Clarendon Press, 1960.

Hardison, Osborne Bennett, Jr. *Christian Rite and Christian Drama in the Middle Ages.* Baltimore: Johns Hopkins Press, 1965.

Muir, Lynnette. *Literature and Drama in the Anglo-Norman Adam.* Oxford: The Clarendon Press, 1973.

Nagler, A. M. *The Medieval Religious Stage.* New Haven: Yale Univ. Press, 1976.

XI. Christ and the Saints in *Life* and Legend

Baillet, Adrien. *Topographie des saints, où l'on rapporte les lieux devenus célèbres par la naissance, la demeure, la mort, la sépulture et le cult des saints* (par Adrien Baillet). Paris: L. Roulland, 1703.

Le Roux de Lincy, Antoine Jean Victor. *Le Livre des légendes.* Paris: Silvestre, 1836.

Furnivall, Frederick J., ed. *Adam Davie's Five Dreams.* EETS, 69. London: Kegan Paul et al., 1878.

Neuhaus, Carl Ludwig. *Adgar's Marienlegenden. Altfranzösiche Bibliothek,* IX (1886). Rpt. Wiesbaden: M. Särdig, 1968.

Donehoo, James de Quincey. *The Apocryphal Legends of Christ.* New York and London: Macmillan, 1903.

Meyer, Paul. "Légendes hagiographiques en français." *Histoire littéraire de la France,* XXXIII (1906), 328-458.

Hulme, W. H., ed. *The Middle-English Harrowing of Hell and the Gospel of Nicodemus.* EETS, C. London: Kegan Paul et al., 1908, pp. 32-60 (xxxii-lx).

Shackford, Martha Hale. *Legends and Satires from Mediaeval Literature.* Boston: Ginn and Co., 1913.

Gerould, Gordon Hall. *Saints' Legends.* Boston and New York: Houghton Mifflin, 1916.

Baker, Alfred T. "Saints' Lives in Anglo-French." *Royal Society of the United Kingdom*, Transaction IV (1924), 119-156.

Fawtier-Jones, E. C. "Les vies de sainte Catherine d'Alexandrie en ancien français." *Romania*, LVI (1930), 80-104.

Delehaye, Hippolyte. *L'Origine du culte des martyrs.* Brussels, Soc. des Bolland., 1934.

Rappoport, Angelo Solomon. *Medieval Legends of Christ.* New York: Ch. Scribner's Sons, 1935.

Hervieux, Jacques. *Ce que l'Evangile ne dit pas.* Paris: Arthème Fayard, 1958.

Saxer, Victor. *Le culte de Marie Madeleine en occident des origines à la fin du moyen âge.* Auxerre: La Société des fouilles archéologiques et des monuments historiques de l'Yonne, 1959.

Kendall, Alan. *Medieval Pilgrims.* New York: G. P. Putnam's Sons, 1970.

Finucane, Ronald C. *Miracles and Pilgrims: Popular Beliefs in Medieval England.* Totowa, N. J.: Rowman and Littlefield, 1977.

XII. The Medieval Ethos
Learned Tradition and Popular Culture

Thorndike, Lynn. *History of Magic and Experimental Science.* London, 1923. Rpt. New York: Columbia Univ. Press, 1958.

Hopper, Vincent. *Medieval Number Symbolism.* New York: Columbia Univ. Press, 1933.

Castelnau Jacques. *La Vie au moyen âge d'après les contemporains.* Paris: Hachette, 1949.

Bernheimer, R. *Wild Men in the Middle Ages.* Cambridge: Harvard Univ. Press, 1952.

Curtius, Ernst R. *European Literature and the Latin Middle Ages.* Trans. Willard R. Trask. Princeton: Princeton Univ. Press, 1953.

Kantorwitz, Ernst Hartwig. *The King's Two Bodies.* Princeton: Princeton Univ. Press, 1957.

La Roncière, Ch.-M., Philippe Contamine, Robert Delort and Michel Rouche. *L'Europe au moyen âge. Documents expliqués.* Vol. II: *Fin IXe siècle-fin XIIIe siècle.* Paris: A. Colin, 1969.

Meyer-Baer, Kathi. *The Music of the Spheres and the Dance of Death.* Princeton. Princeton Univ. Press, 1970.

Pickering, Frederick P. *Literature and Art in the Middle Ages.* Coral Gables: Univ. of Miami Press, 1970.

Grodecki, Louis, F. Mutherich, J. Taralon, F. Wormald. *Le Siècle de l'an mil.* Paris: Gallimard, 1973.

Duby, Georges. *Le Temps des cathédrales; L'art et la société 980-1420.* Paris: Gallimard, 1976.

Frye, Northrop. *The Great Code. The Bible and Literature.* New York: Harvest/Harcourt Brace Jovanovich, 1981.

Woledge, B. and I. Short, "Manuscrits du XIIe siècle en langue française," *Romania,* CI(1981).

Cook, William R., and Ronald B. Herzman. *The Medieval World View.* New York/Oxford: Oxford Univ. Press, 1983.

XIII. Medieval Medicine and Malady, especially Leprosy

Guy of Chauliac. *La Grande Chirugie.* Ed. E. Nicaise. Paris: Bouron, 1890.

Maury, Louis Ferdinand Alfred. *Croyances et légendes du moyen âge.* Paris: H. Champion, 1896.

Amato, Vincenzo d'. *La lebbre nella Storia, nella Geografia e nell' Arte.* Rome: Stabilimento Tipografico Romano, 1923.

Delauney, Paul. "Histoire de la Médecine. De la condition des lépreux au Moyen Age." *Hippocrate,* II (1934), 456-467. Also in Albert Blaise, ed., *Dictionnaire latin-français des auteurs chrétiens.* Paris, 1954. (Strasbourg, *Le Latin chrétien,* dépositaire pour l'étranger Librairie des Méridiers.)

Riesman, David. *The Story of Medicine in the Middle Ages.* New York: P. B. Hoeber, 1936.

Huizinga, Lee S. "Leprosy in Legend and Literature." *Leper Quarterly,* XIII (1939), 178-213.

Rémy, Paul. "La lèpre, thème littéraire au moyen âge." *Le Moyen Age,* LII (1946), 135-236.

Clay, Rotha Mary. *The Mediaeval Hospitals of England.* London: Cass, 1966.

Brody, Saul Nathaniel. *The Disease of the Soul. Leprosy in Medieval Literature.* Ithaca: Cornell Univ. Press, 1974.

Kauffman, Christopher J. *Tamers of Death.* Volume I. *The History of the Alexian Brothers from 1300 to 1789.* New York: Seabury, 1976.

Richards, Peter. *The Medieval Leper and his Northern Heirs.* Cambridge, Engl.: D. S. Brewer; Totowa, N.J.: Rowman & Littlefield, 1977.

253

APPENDIX I

The St. Albans Psalter:

Description of the manuscript as furnished by Dr. Francis Wormald, *The St. Albans Psalter*, The Warburg Institute, London, 1960. (Summarized.)

Vellum; 418 pages (209 folios); pages 1-417 numbered in Arabic numerals in the top right hand corner of the rectos only, probably 19th cent. Full leaf measures 10 7/8 x 7 1/4" (27.6 x 18.4 cm.); the writing space 7 5/8 x 5" (19.3 x 12.8 cm.). 22 lines to a page at most. XII cent.; before A.D. 1123. Executed at St. Albans, England.

Binding. Remains of a medieval binding, pigskin over wooden boards, considerably mended.

Collation. The following is a list of the gatherings. The quires are not numbered, nor are catchwords given.

1.	8 leaves.	ff.	1-8	(pp. 1-16)
2.	8 leaves.	ff.	9-16	(pp. 17-32)
3.	10 leaves.	ff.	17-26	(pp. 33-52)
4.	2 leaves.	ff.	27, 28	(pp. 53-56)
5.	8 leaves.	ff.	29-36	(pp. 57-72)
6.	10 leaves.	ff.	37-46	(pp. 73-92)
7.	10 leaves.	ff.	47-56	(pp. 93-112)
8.	10 leaves.	ff.	57-66	(pp. 113-132)
9.	10 leaves.	ff.	67-76	(pp. 133-152)
10.	10 leaves.	ff.	77-86	(pp. 153-172)
11.	10 leaves.	ff.	87-96	(pp. 173-192)
12.	10 leaves.	ff.	97-106	(pp. 193-212)
13.	10 leaves.	ff.	107-116	(pp. 213-232)
14.	10 leaves.	ff.	117-126	(pp. 233-252)
15.	9 leaves.	ff.	127-135	(pp. 253-270)

No. 8 in the gathering between pp. 266 and 276 has been cut out.

16.	10 leaves.	ff.	137-145	(pp. 271-290)
17.	10 leaves.	ff.	146-155	(pp. 291-310)
18.	10 leaves.	ff.	156-165	(pp. 311-330)
19.	10 leaves.	ff.	166-175	(pp. 331-350)

20.	10 leaves.	ff.	176-185	(pp.	351-370)
21.	10 leaves.	ff.	186-195	(pp.	371-390)
22.	10 leaves.	ff.	196-205	(pp.	391-410)
23.	2 leaves.	ff.	206,207	(pp.	411-414)
24.	2 leaves.	ff.	208,209	(pp.	415-418)

Ruling. Ruled with a sharp point. At the beginning of gathering no. 19 (p. 331) the ruling changes. It is more deeply incised and the page is ruled for two columns of writing.... This system continues until p. 410 when the old system is reverted to.

Contents

    1. p. 1.

Inscriptions on the flyleaf written in the 17th and 18th centuries. They are as follows: a) L[iber] Monast[erii] Lambspring 1657; b) written below in a larger hand "Liber Monast[erii] Lambspring O.S.B. Cong[regationis] Angl [icanae]; c) *S 1* written in the same hand as (b) over an earlier inscription *A 5*, which does not appear to be by the hand of (a); d) Fr. Ben: written in an early 17th cent. hand. It may stand for Fr[ater] Ben[edictus], but if this is so, the name is too common for any certain identification.

    p. 2.

Inscription in a rather thin 18th cent. hand "Liber Monasterii Lambspringensis / Ordinis Sancti Benedicti/

Congregationis
Anglicanae."

The poem is preceded on
p. 57 by a preface beg. "Ici
cumencer [sic] amiable
cancan [sic] e spiritel
raison [sic] di ceol noble
barun eufemien par nun
[sic]. e de la uie de sum
filz boneuret del quel
nus auum oit lire e
canter." [I read:
cumencet, cancun,
raisun, num. See
Appendix II-A for a
photocopy of this page
containing the text in
question.] Above the
preface is the miniature
with three scenes from
the life of St. Alexis.
There are three tituli to
these scenes: a) Beatus
alesis puer electus; b) 0
sponsa beata semper
gemebunda; c) Ecce
benedictus alexis
receptus in naue. At the
top of the page is the

following titulus in verse:

Vltima pudice donantur munera sponse. Anulus et remge uerborum finis et aue.

On pp. 57, 58 the lines are written alternately in red and blue. The beginning of the song on p. 58 is decorated by a large capital B [ons fut li secles....]

5. p. 68.

"[E]cce responsum sancti gregorii secundino incluso rationem de picturis interroganti", beg.: "Aliud est picturam adorare. aliud per picture historiam quid sit adorandum addiscere ... ut pastoris intemeratum nomen excelleret non culpa dispersoris incumberet."

6. p. 68.

"[I]ste uus le respuns saint gregorie a secundin le reclus cum il demandout raison des paintures", beg. "Altra cose est aurier la painture e altra cose est par le historie de la painture aprendre que la cose seit adaurier ...."

This is a translation into French of art. 5.

dixi; Ps. 143.9, Deus
canticum novum; Ps.
144.10, Confiteantur
tibi Domine. The
divisions of the Psalter
are indicated by larger
initial letters and/or by
the use of more
elaborate display script
at the opening of the
psalm, viz: a) The 3-fold
division (Pss. 1, 51, 101);
b) the liturgical division
(Pss. 26, 38, 52, 68, 80,
109). Ps. 97 (p. 267) has
been cut out. The
majority of the psalms
have inscriptions
referring to the initials
written near the initials
or in portions of them....

magna solus ..., p. 412. In
this prayer the words
"sempiterne deus" and
"pretende super famulos
tuos et super" are written
over an erasure. It has not
been possible to read the
lower writing; c) "Pretende
domine famulis et
famulabus tuis ..., pp. 412,
413; d) "Deus a quo sancta
desideria," p. 413; e) "Ure
igne sancti spiritus...", p.
413; f) "Actiones nostras
quesumus domine ...," 414;
g) "A domo tua quesumus
domine spirituales ...," p.
414; h) "Ecclesie tue
domine preces placatus...,"
p. 414....

20. pp. 416, 417

Two full-page
miniatures measuring
9 1/2 x 6" (23.2 x 15.3
cm.) representing a) The
martyrdom of St. Alban;
b) David and his
musicians.

Provenance

The MS. was probably written at St. Albans and
brought together for Christina, anchoress of Markyate,
and after 1145 first prioress of Markyate. The litany has
St. Albans features, ... and the hand which wrote the
"chançon" of St. Alexis is found in a St. Albans MS. B.M.
Harley MS. 2624, and is very close to that of the St. Albans
calendar in B. M. Egerton MS. 3721. It is likely that the
MS. was completed before 1123, since the obit of
Christina's patron, Roger the hermit, on 12 Sept. is an ad-

dition. The circumstances under which the MS. was composed are unknown, though it may be recalled that Geoffrey, abbot of St. Albans from c. 1119 to 1147, was a friend and patron of Christina. The MS. shows a close connection with St. Albans and Christina in the second half of the twelfth century when its calendar received a number of additions in the form of saints and obits, ... written by a St. Albans scribe.... The MS. was still in England, possibly at Markyate, in the sixteenth century, when as the result of the order of Henry VIII the word "pape" was erased from the calendar.... By 1657 the MS. had passed to the Benedictines of Lamspringe near Hildesheim, see inscription on p. 1. How it came there is unknown. If the inscription "Fr. Ben." on p. 1 could be interpreted with certainty it would doubtless assist.

The MS. probably came to St. Godehard's, Hildesheim, to whom it still belongs, in 1803 when Lamspringe was suppressed.

Writing

There are three main hands: 1) the calendar and computus tables, pp. 2-15; 2) The Psalter, Canticles, Litany and Prayers which all seem to be written in the same hand, pp. 74-414; 3) The hand who wrote the "chançon" of St. Alexis, pp. 57-60; the reply of St. Gregory, p. 68; the account of the meeting on the road to Emmaus, p. 69; the description of the spiritual battle; the inscriptions attached to each psalm, canticle, etc.; and the obit of the hermit Roger on 12 Sept.... To these hands there should be added that of the main group of additions to the calendar and of the obits.... All these hands are of the twelfth century. The additions were made after 1155, since Christina of Markyate was still alive in that year, and her name is found amongst the obits....

Decoration

This consists of a) Full-page miniatures, b) tinted drawings, c) calendar illustrations, d) historiated initials, e) decorated initials.

a) Full-page miniatures. These consist of forty full-page miniatures measuring 7 1/4 x 5 1/2" (18.4 x 13.9 cm.) in full colour by the chief artist, viz:

1)	p. 17.	The Fall.
2)	p. 18.	The Expulsion from Paradise.
3)	p. 19.	The Annunciation.
4)	p. 20.	The Visitation.
5)	p. 21.	The Nativity.
6)	p. 22.	The Annunciation to the Shepherds.
7)	p. 23.	The Magi before Herod.
8)	p. 24.	The Magi guided by the star.
9)	p. 25.	The Adoration of the Magi.
10)	p. 26.	The Dream of the Magi.
11)	p. 27.	The Return of the Magi.
12)	p. 28.	The Presentation in the Temple.
13)	p. 29.	The Flight into Egypt.
14)	p. 30.	The Massacre of the Innocents.
15)	p. 31.	The Return from Egypt.
16)	p. 32.	The Baptism.
17)	p. 33.	The First Temptation.
18)	p. 34.	The Second Temptation.

At the end of the MS. are two miniatures, each measuring 9 1/8 x 6" (23.2 x 15.3 cm.), painted by the hand of the historiated initials, viz:

1)	p. 416.	The Martyrdom of St. Alban.
2)	p. 417.	David and his musicians.

The position of these two miniatures is remarkable and it is highly probable that they were intended originally to come before the Psalter. When the full-page miniatures and the life of St. Alexis were introduced they were put at the end. Their style fits with that of the illuminated page containing the first verse of Ps. I on p. 73. If this were so it must be assumed that a large initial B has been either lost, abandoned, or never executed.

b) Tinted Drawings

Five tinted drawings by the chief artist, viz:

1)	p. 57.	Scenes from the life of St. Alexis.
2)	p. 69.	Christ on the road to Emmaus.
3)	p. 70.	Christ breaking bread at Emmaus.
4)	p. 71.	Christ disappears from the table at Emmaus.
5)	p. 72.	Two armed warriors on horseback in combat illustrating the dissertation relating to the spiritual battle which is written in the margins on pp. 71, 72.

c) The Calendar illustrations consist of the labours of the months painted in medallions at the top of each month, [and] the signs of the Zodiac.

d) Initials. They may be divided into two groups: 1) Historiated initials; 2) Decorative initials.

   I. *Historiated initials.* These consist of a) the large initial [B]eatus vir at the beginning of the psalter on p. 72 representing David.... It was executed by the chief artist; b) Initials at the beginning of the psalms, etc., executed by the artist of the initials ...; c) the initial on p. 285 before Ps. 105 which was added by a rather later hand on a separate piece of vellum and then stuck on to the page....

   II. *Decorated initials.* At the beginning of the psalter on p. 73 there is a page of initials containing the opening of Psalm I.... On p. 68 are two penwork initials in red and green executed probably by the main artist. The small initials at the beginning of each verse of the psalms are in green, red, blue and purple.

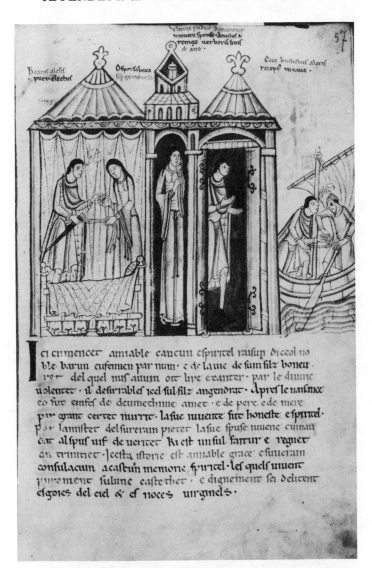

p. 57. Life of St. Alexis. The St. Albans Psalter.
From C. Pächt, C. Dodwell, F. Wormald, ed.,
The St. Albans Psalter, London 1960. Reproduced
by permission of the Warburg Institute, University
of London.

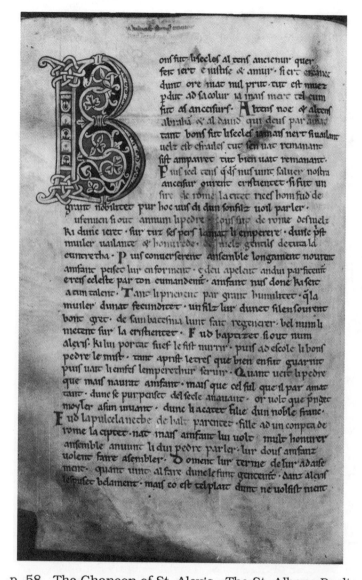

p. 58. The Chançon of St. Alexis. The St. Albans Psalter.
From *The St. Albans Psalter*, O. Pächt, C. Dodwell,
F. Wormald, ed., London, 1960. Reproduced by permission
of the Warburg Institute, University of London.

p.72. The St Albans Psalter. From Pächt, Dodwell, Wormald ed., *The St. Albans Psalter*, London, 1960. Reproduced by permission of the Warburg Institute, University of London.

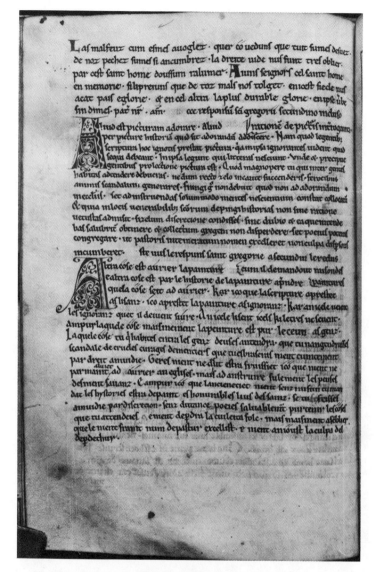

p. 68. St. Gregory's Reply to Secundinus. The St. Albans
Psalter. From Pächt, Dodwell, Wormald, ed., *The St.
Albans Psalter*, London, 1960. Reproduced by permission
of the Warburg Institute, University of London.

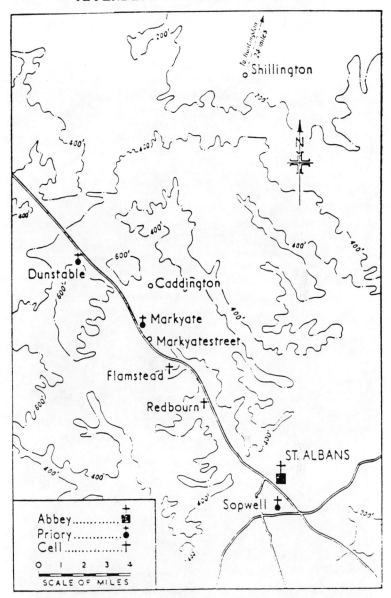

From C.H. Talbot, The Life of Christina of Markyate, Oxford, 1959. Reproduced by permission of the Oxford University Press.

Avranches, Bibliothèque municipale Edouard Le
Héricher. Ms. 72, f. 97.

Frontispiece: "Alpha and Omega" - Bibliothèque Nationale
MS. Lat. 9438

APPENDIX IV: EPITRE FARCIE: "IN DIE S. STEPHANI ESPISTOLA"

from l'Abbé Lebeuf,
*Traité historique et
pratique sur le chant
ecclésiastique*, Paris,
1741.

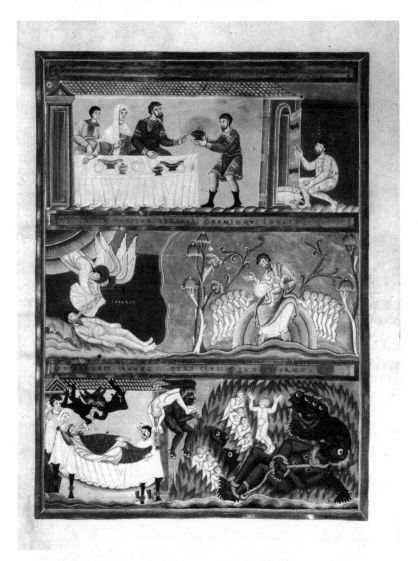

Echternach. *Codex aureus Epernacensis*: Scenes from
Luke XVI. Nuremberg, Germanisches National museum,
Hs. 2⁰ 156142, fol. 79 r⁰.

I-ci cu-men-cet I la-mia-ble cancun
E Spir-tel rai-sun I dicel no-ble ba-run
Eu-fe-mien par num.

E de la vie de sum I filz bo-neu-ret
Del quel nus a-vum o-it I lire e canter
Par le I di-vine volentet.

(Il de-sir-rables i-cel sul filz
an-gendrat

A- I pres le nai-sance co fut I em-fes
de I de-u me-thim-e amet
e I de pere e de I mere
nur I -rit par grant certet.

(la sue ju-ven-te fut honeste e
spi-ri-tel.)

Par la-mis-tet del suv-rain pi-e-tet
la sue spu-se ju-ven-e cu-man-dat
al spus vif de ve-ri-tet

(Ki est un sul fai-tur e regnet
an tri-ni-ti-et.)

I-ces-ta his-to-rie est a-mi-able grace
E-su-ve-rain con-su-la-ciun a cas-cun
me-mo-rie spi-ri-tel
Les quels vi-vent pure-ment su-lunc
cas-te-thet
e digne-ment se-i delitent/
es goies del ci-el ed es noces
vir-gi-nels.

276

APPENDIX VII: GENEALOGY OF ALEXIS MSS., after
GASTON PARIS,
La Vie de Saint Alexis, Paris, 1872.

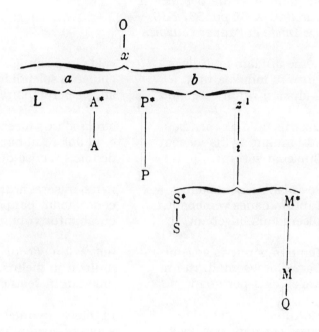

B = cod. 8860-8867 bibliothecce Burgund.
Bruxellencis saec. X in f. 75 - 76   Homo
quidam erat dives.

Mon. Germ. Hist.; Poetarum
Latinorum Medii Aevi, Tom.
IV.
Rhythmi Aevi Merovingici et
Carolini. XXV, pp. 537-539.
De Divite et Paupere Lazaro.

1. Homo quidam erat dives   valde in pecuniis.
   Purpura induebatur.   epulabat splendide:
   Caducam vitam diligendo   amisit perpetuam.

2. Lazarus quidam mendicus,   circumdatus ulcera,
   Ad ianuam divitis iacebat   cum dolore nimio;
   Cupiebat saturari   de micis mense divitis.

3. Postulabat: nemo dabat,   nemo miserebatur;
   Tantum canes veniebant,   consolabant pauperem,
   Ulcera eius lingebant,   curabantur vulnera.

4. Tempus pauperis advenit,   migravit a saeculo;
   Caruit praesentem vitam,   mutavit in melius:
   Angeli eius portabant   animam in requiem.

5. Mortuus est autem dives,   in infernum ducitur:
   Misericordiam non fecit,   eam non merebitur.
   Pro epulas poenas recepit,   cruciatur anxie.

6. In tormentis cum adesset,   elevavit oculos,
   Habrabam a longe cernit,   in sinu eius Lazarum;
   Ut recognovit, quem dispexit, in nullo consolabitur.

7. Patrem Habraham vocavit,   ut emittat Lazarum,
   Digiti extrema sui   guttam aquae tribuat,
   Ut refrigeret linguam cuis   in flammis ardentibus.

278

8. Filium eum non cupevit,   quod esse debuerat:
   'Recepisti in vita tua   valde bona plurima,
   Lazarus econtra mala: modo consolabitur.'

9. 'Quinque fratres se fatetur   habere in saeculo;
   Illis curam providebat,   quod sibi non poterat:
   Pro micas panis, quas negavit,   in infernum torquitur.'

10. 'Habent Moysen et prophetas,   si uellent, illis audiant;
   Si quis eos contempserit,   cuncta bona perditur;
   Perpetuas dantur ad poenas,   usque in novissimo.'

11. Chaus magnum est firmatum   inter nos et impios:
   Nullus valet transmeare   inde huc ad dominum;
   Impii dantur ad poenam   et iusti laudant dominum

12. Christiani qui adestis,   cavete divitias,
   Ne sicut dives ille fecit,   pereatis invicem;
   Perpetuam mortem fugite,   vitam concupiscite.

13. Gloria et honor deo   usquequo altissimo,
   Uno patri filioque   inclito paraclito,
   Cui est laus et potestas   per infinita saeculo.

Rhythmi ex variis codicibus collecti.

Eos rhythmos, quos ex codicibus deprompsi
aut in monasterio S. Galli exaratis aut cum illa
sylloga Sangallensi cohaerentibus....

                    p. 614

    Ex his codicibus ... in Monasterio s Galli
scriptisint, ante annum 800....

    Sed hi rhythmi in monas. S. Galli collecti,
non conditi sunt: Multos certe a poetis
Francogallocis sive Italicis compositos esse ex usu
poetico atque intellegitur....

                    p. 454

JOB

1 Come all you worthy Christian men
That dwell upon this land,
Don't spend your time in rioting;
Remember you're but man.
Be watchful for your latter end;
Be ready for your call.
There are many changes in this world;
Some rise while others fall.

2 Now, Job he was a patient man,
The richest in the East:
When he was brought to poverty,
His sorrows soon increased.
He bore them all most patiently;
From sin he did refrain;
He always trusted in the Lord;
He soon got rich again.

3 Come all you worthy Christian men
That are so very poor,
Remember how poor Lazarus
Lay at the rich man's door.
While begging of the crumbs of bread
That from his table fell.
The scriptures do inform us all
That in heaven he doth dwell.

4 The time, alas, it soon will come
When parted we shall be;
But all the difference it will make
Is in joy and misery;
And we must give a strict account
Of great as well as small.
Believe me, now, dear Christian friends,
That God will judge us all.

From *The Oxford Book of Carols*, ed. by Percy Dearmer, R. Vaughan Williams, Martin Shaw, London, 1965. Reproduced by permission of Oxford University Press.

57 DIVES AND LAZARUS
(GENERAL)
SECOND TUNE

Traditional   Ibid.

1. As it fell out up - -
2. Then La - za - rus laid him
3. 'Thou'rt none of my bro - thers,

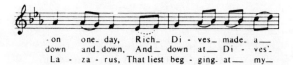

- on one day, Rich Di - ves made a
down and down, And down at Di - ves'
La - za - rus, That liest beg - ging at my

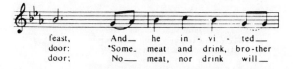

feast, And he in - vi - ted
door: 'Some meat and drink, bro-ther
door; No meat, nor drink will

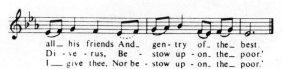

all his friends And gen-try of the best.
Di - ve - rus, Be - stow up - on the poor.'
I give thee, Nor be - stow up - on the poor.'

4 'Then Lazarus laid him down and down,
   All under Dives' wall:
   'Some meat, some drink, brother Diverus,
   For hunger starve I shall.'

5 'Thou'rt none of my brothers, Lazarus,
   That liest begging at my wall:
   No meat, nor drink will I give thee,
   For hunger starve you shall.'

From *The Oxford Book of Carols*, ed. by Percy Dearmer, R. Vaughan Williams, Martin Shaw, London, 1965. Reproduced by permission of Oxford University Press.

6 *Then Lazarus laid him down and down.
   And down at Dives' gate:
   'Some meat! some drink! brother Diverus,
   For Jesus Christ his sake.'

7 *'Thou'rt none of my brothers, Lazarus,
   That liest begging at my gate;
   No meat, no drink will I give thee.
   For Jesus Christ his sake.'

8 *Then Dives sent out his hungry dogs,
   To bite him as he lay;
   They hadn't the power to bite one bite,
   But licked his sores away.

9 *Then Dives sent to his merry men,
   To worry poor Lazarus away;
   They'd not the power to strike one stroke,
   But flung their whips away.

10 As it fell out upon one day,
   Poor Lazarus sickened and died;
   There came two angels out of heaven,
   His soul therein to guide.

11 'Rise up! rise up! brother Lazarus,
   And go along with me;
   For you've a place prepared in heaven,
   To sit on an angel's knee.'

12 As it fell out upon one day,
   Rich Dives sickened and died;
   There came two serpents out of hell,
   His soul therein to guide.

13 'Rise up! rise up! brother Diverus,
   And come along with me;
   There is a place provided in hell
   For wicked men like thee.'

14 *Then Dives looked up with his eyes
   And saw poor Lazarus blest;
   'Give me one drop of water, brother Lazarus,
   To quench my flaming thirst.

15 *'O, was I now but alive again
   The space of one half hour!
   O, that I had my peace again
   Then the devil should have no power!'